RETIRED

Dear Friends:

It is my pleasure to present you a copy of *North Carolina, New Directions for an Old Land*, which features the educational contributions of Louisburg College, the oldest two-year, coeducational, church-related college in the nation.

We sincerely hope that you enjoy your copy of this book, which has been given to you as a token of appreciation for your support and service to Louisburg College. Our loyal alumni and friends are the living history of the college, and we hope you are proud of your role in the continued success of this historical institution.

As Louisburg College's 220th anniversary approaches in 2007, we are excited to have our story represented in this wonderful volume of North Carolina's history. We hope you enjoy this gift.

Sincerely,

Reginald W. Ponder
President

NORTH CAROLINA

Facing page
Wright Brothers Glider Flight. *Orville and Wilbur Wright from Dayton, Ohio brought considerable publicity to North Carolina by their aeronautical experiments at Kill Devil Hills on the Outer Banks. Following their glider experiments on December 17, 1903, they achieved a powered flight of twelve seconds that ushered in modern aviation. Courtesy, Samuel D. Bissette*

American Historical Press
Sun Valley, California

NORTH CAROLINA

NEW DIRECTIONS FOR AN OLD LAND
AN ILLUSTRATED HISTORY

David E. Brown & Shepherd W. McKinley

Library of Congress Catalogue Card Number: 2006928109

ISBN 13: 978-1-892724-51-9
ISBN 10: 1-892724-51-0

Bibliography: p. 256
Includes Index

The Blue Ridge Parkway contains vistas of both manmade and natural beauty. One of the most complicated concrete bridges ever constructed, the 1,243 foot long Linn Cove Viaduct, pictured here, hugs the side of Grandfather Mountain. Courtesy, N.C. Division of Tourism, Film, and Sports Development

The University of North Carolina at Chapel Hill was the first state university in the nation to accept and graduate students. Courtesy, N.C. Division of Tourism, Film, and Sports Development

CONTENTS

INTRODUCTION

As significant as the Revolutionary and late antebellum years, the past few decades have proven to be one of the most important eras in North Carolina's long history. Often characterized as isolated—and once labeled "the Rip Van Winkle state"—North Carolina emerged during the 1980s and 1990s as a progressive leader in business, religion, sports, tourism, education, and a variety of other categories. The authors' goals are to acquaint the reader with the history and traditions of the state, as well as with newer trends and developments. From barbecue to industry and geography, North Carolina has always been a diverse and unique state. Ample historical and modern photographs throughout the book provide evidence of the state's beauty, vigor, and pride.

Chapter one introduces North Carolina's history starting with its "discovery" and exploration by Europeans in the 1500s. The state's colonial and early national economy was best described by "Turpentine, Trees, and Tobacco," but the foundations of industrialization were laid during the antebellum period. The state struggled after Confederate defeat. In "The Aftermath of War," textile, tobacco, and furniture manufacturing emerged to resuscitate and reorganize society. When North Carolina moved into the twentieth century, "Good Roads and Cheap Labor" brought further industrial development and growth in banking, insurance, and utilities. Labor unrest emerged during the first three decades of the new century, and increased during the Great Depression when falling crop prices drove many "From the Farm to the Town." The New Deal and World War II brought significant changes to the economy, and the state's postwar leaders built the groundwork for a modern economy. Entitled "Basking in the Sunbelt," chapter five describes the birth of the future in Research Triangle Park, as well as the continuing importance of the state's traditional manufacturing industries. "Preservation and Innovation" continues the theme of the past meeting the future. North Carolinians sought to preserve the place of folkways and religion, and enhance the place of education and the arts. Tourism steadily developed throughout the twentieth century as visitors flocked to "The Goodliest Land." Chapter eight focuses on "A Time of Change" for the industrial and agricultural sectors from a 1980s perspective. Tobacco, textiles, fishing, and furniture were in decline. Banking was taking off, and the government was attracting new industries and companies to the state. While high-tech companies moved to North Carolina, state and local leaders renewed their efforts to improve education. "Moving Forward" into the new century, the surging economy remains the biggest story, but growth in education, religion, sports, and tourism highlights the period of great change. "Chronicles of Leadership" introduces the reader to some of North Carolina's businesses and organizations that have made significant contributions to the state. Each entry describes the business's history, the people who built it, and its importance.

North Carolina: New Directions for an Old Land offers the reader an introduction to the state's history, a wide-ranging analysis of the modern state, and a look at some of its business leaders and their organizations. This book provides a working knowledge of North Carolina for those who know little about the state, as well as those with some familiarity. See the bibliography for additional sources and suggested readings. All readers will come to understand why North Carolinians, native as well as adopted, love this state, are so proud of its past, and have so much confidence in its future.

Brightleaf Square in downtown Durham is a turn-of-the-century, neo-Romanesque tobacco warehouse renovated as a unique shopping, dining and entertainment district. Courtesy, 1994 Durham Convention & Visitors Bureau

1

TURPENTINE, TREES, AND TOBACCO

The Cradle of Forestry, located in Pisgah National Forest, explores the history of forestry in the United States. Courtesy, N.C. Division of Tourism, Film, and Sports Development

At various times during his career, he was a land developer, farmer, homebuilder, soldier, mill operator, salesman, inventor, and furniture designer. He dabbled in metal working, beekeeping, and winemaking.

She was known best for her work in textiles, but also distinguished herself in animal husbandry, food processing, and the manufacture of soap and woven baskets.

They were among the greatest industrialists North Carolina has ever known. But really, they didn't have any choice. Had they not developed skills with the plow and the handmill, they would have gone hungry. Without expertise at the loom and the spinning wheel, they would have had nothing to wear.

They were the first citizens of a land which was at once abundant and confining. Fertile soil was everywhere. Trees in the vast forests yielded turpentine while they stood—and lumber, tar, and pitch when they fell. There were ready buyers for all. Yet, a treacherous coastline unsuitable for ports and rivers too shallow for heavy navigation made the distant markets hard to reach. For the settlers of the "backcountry" west of the coastal plain, good roads were scarce and, as the agrarian colony grew, capital for development of more sophisticated manufactures was scarcer still.

Thus, until well past the American Revolution, North Carolinians cultivated tobacco, cotton, corn, peas, wheat, and rice. They also raised hogs and cattle, and derived most of their other needs from the land around them—pins from prickly pears, cups and bowls from gourds, sugar from maple trees.

But while industry was limited to the thriving extraction of naval stores in the coastal region, "homespun" products were booming everywhere. Hardly a household in the state lacked the tools for making woolen and linen cloth and shaping them into shirts, dresses, and blankets. Home manufacture was so extensive that by 1810, the value of North Carolina textiles exceeded that in all of New England—this, three years before construction of the state's first significant cotton mill.

What farm woman, laboring at her loom,

As North Carolina's only water route capable of handling large trade vessels, the Cape Fear River fostered Wilmington's commercial growth. Courtesy, N.C. Division of Archives & History

could have known her simple process was a precursor of an industry in which North Carolina would have no American peers.

* * *

The 300-mile shoreline of North Carolina, from the unspoiled park lands of its Outer Banks to its busier vacation beaches, sparks pride in all citizens today. For those who, like the settlers of Virginia and Maryland, once hoped to use the coast to commercial advantage, it was a nuisance.

The Outer Banks could have been called the Outer Barrier—they close off access to the coastlines of the large sounds, and their small inlets, many of which were created relatively recently by major storms, prove navigationally hazardous. Of several rivers, only the Cape Fear at the state's southern tip can handle large ships. Small boats must be used to ply the other rivers.

Mother Nature seems to have compensated on the mainland. The first arrivals found the coastal plain thick with pine forest. Its soil and climate also yielded a variety of crops, and while the rivers weren't much use to commercial

Even in colonial times, the turpentine industry was an important and labor-intensive business. "Dipping crude"— gathering the resin from pine trees—initiated the process. Courtesy, N.C. Collection, UNC Library, Chapel Hill

shippers, they were superhighways for farmers and naval stores producers. In the rolling hills of the Piedmont, the rivers became obstacles to early intrastate commerce. Since they run mainly northwest to southeast, construction of east-west roads was difficult, and backcountry settlers often favored markets in neighboring states. Nevertheless, those same rivers and a web of smaller streams later made the state attractive to industrialists as sources of power.

Fertile soil and usable timber still run through the Piedmont and into the Appalachian mountains. Underneath the surface are mineral deposits including (in various parts of the state) one of the world's largest supplies of phosphate rock, as well as substantial deposits of clay, mica, feldspar, lithium, granite, pyrophyllite, and talc. Gold and iron also were discovered during antebellum days.

European settlers were not the first people to behold all of this richness. The land had been inhabited for more than 10,000 years, and the explorers who began arriving by ship in the early 1500s found Indian tribes everywhere.

The Indians traded among themselves for what they needed, but generally resisted any more formal commercial activity until the white settlers exposed their culture to tools, cloth, and other products of European technology. The burgeoning trade between the Indians and the newcomers was a source of frequent conflict. One of the first commercial regulations in the colony prohibited whites who were not landholders from conducting commerce with the Indians, an effort to cut competition for this trade.

As they were pushed off their lands, the Indians left an important contribution to the settlers' livelihood. The many open, meadow-like lands of which early explorers like John Lawson boasted actually had been forests until cleared by native tribes many years before. Although the Indians cultivated the future state's biggest staple, tobacco, the settlers' interest in the crop probably is attributable more to its introduction by Virginians who migrated south in the mid-1600s looking for new lands.

Of one commodity, land, there was a seemingly endless supply, and although the colonial

After the distillation of turpentine, the remaining rosin was drained into barrels and moved about with the aid of a horse-drawn mobile crane. Courtesy, N.C. Collection, UNC Library, Chapel Hill

government granted a few tracts of between 5,000 and 10,000 acres, most of it went in small parcels to settlers who farmed it themselves. The farmers tried and failed with European crops like silk and olives, settling instead on corn, peas, beans, and rice, which could be consumed at home in the temporary absence of outside markets. For tobacco, however, there was a strong market in England, and it soon became the major money crop.

The tobacco industry's beginnings in North Carolina were imported from Virginia—cultivation, shipping, and marketing methods. Most of the tobacco grown in the colony was transported to England, but some went to Virginia markets. The farmer hauled the leaf by wagon where possible; however, he more often packed it in a hogshead, inserted an axle, and rolled his product to market behind a horse.

If the mother country was hungry for tobacco, she was starving for the products of North Carolina's "piney woods," and it was the naval stores and lumber industries which made the colony a star in the British mercantile system. During the early 1700s England moved to cut her dependence on imports of naval stores from unreliable countries. North Carolina was the chief beneficiary of this decision. As long as turpentine, tar, pitch, and resin were needed for wooden ships, the colony prospered.

For the settler who in many cases owned, managed, and worked the land, the production of naval stores proved beautifully simple. Turpentine was extracted by making a long, V-shaped incision in the trunk of the tree and waiting through the spring and summer. The liquid slowly bled into a box at the tree's base, and was then ladled into barrels for shipment.

"Lightwood" cut from the centers of the dead trees was slow-burned in wooden and earthen kilns to produce tar, and the tar boiled to make pitch. This was simply barreled and hauled to the coast for shipping.

So plentiful were the trees that naval stores producers often subscribed to wasteful methods, taking the best from each tree and then moving on, so that by the late 1800s the industry had receded deeper into the South.

Travelers often feared injury from the sudden fall of a dead tree, and in 1854 one of them offered a requiem for the pines destroyed by the industry:

... They show their white faces around you on every side a great way up, and at night as you ride along they look for all the world like a great army of spectres ready to pounce upon you at every step and bear you away. Some of them from appearance have yielded their last supply and now stand like old martyrs awaiting the axe of the woodman ... No wonder that the pines here sigh through all their leaves to every breeze that whispers by ...

Another remnant of the pine tar industry is found in the state's nickname. During a Civil War battle, troops supporting a North Carolina regiment were driven back, leaving the regiment to fight alone. The lone soldiers later derided the beaten troops by threatening to put tar "on you'uns' heels to make you stick better in the next fight," whereupon General Robert E. Lee is said to have declared, "God bless the Tar Heel boys."

The naval stores industry had its greatest impact in the antebellum period, providing stability to the state's economy during the up-and-down vacillation of cotton prices. This growing enterprise also hastened the improvement of interstate transportation routes, and pine tar income helped build the public schools which at one point were the best in the South. By the time naval stores production declined in the mid-1800s, the state had led the world for 150 years.

The barrels for shipping naval stores were made in North Carolina, advancing a lumber industry which, as of the early eighteenth century, had grown from household to commercial status. With lumbering came the cooperage and sawmill trades, and the state became a significant manufacturer of barrel and hogshead staves, casks, and shingles. All of this commerce was concentrated in the East, where rivers made the products easier to transport.

For a coastal state, North Carolina never was much of a shipbuilder, trailing the New England states and Virginia in production. Surprisingly, perhaps, there also is no evidence that commercial fishing held much status in the state before the Civil War; in fact, even on the Outer Banks, few earned a livelihood directly from the sea.

While commercial centers were growing in the mid-eighteenth century around coastal towns like Edenton, Halifax, New Bern, Wilmington, and Cross Creek (Fayetteville), the Piedmont and the western regions remained sparsely populated, inhabited only by small pockets of farmers. Travelers from the Northeast often interpreted the scarcity of towns and the hand-to-mouth economy of the backcountry as a rural slovenliness. But many newcomers stayed, notably those who trekked the Great Wagon Road from Pennsylvania to Salisbury. As the population growth

Old Salem was a small community of industrious Moravians in 1824 when Daniel Welfare painted this landscape featuring Blum's mill (foreground). Courtesy, Wachovia Historical Society

Coastal North Carolina prospered more than the interior in colonial days. This busy wharf scene decorated an early map of the Carolina region. Courtesy, N.C. Collection, UNC Library, Chapel Hill

accelerated in the second half of the century, so did a zest for common enterprise. There is no better example than the Moravians, who settled Wachovia in the area around present-day Winston-Salem.

These intensely industrious Pennsylvanians were unimpressed with the general economy of North Carolina, and dismayed that farm products were marketed in other states. "Of handicrafts I have seen practically nothing in the 150 miles we have traveled across this province," commented their leader upon arriving in 1752. "Almost nobody has a trade." The Moravians

were big believers in specialized labor; thus, their new town soon attracted surrounding settlers who sought the services of its doctor, tailor, and blacksmith.

Wachovia became a trading center for the backcountry, and its citizens led wagon trains to the markets of Charleston, South Carolina, and the larger Cape Fear Valley towns. But throughout accounts of the state's colonial history, the Moravians are exceptions to the primitive subsistence west of the coastal plain.

The agonizingly slow development of commerce in North Carolina can be attributed largely to the dearth of transportation systems. For a backcountry farmer a trip to market often was an arduous, expensive ordeal over crude paths which could hardly be called roads. By 1764 the county courts were responsible for adequate roads, bridges, and ferries, but the law went unenforced in most places. Fifteen years after its passage, the state's main post road was described as a horror of mud, holes, and obstacles like fallen trees.

The rivers made the coastal planter and merchant better off, and to them boats—small canoes or perriaugers (barges) that could carry 100 barrels—proved indispensible. Still, the rivers were plagued by obstructions. They ran shallow in times of drought, and to an overland traveler in the coastal plain, they were an even bigger headache than in the backcountry. These problems, coupled with a coastline that was usually dangerous and always inconvenient for shippers, hindered even the best trading centers in the East.

As the population of the coastal plain grew, there evolved in the port towns a class of merchants who accumulated great economic and political power. This elevated status derived mainly from the fact that there were so few traders and that other participants in the economy depended on them so much. Just as the frontier settler was a jack-of-all trades for his family's needs, the merchant became a versatile creature of the marketplace.

Maybe he started as a planter who set up a store alongside a road or stream on his land. When business grew, he opened a shop in town, and expanded beyond the products of his plantation to include imported clothing, tools, and food. As he acquired capital, other functions of the infant economy naturally fell to him—he assumed the positions of both wholesaler and retailer; he began to service the transportation needs of the surrounding farmers by blacksmithing and repairing wagons; and he started a cooperage to make barrels for naval stores. The merchant then found it profitable to own and dispatch ships. With capital and connections to so many local commercial establishments, he also was the most likely moneylender.

From all of these enterprises, many merchants amassed small fortunes. In the early part of the eighteenth century some were known to charge between 2,000 and 3,000 percent above the initial cost of British products; later, increasingly sophisticated trade with England and the growth of commercial competition within the colony halted such outrageous profiteering, but merchants rarely were immune to charges of gouging.

Wealth and standing in the community led to political power, and the colonial government typically was dominated by merchants and planters. Since these groups were concentrated in the East, backcountry settlers rightfully doubted that they had much of a voice in the legislature. Even in the new state constitution of 1776, representation was stacked in the easterners' favor. Cries of the backcountry for transportation improvement often fell on deaf ears.

Trade in the rural areas was ruled much less by class division—the more rugged living conditions tended to equalize settlers. The hub of their economy was the country store, and, like the town merchant, its owner could not afford to specialize.

The store's shelves held everything the settler would ever need beyond what he, himself, could make: calico, perfumes, ribbons, looking glasses, schoolbooks, wood screws, writing paper, liniments, coffee, boots, and suspenders. If the settler lacked the cash or goods to trade, at least he and his family had the right to dream about them.

Coastal ports handled large-scale farm exports, but it fell to the country store owner to handle small amounts of crops and livestock and pay the farmer from his inventory. A majority of store owners offset the bulk of their wholesale bills more with farm products like wool, beeswax, and pork than with cash.

Just as this fledgling commerce was struggling to its feet, the Revolutionary War commenced. To her good fortune, North Carolina largely evaded the physical destruction other colonies suffered because relatively few battles were fought on her grounds. The later years of the war, however, brought the colony's trade almost to a halt, as the occupation of Wilmington closed the Cape Fear port of entry. In addition, various bands of raiders stripped the backcountry of provisions. The already established tradition of self-sufficiency ultimately buoyed the settlers. When need arose, they simply went back to living off the land, fending for themselves.

The aftermath of war was remarkable not for changes in the old order, but for similarity to it. Trade quickly returned to normal pre-war levels, and regulations and practices were essentially the same in the new state as they had been in the colony. This is a good illustration of how little the colony had been affected by British trade policies.

But long after Yorktown, a battle raged in North Carolina over adoption of the new federal constitution. The heart of the disagreement centered on commercial issues which exacerbated the differences between the state's mercantile East and its agrarian backcountry. Eastern merchants feared the infusion of too much paper currency, and favored a clause in the constitution which barred states from issuing bills of credit. They also realized that as a non-Union state, they would be considered "foreigners" for trade purposes, and would suffer higher duties. The farmers, who clamored for more money, believed that ratification would bring them under even tighter control of the merchant powers. Therefore, they did not back the constitution.

North Carolina remained independent for a year after the constitution was adopted. The reasons the state's two divergent groups came to agree on ratification were many, all adding up to a realization that North Carolina had too much to lose by remaining apart from the Union.

For other states, perhaps, the Revolution was a turning point, a clarion of brighter days and bigger things to come. For North Carolina, it seems to have signaled hibernation.

The first third of the nineteenth century was an embarrassing chapter in the state's history. "The Rip Van Winkle State" is the most popular—and probably the kindest—label applied to North Carolina during the period. Let factories and railroads spread throughout the Northeast.

Let Virginia and South Carolina build impressive markets. North Carolinians seemed incredibly indifferent to progress; poverty, ignorance, and sloth hung over them like a thick fog. Those still swayed by ambition departed in droves: nearly half the state's counties lost population during the 1830s. North Carolina's national rank fell from fourth in 1790 to twelfth by 1860.

Even the leaders of the day were complacent. Consider the views of Nathaniel Macon, a Warren County planter and a congressman of thirty-seven years, who pessimistically viewed economic development and thought the growth of capitalism was based on "gambling." Macon asserted that the South should withdraw from the Union and become entirely self-sufficient, shunning foreign trade and ties to the North. This morass was not without explanation. North Carolina was deeply imbedded in the plantation and slave labor systems; crop prices which were generally favorable in the period after the War of 1812 made men of means reluctant to try anything else. The invention of the cotton gin in 1793 solved the problem of separating the seeds from the lint, and North Carolina planters

Nathaniel Macon (1758-1837) supported American independence and continuously represented North Carolina in the U.S. Congress for thirty-seven years. A staunch Jeffersonian Republican, he fought all plans to have government promote internal improvements or stimulate economic growth. Courtesy, Southern Historical Collection, Wilson Library, UNC, Chapel Hill

turned from tobacco and other crops to the more profitable cotton. Domestic spinning and weaving boomed along with the surge in cotton growing, but there was little appetite for more sophisticated manufacture.

When, in 1810, prominent men were asked to describe the industrial offerings of their counties, one Wayne County representative stated: "There is two or three Spinning Machines with 30 or 40 Spindles each but from the difficulty of abandoning old & Established habits they are not very much used."

Finally Archibald D. Murphey, a Hillsborough lawyer and state senator, let the senate have it in a series of reports during 1815-18, highlighted by the words "lazy, sickly, poor, dirty, and ignorant." Murphey's was a positive approach—the state had the resources and the character to keep pace with the rest of the Union, he said, and its failure was in never having spent money on internal improvements. His call for the deepening of coastal inlets, a north-south canal to connect the eastern rivers, and good roads which would open the backcountry to markets met with the same general apathy and smug complacency in the East. But he had gotten the ball rolling.

In 1828 another state senator, Charles Fisher, went a step further, saying radical changes were needed and that the answer was cotton manufacturing. Fisher seemed to know what he was up against: "Our habits and prejudices are against manufacturing," he stated, but "the policy that resists the change is unwise and suicidal." The state's advantage over the North, Fisher stressed, was its ability to grow, as well as process, the raw material.

Like Murphey, Fisher had done his homework. He estimated the income from the North Carolina cotton crop of 80,000 bales could be quadrupled if manufactured at home rather than selling the raw product to northern factories.

Newspapers across the state took up Fisher's cry, but they had no easy time. There remained a widely held feeling that agriculture was pure, manufacturing evil. Working people, to whom a wage was the same whether it came from farm

Looking ahead when very few other North Carolinians chose to do so, Archibald DeBow Murphey sought internal improvements which would have revolutionized commerce and transportation as early as 1815. Courtesy, N.C. Division of Archives & History

or factory, detested the more ordered and confining atmosphere of mills. Many farmers dreamed of becoming planters, and to turn to industry was to give up that ambition.

Moreover, land and slaves still abounded. Slavery made large-scale farming profitable, and not until after abolition did great numbers of capitalists turn their attention to manufacturing. Yet, throughout history there are those who went against the grain, who saw opportunities and refused to wait for a more supportive atmosphere. Such men were Michael Beam and Michael Schenck.

In 1804 Beam, then twenty-two, left his home in the Piedmont foothills and visited a Cincinnati cotton mill. There he studied and sketched the equipment. Upon his return to North Carolina, Beam constructed a crude textile machine. Newspapers hailed his small mill in present-day Cleveland County as the state's first cotton factory. Using Beam's inspiration and some of his machinery, Schenck built a mill on the Catawba River in Lincoln County in 1813. He later was joined by Absolom Warlick, and the Schenck-Warlick cotton factory is usually cited as North Carolina's first such operative, probably because it continued to do business for fifty years.

Schenck had been a Lincolnton merchant, and before coming to the state, he had been a tailor. Like most of the early mills, his was engaged in spinning cotton into yarn, which still had to be woven into fabric, either in northern mills or on home looms.

The factory was hailed as a sight "worth fifty miles of travel to see." A later account described trade at the early mills:

Much of the business of this early mill was done by barter. People came to Lincolnton from as far away as a hundred miles to trade cotton for factory-spun yarn.

This model of a typical 1830s cotton factory shows carding and twisting machines on the first floor, spinning frames on the second, and weaving looms on the third. Courtesy, N.C. Division of Archives & History

During the busy season it was customary for them to camp near the mill to wait their turn for yarn to come off the machinery ... Great, gayly painted Conestoga wagons, eleven feet high and drawn by six horses, brought raw cotton and merchandise for sale in Schenck's store, and took away loads of yarn for the chief cotton market in Fayetteville ... In these ways much of the product of the Shenck cotton mill found its way into the town and farm homes of the South to be colored with vegetable dyes heated on the kitchen stove, and woven on the home hand looms ...

Though manufacturing did not gain momentum during this early period, pioneer mills were built in the next twenty years by Joel Battle and Henry A. Donaldson in Rocky Mount, Henry Humphries in Greensboro, John W. Leak in Great Falls (Roanoke Rapids), E.M. Holt in Alamance Creek, John W. Morehead in Leaksville, and Francis Fries in Salem. By 1840 the census listed twenty-five mills in the state, most of them in the northern Piedmont.

These early entrepreneurs were gamblers of sorts—there were many ways to fail, as Schenck discovered when the water-powered dam for his first mill was washed away. In addition, planters defrauded the operators by watering cotton bales; water shortages cut off the power source; week-long religious revivals, a deep seated tradition, shut down mills for their duration; and the most feared enemy, fire, wiped out several early factories.

Meanwhile, long held attitudes and market forces continued to inhibit North Carolina from becoming a manufacturing state. Though the newspapers almost unanimously pushed industry, when cotton prices were favorable, the people with capital concentrated it on more land and slaves. Later in the period, these same individuals became preoccupied with the growing conflict between the nation's North and South.

Conversely, hard times for the crop often spurred mill construction, as in 1826 when a bumper crop glutted the market. The varying fortunes of other commodities—notably declines

Pine Street in Kannapolis showed the bleak uniformity of mill villages built to house workers. Here, Cannon Mills dominated the skyline. Courtesy, N.C. Collection, UNC Library, Chapel Hill

in demand for lumber and tobacco—also suggested the need for manufacture. With more cotton being grown at less expense in the new farmlands of the Southwest, North Carolina planters risked being undercut at market.

Bad times for cotton trickled down to the laborer in the form of poverty and even starvation, sharp reminders of the dangers of a strictly agrarian economy. And it didn't take a tycoon to calculate that it was just as cheap to transport $40,000 worth of a finished product to distant markets as it was to ship $10,000 worth of raw cotton. Manufacturing was starting to make

sense.

The fact that North Carolinians produced more textiles than all of New England in 1810 begs the question, why did New England get the jump on manufacturing? In addition to all the aforementioned liabilities, the transportation problem continued to restrain progress. Finally, in the early 1830s, there was movement toward railroad building, and shortly thereafter, the construction of plank roads developed.

Joseph Caldwell, president of the University of North Carolina, wrote a series of newspaper articles in 1827, touting railroads as prerequisite to progress. A few years later the state got another jolt when Virginia's Petersburg Railroad passed near enough to Halifax to lure some trade away from the Roanoke River Valley. Almost immediately, the legislature chartered ten railroad building companies.

With state financial aid to the struggling companies, the first lines were built from Wilmington to Weldon and from Raleigh to the old Roanoke River town of Gaston in 1840. Later tracks connected Hillsborough, Salisbury, Concord, Charlotte, Stesville, and Morganton, and Kinston, New Bern, and Beaufort. By 1860 North Carolina had 891 miles of railroad.

As good as trains were for commercial transport, they didn't quite solve the farm-to-market problem. Plank roads, constructed of pine boards laid end-to-end, cut days off the farmer's travel time. Built by private companies which levied tolls, most of the main roads branched from Fayetteville. The Fayetteville-High Point-Salem Road, ending in the old Forsyth County town of Bethania, was the longest plank road in the world, covering 129 mills. But the "farmers' railroads" wore out faster than expected, and by 1860 most of them were gone.

Textile mill owners, of course, welcomed the transportation improvements. The first mills generally were very small, often family-managed in much the same way as was the farm. The hands-on, paternalistic methods practiced by operators bore little similarity to the conventional approach to industrial management. Yet, the fact that these businesses were passed on from one generation of owners and managers to the next gave the later, larger mills a distinctly North Carolina flavor. For one thing, this custom negated the need to import expertise from the northeastern states. For another, it perpetuated into the twentieth century the idea that smaller mills were more profitable, leaving North Carolina with more, but smaller, factories than the other southern states.

Few of the antebellum mills were islands unto themselves; more likely, a man bought one mill and invested its profits into other factories at different locations. The people he employed and trained, meanwhile, might have been thrifty enough to set out on their own. Marriage proved another common means of sharing the wealth with many people. Raised in Cedar Falls in Randolph County, John Milton Odell worked in the local mill. He then bought a factory in Concord. Odell married the daughter of a prominent pioneer in the industry and later was a principal in some nine other cotton works. The Cedar Falls mill, wrote Elizabeth Yates Webb, "seems to have been a training ground for some of the most prominent early and post-war manufacturers."

After establishing his first factory, E.M. Holt of Alamance established all his sons and sons-in-law in textile ventures elsewhere; to save money and time, Holt and Francis Fries of Salem alternated the task of taking trips to the Northeast to buy machinery and assess the markets. A few founders of the Pinhook factory (1847) in Gaston County later went their separate ways, spreading knowledge to those who ultimately became responsible for all of the 1880-1900 textile mill development around Gastonia.

Women dominated the labor force in the antebellum cotton mills. The transition from home spinning to similar work on larger machines was natural, but the relative wages for men and women probably emerged as a bigger factor in an owner's choice of employees: average wages in the mills in 1850 were $11.65 a month for men and $6.13 for women (and these were substantially below other southern states—South Carolina mills paid $13.94 monthly to men and $8.30 to women). There is little record of the number of youngsters the mills employed, but census figures which show suspiciously small numbers of people engaged in manufacturing indicate that many mill workers were children not counted in the "occupation" category. Children were paid as little as twelve and one-half cents a week.

The use of slaves in the work forces of the early factories was relatively insignificant. Their owners needed them on the farms, and there are only three known instances of regular employment of slaves in antebellum mills.

Hours in the plant were long—sunup to sundown in the summer, and usually twelve-hour days in winter. As if the workers needed further restrictions on their lifestyles, the state at one point tried to regulate morals when chartering mills; one charter forbade the selling of liquor within a mile of the factory.

Most mills were built of brick, usually away from towns and along rivers or creeks which provided the power. The rural location, and the paternalism of early owners, led to the formation of factory villages. The owners built and, in many cases, maintained the workers' houses; some even provided churches, schools, and ball fields.

A typical mill village description in a Wilmington newspaper pays high compliments to the owner, or, perhaps, celebrates the plant's impact on the local economy :

There have been at least a dozen new cottages built lately for the 'hands'. They are extremely neat and pretty, all painted white, and nicely finished off, containing three or four rooms, a porch, and an entry. Besides these new houses, the old ones having been renovated, make up quite a thriving little village; and the flower plots, flourishing beds of vegetables, and graceful flowering vines give it an appearance of taste, comfort and beauty.

The mills' main product was yarn, most of which was sold to domestic weavers. Another major product was osnaburgs, or coarse cloth, used mainly to clothe slaves. Heavy production of osnaburgs, as opposed to more finely textured fabric, indicates the low level of sophistication in the antebellum North Carolina mills. Products made in lesser quantities included sheeting, batting, tweeds, and denim. By far the biggest markets were local.

In 1869, *Branson's North Carolina Business Directory* listed forty-five cotton mills operating 54,575 spindles and 1,126 looms, representing a capital investment of $2.2 million. Approximately seventy mills were built before 1865; some burned, some failed financially, and twelve met destruction during the Civil War. The forty-five that remained employed 1,987 people. When dependents are taken into account, roughly 9,000

people owed their support to the textile industry. There were mills in some twenty counties from the coast to the foothills, with the heaviest concentrations in Alamance, Randolph, Cumberland, and Gaston.

In the first half-century of textile mill development, expertise and financial backing came from North Carolina natives. The state's first incorporation law, enacted in 1828, greatly boosted capital growth. Business pioneers subsequently were able to raise funds by selling stock certificates to several investors. However, statewide industry still lagged behind that of South Carolina at the dawn of the Civil War, and national leader Massachusetts had four times as many mills.

Another major North Carolina industry evolved when the war erupted. The manufacture of tobacco products developed very slowly, partially because farmers were unable to cultivate a bright-leaf strain to replace the dark, coarse tobacco grown during the mid-nineteenth century.

Lunsford Lane, a remarkable entrepreneur, earned the $1,000 price for freedom by selling his homemade smoking tobacco mixture in Raleigh, Fayetteville, Salisbury, and Chapel Hill. He eventually freed his wife and six children and moved North, where his ambition and accomplishments were less frowned upon. Courtesy, N.C. Division of Archives & History

Then one rainy night in the early 1850s on a Caswell County farm, a slave named Stephen fell asleep while watching tobacco curing over a wood fire. The fire nearly went out. When Stephen awoke and scrambled for something to rekindle the flame, he turned to the pit where he made charcoal for the forge. There he found several charred logs, which he placed under the tobacco.

As Stephen said, "To tell the truth about it, 'twas a accident," but he had accomplished what 250 years of experiments in curing and soils had not: the drying heat from the charcoal produced the unique flavor of what came to be known as bright-leaf tobacco.

Throughout the antebellum period, the state's heavy production of tobacco was limited to the Piedmont counties along the Virginia border. Little is known about North Carolina tobacco manufacturing before 1840, but the industry grew steadily until the dawn of the Civil War. Almost exclusively, Caswell, Rockingham, Stokes, and Granville counties were the sites of this manufacturing upsurge.

One of the first entrepreneurs, Lunsford Lane, began his ventures in Raleigh. Lane's father had taught him how to prepare tobacco with a flavor that other local producers couldn't seem to match. In the mid-1800s Lane began selling tobacco to state legislators, about a quarter pound for fifteen cents, and he also invented a special pipe. He peddled his wares in the early evening and manufactured later at night, as he was otherwise occupied—as a slave. After taking Raleigh by storm, Lane marketed his smoking mixture in Chapel Hill, Salisbury, and Fayetteville, declining partnerships with others because he knew his smoke was a "cut above."

Most tobacco factories were very small and very simple, usually started by planters as adjuncts to their farms. About 98 percent of their product before 1860 was for chewing, and crude, hand-operated presses converted the raw material into plugs and twists. What the factory couldn't sell locally was carried away by northern agents and backcountry peddlers.

In contrast to the textile industry, most farm labor was done by slaves. Tobacco manufacture

North Carolina's gold rush began in 1825, although the real commercial activity came about two decades later. This picture features "Main Street" of a boomtown, Gold Hill, at the turn of the century. In its heyday the small city housed 3,000 people, seven saloons, three doctors to patch up the victims of fights, and three jails, "which were always full." Courtesy, N.C. Division of Archives & History

*Illegal liquor stills have long presented law enforcers with
a challenge: tracking them down. Here, a moonshiner
checks his equipment, hidden deep in the mountains.
Photo by Margaret W. Morley. Courtesy, N.C. Division of
Archives & History*

thus provided a market for the planter's crop and a workplace for any field hands he could spare. By 1860 there were ninety-four factories in North Carolina, employing just less than 1,500 people. The annual value was $1.1 million.

As with textiles, the glory days for the state's tobacco industry were yet to come. The Duke family of Durham would not pioneer the cigarette industry until after the war, but in a curious way, Durham proved largely responsible for the spread of bright-leaf tobacco to other parts of the country. A factory built there in 1858 was accessible to both Union and Confederate armies during the war. The soldiers became fond of the bright leaf, and the tobacco habit followed them to their far-flung homes at war's end. This amounted to free advertising for bright-leaf tobacco beyond the manufacturer's wildest dreams.

A handful of other pre-Civil War industries deserve mention. For example, North Carolina had its own gold rush after the discovery of the Reed Mine in Cabarrus County in 1799. The first miners found nuggets as large as twenty-eight pounds, and at the height of the boom, there were fifty-six mines in the area around Charlotte and Gold Hill in Rowan County, and some 1,000 people working them. North Carolina produced all of the nation's gold before 1829, but there was little left of it by the time of the California rush.

Iron was mined and pig iron processed in Lincoln, Nash, and Johnston counties during the antebellum years. The industry never boomed, being an economic risk, but it was used as a selling point for the first railroads.

The state's welding industry remained small due to the severe scarcity of hard money—barter was the rule in trade and, except for the Bank of the United States, notes from North Carolina were subject to depreciation outside the state. No lending institutions existed until the start of the nineteenth century, when the Bank of New Bern, the State Bank of North Carolina in Raleigh, and the Bank of Cape Fear in Wilmington were chartered. By 1860 thirty-six state-chartered banks conducted business, but their holdings attest to the state's poverty:

less than seven million dollars in capital stock and less than $1.5 million in deposits.

One of North Carolina's most legendary enterprises was built by shrewd, colorful men who never came out of the backwoods, and didn't care to, as long as their stills were pumping out liquor. At the close of the nineteenth century the state had 733 licensed grain and 1,300 legal fruit distilleries producing more than a million gallons of whiskey and brandy a year. Nevertheless, it was entrepreneurs like Amos Owens who gave the business, shall we say, a reputation.

From his secluded perch on Cherry Mountain in Rutherford County, Amos produced a notorious mixture of corn whiskey, sourwood honey, and cherry juice that earned him the title "the Cherry Bounce King." Amos was not fond of paying taxes on his export, however, and made several trips down the mountain to federal court.

On one occasion the judge held himself up as an example of sober virture. "Waal, jedge," Amos drawled, "you've missed a durned lotsa fun if you hain't naver made, drunk, nor sold no likker."

Any discussion of industry in pre-Civil War North Carolina should not overshadow the fact that the state was still largely agricultural. The 1860 census listed 87,025 farmers in contrast to 110,594 people employed in all other occupations combined.

North Carolina was a long way from prosperity. She was the last colony to establish banks, she scoffed at internal improvements, and she was painfully slow to nurture a major industry which practically waited on her doorstep. Rarely was there a truce in the bickering between her eastern and western regions.

And the plantation—the peculiar phenomenon in which she and her southern neighbors had so invested—gradually became a burden that was about to come tumbling down. Gone would be a labor system based on chains. Farms, rail lines, and factories would have to be rebuilt from scratch. Gone would be many of the ablest citizens—for good. Only the bitter awareness of the necessity of modern manufacture would remain.

2

THE AFTERMATH
OF WAR

During busy market days in the 1890s, much of a region's produce and news were exchanged. Here, buyers and sellers of firewood crowd the Fayetteville town square. Courtesy, N.C. Collection, UNC Library, Chapel Hill

Weary and disheartened, the North Carolina farmer trudged back from the battlefield in 1865. If he was lucky he was all in one piece, but any elation he might have felt at the end of the fighting was tempered by what he found at home—cattle and pigs gone; barns and smokehouses barren; and field, fences, and tools tattered from years of neglect. If he had been wealthy in the old order, he was reduced to poverty in the new; if he had struggled before, he would resume the struggle from scratch.

On a larger scale, his state was no less ravaged. The fledgling banks were collapsing along with the money system, the railroad network lay in disrepair, and political operations dominated by outside influence were rife with corruption.

Suddenly 350,000 black people and 650,000 white people were forced to interact with each other on completely different terms. The economic order which had concentrated riches in the hands of a very few, while keeping so many down, was history. The ensuing despair found release in ugliness like the Ku Klux Klan.

North Carolina was in social and economic shock. Radical reforms were inevitable, and the traditional voices for change seized on the ruin of war to plead louder than ever that the state should take advantage of her natural assets.

One of the loudest crusaders for industrialization, *The News and Observer* of Raleigh, declared in 1880:

It is idle to talk of home independence so long as we go to the North for everything from a toothpick to a President ... We may look in vain for the dawn of an era of enterprise, progress, and development, as long as thousands and millions of money are deposited in banks on four per cent interest, when its judicious investment in manufactures would more than quadruple that rate ... Out of our political defeat we must work out a glorious material and industrial triumph.

Just five years later, the same newspaper could be charged with understatement for saying, "Everywhere signs of improvement are becoming visible."

James Albert Bonsack of Bonsack, Virginia utilized a room in his father's wood mill to invent this cigarette-making machine. Although the prototype burned while being shipped to Richmond for a "trial run," Bonsack eventually found a Parisian who was willing to manufacture the invention. Courtesy, N.C. Division of Archives & History

The collapse might have been less disastrous had the plantation system not enjoyed such prosperity in the 1850s. With cotton and tobacco prices rising, the state chose to use the new railroads to expand the agrarian economy rather than to switch to manufacturing. The coming of the railroads merely opened routes from the North Carolina farm to the New England mill.

At the war's end, the material losses to Sherman's bummers were only the first of the planter's worries. Farm laborers might wander off to the next county to work for someone they liked better, or to seek their fortunes on their own. If they did stay, the planter never could be certain of their status, and he couldn't control their output like before. The wages he had to start paying often were worth more than the work he got for them. Add to this high interest rates, and one by one the plantations fell into the open market for whatever price they would bring.

Men with the means to continue the textile mill surge suffered similarly. Many of these people had been exempted from joining the army, and in return had agreed to devote much of their production to blankets, uniforms, and other needs of the war effort. When the smoke cleared, twelve mills in the state had been destroyed; the economic collapse during Reconstruction doomed several more. Counting mills built between 1860 and 1870, there was a net loss of six during the decade.

Those who managed to insulate themselves from the demise of the Confederate money system faced such economic and political uncertainty that they were skittish about investing in new plants, and northerners were equally afraid to pour capital into the South. The mill-building boom would have to wait almost fifteen years after the war was over.

Destruction of train lines and the surrounding property probably didn't set North Carolina back as much as it did other states. The rail system was in good shape at the start of the war, and the Union armies which seized the lines utilized and maintained them. Although repairs to burned railroad warehouses and bridges added to the state's money problems, most of the major routes were restored before the end of 1865. Ironically, the railroads probably suffered more from underuse due to the general poverty than they did from wartime conditions.

As the state struggled to recapture some of the optimistic boom of the 1850s, its people fell back into asking the same nagging question: to farm or to manufacture? Cotton and tobacco growing still was attractive—it required the least capital, it was the only thing many people knew how to do, and cotton prices remained high. The labor supply proved less reliable, but emancipation didn't relieve anybody of the need to work.

Pulling in the opposite direction were stark reminders from the war years: the South's inablility to supply herself when lines to the North were cut off figured heavily in the outcome, and there was no reason to believe the absence of industry wouldn't return to haunt the region again.

Besides Charlotte-based cotton and oil mills, D.A. Tompkins produced machinery, as this advertisement illustrates. Courtesy, N.C. Division of Archives & History

In North Carolina, the common suffering during the war and Reconstruction had done a lot to ease the differences that had kept the East and West apart for so long. The break may be traced to 1872. Overproduction glutted the cotton market and the price plummeted to ten cents a pound, where it would hover for the next forty years. Gradually, those with capital began to take the editorial writers seriously.

By the time the cotton price slump hit the South Carolina plantation where Daniel Augustus Tompkins was born, he was well on his way to becoming innovator, capitalist, and proponent for Southern industrialization. It is difficult to say which of those roles was more important to North Carolina's manufacturing swell in the last two decades of the nineteenth century.

While many would-be builders of the New South were preoccupied with Reconstruction politics, Tompkins' fascination rested in machinery and what made it work. His mastery of engineering was exceeded only by his forceful personality—in 1873, at age twenty-two, this son of a Confederate soldier and slaveholder was elected student body president of a technical institute in New York. Tompkins' apprenticeship then took him to the Bethlehem Iron Works in Pennsylvania, where he learned the machinist's trade so thoroughly and so quickly that he was sent to Germany to train workers and to set up a rolling mill. When he returned, he was ready to go into business for himself, and he longed for the South. It is not known why he chose Charlotte as the place to hang his shingle in 1882, but one could surmise that the abundance of streams and rivers to power industrial machines made it as attractive as anywhere.

With his knowledge of engines, he started as a southern agent for companies like Westinghouse, dividing his time between his home base in Charlotte and horse-and-buggy trips to other western Piedmont towns and South Carolina. During these excursions, he sold, delivered, and installed machines. He also was becoming interested in making use of cottonseed, one of the greatest examples of plantation wastefulness. Cottonseed oil could be used as a food additive and cottonseed meal could nourish livestock, but all over the South this potentially versatile product was left to rot in mountainous piles beside the cotton gins.

Tompkins is perhaps the best example of what could be accomplished in those days by a tireless worker who carefully plowed his profits into industrial expansion. By 1895 he had had a hand in building some fifty cottonseed oil mills all over the South; he constructed more than 150 electric light plants; and he helped to establish many textile works, including three in Charlotte and one in Salisbury. But Tompkins was more widely known for prodding the sleepy South toward industrialization through his writings and speeches—and demonstrating ways to go about modernization. He was that rare combination of talker and doer. In a speech to the Southern Industrial League, he said:

All the cotton now made is manufactured by somebody. The world's requirement seems to be increasing, and we seem to be as well situated to make the yarn and cloth as to produce the cotton. It would seem as if the limit of our manufacturing interests is simply the labor we have ... For the coming generation the way to prosperity is wide open and plain. The passing generation has won the fight against anarchy and left to their children a heritage more valuable than any riches. It is now simply a question of redemption from poverty. To do this we must combine farming and manufacturing.

In the last years of the century Tompkins focused on the region's most urgent industrial development need. It was fine for the Holts and the Frieses to put their wealth into cotton mills wherever they saw fit, but what of the communities which had no such rich men? Every community should have a mill, Tompkins said, and he preached cooperative arrangements among groups of small investors. These enterprising individuals would pay for the stock in installments; as the money rolled in bit by bit, the land gradually would be purchased, the building built, and the machinery added. In North Carolina capital investment in cotton mills tripled in the last decade of the 1800s, from 10.7 to thirty-

Founder of a family empire built on cotton manufacture, railroads, and banking, Edwin M. Holt learned to color yarn from a Frenchman who charged one hundred dollars plus board to share this knowledge. The resulting "Alamance Plaids" became hallmarks of the American textile industry. Courtesy, N.C. Division of Archives & History

three million dollars. And the sources were overwhelmingly local.

Before his death in 1914, Tompkins turned to industrial education. He promoted trade schools, was a leading national organizer of industrial expositions, and founded the School of Textiles at the State College of Agricultural and Mechanical Arts, now North Carolina State University.

Everything about the textile industry in North Carolina from 1880 to 1900 said "boom." Investment growth was even greater in the 1880s than in the 1890s—capital investment jumped from $2.8 million to $10.7 million. The number of mills climbed from forty-nine in 1880 to 177 in 1900; the average size of the mills more than tripled, from a mean of 1,885 spindles in 1880 to 6,400 ten years later.

Capital investment in textiles during the last decade of the century shot up 205 percent in North Carolina, compared with 14 percent in New England and 32 percent in the entire country. Northern mill builders conceded that conditions like labor and natural resources were more favorable in the South and, predictably, they began studying the possibility of moving into the region. The physical migration of mills would

wait until the twentieth century, but during the post-war boom, northern capitalists did make more and bigger investments in the South. At the close of the century, South Carolina had grown at least as fast as North Carolina, and still led her sister state in textile production.

This movement toward growth was fairly well insulated from economic hard times. The depression of 1893-94 had little effect on the mills, and although a more serious slump in 1896 shut down nineteen of them, it didn't even slow construction of several new plants.

Mill building spread in every possible way.

The giants of the industry reinvested their profits in more factories—John Milton Odell used the rewards of his 1877 Concord Cotton Mill to build others in 1882, 1886, 1890 and 1894; the Holt family eventually owned thirty-five plants; and the Fries family had ten.

Some businesses, like the Salisbury Cotton Mill in 1887, were started simply to take advantage of idle pools of labor. Several communities used Tompkins' cooperative investment plan to satisfy jealousies—if one town had a mill, the leading capitalists of a neighboring town might start one in order to keep up with the Joneses.

From the original centers of Alamance, Randolph, Cumberland, and Gaston counties, the industry began to find other havens like Mecklenburg, which was spurred by Tompkins' influence, Gaston's success, and Charlotte's general growth; Rutherford, a spinoff of the huge Henrietta mill; and Durham, established with capital overflow from the highly profitable tobacco enterprises.

Of all these mill centers, one, Gaston County, stands out. In the late 1840s Henry Humphries of Greensboro had tired of the expense of powering his Mount Hecla mill with coal, and went looking for a good fast-running stream. He settled on Mountain Island on the Catawba River in Gaston, and moved his operations there. It was the first of more than 200 mills in an area that would become a world textile center on the order of the pioneering models in Manchester, England and Lowell, Massachusetts.

Why Gaston? The profusion of rivers and streams seems reason enough for the early development (Gaston had thirty mills by 1904), when most factories were water-powered. It also was close to the influential presence of Tompkins, textile entrepreneurs, and the growing centers of

South Carolina. Finally, Gaston boasted more than its share of determined builders, men like Caleb Lineberger, Jasper Stowe, and A.P. Rhyne, as well as Rufus McAden, who doubtless was inspired during eight years spent in Alamance County.

In Lineberger's Pinhook mill (1852) near present-day McAdenville, a ten-year-old boy named George Gray found work as a floor sweeper in 1861. He had no plantation upbringing like Tompkins, but seems to have shared most of the pioneer's other traits. Gray rose fast, and by nineteen was assistant superintendent. Nine years later he was charged with equipping and starting Charlotte's first cotton mill, and ten years after that, he became a principal in Gastonia's premier textile manufacturer. The boy who

Both Washington Duke's mansion, "Fairview," and his second tobacco manufacturing plant, erected in 1885, replaced simple frame structures. Neither of these buildings still stands, but the Main and Peabody Street locale has become a busy part of downtown Durham. Courtesy, N.C. Collection, UNC Library, Chapel Hill

Washington Duke stands outside the door of the first Duke of Durham tobacco factory, a log shed on his Durham County farm. Courtesy, N.C. Division of Archives & History

started out earning ten cents for a fourteen-hour day came to organize nine of the first mills in Gastonia alone.

But, of course, the vast majority of those who started like George Gray never were anything but mill hands. Farmers for whom the economic disaster continued long after the war's end flocked to places like Gastonia. A year's worth of long, hard labor earned a man $254 in 1890; his wife, $159; their child, $90. These meager wages were sometimes supplemented by various benefits. Many mill owners, for example, provided free or subsidized housing; cared for the sick and injured; and built schools and churches. As industrialization grew increasingly sophisticated, however, the rising pressures on managers eroded this paternalism, and workers who had been grateful for deliverance from failing farms gradually became more and more disgruntled. The plight of mill workers will be discussed at length in later chapters.

It was the textile movement's success and the jump-start that made the newspapers ecstatic over its prospects. *The News and Observer* of November 28, 1895 was not the place to look for a discouraging word. The "Cotton Mill Edition" gushed column after column of long, glowing articles on every prominent mill, mill builder, and nuance of the trade. One page featured "Facts And Fancies About Cotton Mill Bachelors," and addressed the ladies: "If they should conclude to take advantage of their right during Leap Year, and, arming themselves with Cupid's bow and arrow, go husband-hunting, they will wish to know where the best game can be found." The publication date—Thanksgiving Day—was no coincidence. North Carolina's textile industry was on its way to prominence.

So was tobacco manufacturing. Virginia still dominated the industry in 1885, but for ten years the small North Carolina factories had been gaining. The simple processes of making smoking and chewing tobacco had not required nearly the capital or skilled labor demanded in textile manufacture, and thus had developed more primitively, never enjoying the rousing newspaper editorials or the rallying cries of orators. What the industry could be sure of was local markets, since its product was immediately ready for sale to consumers. That fact wasn't lost on men like Washington Duke and his ambitious son Buck.

Broke except for a fifty-cent piece when released from a Civil War prison, Washington Duke walked the 120 miles from New Bern to his farm near Durham. There he found his three sons, two blind mules, one old wagon, and a farm in looted ruins. Not the stuff of an industrial empire—or was it?

Father and sons declared a small log barn their factory, and set about beating, sifting, and packing "Pro Bono Publico" ("for the public good") smoking tobacco. Dukes, mules, and wagon began peddling this product all over the state, and success came quicker than the family could have imagined. These budding entrepreneurs processed 15,000 pounds in the first year, and by 1874 they had built a three-story factory in Durham.

It was the youngest son, James Buchanan, better known as Buck, who recognized that the Dukes weren't gaining on the well-established Bull Durham tobacco of John Green, W.T. Blackwell, and Julian Carr. Cigarette manufac-

turing had been limited to New York and Richmond, and in 1881 Buck Duke decided to bring it to Durham. In order to achieve his goals, he hired Russian Jews who knew the art of cigarette rolling.

Buck's first bold move came two years after he started production. Congress reduced a heavy tax on tobacco products, but Duke didn't even wait for it to take effect before he cut his price from ten cents a pack to five; he suddenly had the cheapest cigarettes on the market, and business soared. Duke's adoption and perfection of the Bonsack rolling machine in 1884 understandably upset the hired rollers, yet he was able to multiply by fifty the output of the hottest item on the market. Soon the tobacco magnate was off to New York to astonish and later conquer the big boys of cigarette production.

While the Duke and the Bull Durham factories were bringing growth to Durham, the manufacture of chewing plugs was taking off in Winston. Hamilton Scales started the first plug plant in 1870, but it was a couple of tobacco peddlers, P.H. Hanes and R.J. Reynolds, who would make the town famous. Both built chewing tobacco empires—Hanes was the giant at first, but by 1900 he was ready to sell out to Reynolds and switch to textiles, where his name became synonymous with men's underwear.

Meanwhile J.E. Liggett and George Myers were helping to establish St. Louis as a plug manufacturing center and Pierre Lorillard was building a snuff business in New York City. Their names would be prominent in the twentieth-century North Carolina tobacco industry.

From the backroads peddler's wagon to the New York advertising offices, the early tobacco industry was as colorful as it was bitterly competitive. Salesmen would load a large wagon and hit the road for a month at a time, taking their food with them and camping along the way to

Richard Joshua Reynolds, pictured here with family members, began manufacturing chewing tobacco in 1875. The R.J. Reynolds Tobacco Company of Winston-Salem became famous for products like Prince Albert pipe tobacco and Camel cigarettes. Courtesy, Reynolda House, Inc.

Wagons and horses crowded the cobblestone streets of Winston-Salem during the 1890's, particularly at the height of tobacco-selling season. Courtesy, R.J. Reynolds Tobacco Company

keep expenses down. The shrewd R.J. Reynolds was a wizard of barter. When the tobacco was gone, he was known to deal horses, bridles, and wagon; if the price was right, he returned home on foot. Manufacturers weren't fond of the federal revenue tax, and the peddlers spent a lot of their time dodging agents who hadn't discovered the tax-evasive tobacco before it left the factory.

Tobacco advertising and gimmickery reflected the fierce competition among hundreds of different brands. Buck Duke placed celebrities' photographs in his cigarette packs, and he was

the first to give coupons redeemable for gifts. His liberal use of billboards, theater programs, and newspaper space also contributed to the rise of big-time advertising by other businesses.

No campaign was more imaginative than Carr's Bull Durham gimmicks. He had four teams of painters who made the bull famous on huge signs all over the countryside, sometimes drawing the attention of art critics. In typical fashion, Carr once provided thirteen four-horse wagons, all emblazoned with the bull, to haul convention guests from Durham to the University of North Carolina commencement exercises

James B. Duke threw lavish parties to celebrate his business triumphs. On the front of a fancy banquet menu, Duke proclaimed the closing of a British-American tobacco deal. Courtesy, N.C. Division of Archives & History

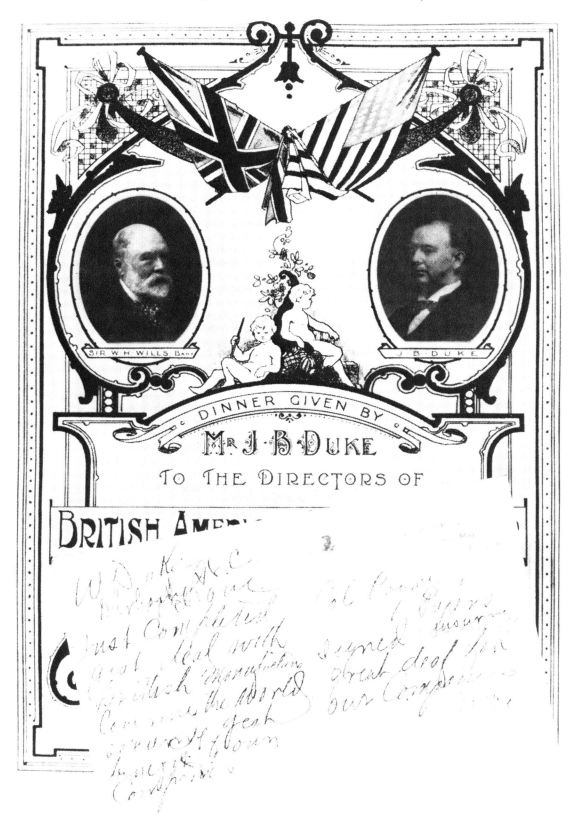

This pair of parlor rockers, with their characteristic carved hand grips, are products of Thomas Day, a free black cabinetmaker from Milton. He sold directly to customers and other retail merchants, made custom furniture and coffins, *and did interior carpentry from the 1820s through the 1850s. Day's business grew to be one of the largest of its type in the state, and today his pieces fetch handsome prices. Courtesy, N.C. Division of Archives & History*

and later to a barbecue sponsored by his company. A newspaper account added: "Near Chapel Hill the procession was met by the Salem Cornet Band, which accompanied the procession making music, each person smoking the 'Bull' brand of tobacco in long-stemmed pipes."

Commercial brand names showed the same sort of imagination. While smokers enjoyed Richmond Gems, Opera Puffs, Pin Heads, Old Rips, and Vanity Fairs, chewers chose from among Rebel Girl, Georgia Home, Molly Cotton Tail, and Honey Dew.

Competition among the big cigarette makers

proved to be of a more serious nature, and by 1890 the time was ripe for a monopoly that could grow and absorb the smaller manufacturers. Buck Duke formed the American Tobacco Company from the five corporations which had controlled 95 percent of the cigarette industry. Cigarette-making in North Carolina soon stopped, however, as it was better suited to the more mechanized northeastern factories. Duke's home companies then concentrated on smoking and chewing tobacco. Smaller North Carolina producers, like those everywhere, either joined this most successful of trusts or shut down. By

1904 the conglomeration had complete control of the U.S. tobacco industry, with 150 companies under its umbrella. The American Tobacco Company, formed in the very year that the Sherman Anti-Trust Act was passed, finally was broken up by the Supreme Court in 1911.

A lot of North Carolinians got rich off the early tobacco industry and a lot of the money was spread around the state in the form of capital for textile mills and other industries. Numerous philanthropic causes, notably those of Duke and Reynolds, also flourished, with many hospitals and schools statewide owing their existence to the golden leaf. Washington Duke and Julian Carr led the move of Trinity College from Randolph County to Durham, and Buck Duke later left forty million dollars to the university that adopted his name.

While Daniel Tompkins was showing the way for mill builders and Buck Duke was pondering a tobacco monopoly, the state's third major industry was beginning to bring the craft of the traveling cabinetmaker uptown. Commercial prosperity was almost a sure bet for the place where the North Carolina Railroad intersected with the Fayetteville and Western Plank Road. Being the highest point of elevation on the train line, natural drainage guarded it against malaria and gave it a reputation as somewhat of a health resort.

That is why a Vermonter, "Captain" W.H. Snow, settled in High Point in 1871. Snow began making shuttle blocks and bobbins for New England textile mills from North Carolina trees, and his work over the next thirty years kindled others' awareness of the possibilities to be found in the untapped stands of white oak, yellow poplar, and other Piedmont and lower Blue Ridge hardwoods.

With small furniture operations already underway in Thomasville, Salem, Charlotte, and Archdale, the area possessed a pool of skilled woodworkers. Completion of the High Point-Randleman-Asheboro Railroad and the extension of the Southern Railroad System further opened up the forested lands, and among a growing population were the decendants of settlers who had made their own furniture. These late nineteenth-century North Carolin-

Currently a state transportation museum, Spencer Shops opened in 1896 to serve as the central repair facility for J.P. Morgan's Southern Railway. In the 1930s workmen refurbished this antique train, "The Best Friend of Charleston." Courtesy, N.C. Division of Archives & History

Commerce in Mt. Airy during the 1890s was bustling, and covered wagons brought the country folk to town for a day of trading and socializing. Courtesy, N.C. Collection, UNC Library, Chapel Hill

ians wanted someone else to make their tables, chairs, and beds—and make them cheap.

Snow's son, E.A. Snow, started a lumber company in 1881. It wasn't long before he realized the wood he was selling elsewhere could be made into finished products right at home. Snow teamed with two local merchants, John Tate and Thomas Wrenn, to start the High Point Furniture Company in 1889. The company's immediate success in making simple beds, dressers and washstands—and selling a lot of them for under five dollars—sparked optimism in the fast-growing town. Not only did the

three founders quickly form new companies, but High Point seemed to catch a drop-everything-and-go-make-furniture fever. Four physicians even left their profession to join the new industry.

Of some forty-four furniture factories built in the state in the 1890s, twelve were in High Point. By the turn of the century, the boomtown of 6,000 people was the furniture capital of the South. Neighboring Thomasville, too, was well on its way to achieving similar distinction in chairmaking. The fever also spread into the foothills and little towns throughout the Pied-

A high school band visited Spencer Shops in 1952 as part of the Rowan County bicentennial celebration. The shops serviced trains until 1960. Courtesy, N.C. Division of Archives & History

mont, but, unlike textiles and tobacco, the North Carolina furniture industry would not become truly national until the 1920s.

High Point is a perfect example of what the expansion of railroads meant to the state's manufacturing sectors. North Carolina discontinued aid to railroads in 1870, leaving big building to private investors, many of them northern capitalists. At the same time, numerous small companies consolidated into a few major rail systems.

Before 1880 train lines were built from Charlotte to Shelby and to within seven miles of Asheville. By 1900 there were new lines from Raleigh to Hamlet and from Monroe to Atlanta. Consolidations by the Atlantic Coast Line in the East, the Southern Railway System in the Piedmont, and the Seaboard Airline Railway between them completed crucial north-south connections to other states. Railroad mileage more than doubled in the 1880s, and in 1900 the state claimed 3,831 miles of track. The physical patterns of North Carolina's future economic development were pretty well laid out along the routes and at the depots of the railroads by this time.

Most of the state's 1.9 million people still lived outside the towns at the turn of the century, but the urban percentage had risen from 3.9 in 1880 to 9.8 in 1900. The snail's pace of urban growth manifested itself in the small number of towns with a population over 10,000. After twenty years of industrial development, only six such cities existed: Wilmington, Charlotte, Asheville, Winston, Raleigh, and Greensboro.

The collapse of the Confederate currency system wiped out the state's infant banks, and for several years afterward the finance structure was not far removed from that of a colonial economy. Very little money circulated, and barter still was the most common means of exchange.

By 1870, however, the beginnings of a new banking system were in place with six national, three state-chartered and several private institutions in operation. Farmers could not yet rely on the banks—crop loans were too dangerous— and their collective efforts to organize their own lending institutions were unsuccessful. Thus, they continued to turn to the merchant and his often-excessive interest rates for financing. It has been shown that industrial development capital came from the North and from those natives fortunate enough to be insulated from the Reconstruction disaster—the banks were in no shape to help. The most positive thing that can be said about banking before 1900 is that by that year, the foundation for the permanent system had been laid: 120 banks held thirty-three million dollars in resources.

Hard times were over for a while. North Carolina finally had begun to exploit her assets, and the manufacture of three things that sprung from the soil—cotton, tobacco, and trees—was pushing her toward the industrial leadership of the South. Ahead lay a long period of improvement, expansion, and prosperity.

3

GOOD ROADS
AND CHEAP LABOR

By the turn of the century, tobacco manufacturing employed many men and women at the Reynolds Company in Winston-Salem. Courtesy, R.J. Reynolds Tobacco Company

It has been said that the reason Sherman's army did comparatively little damage to North Carolina was that the roads were so bad he couldn't get through.

That was a joke, perhaps, but there was nothing funny about the condition of the state's travel and shipping arteries at the turn of the century. While the commercial momentum of the 1880s and 1890s promised great things, the muddy, rutted paths between the growing towns served as a strong symbol of backwardness. The about-face in that condition during the 1920s shows how the state took advantage of good times to make life easier for the farmers and others who couldn't use the trains, and built a solid foundation for the days when the railroads would decline.

It also has been said that North Carolina's industries are the least unionized and lowest paying, no joke to thousands of mill workers who helped push the state to the manufacturing leadership of the South. Industry grew and matured in the first three decades of the new century; the economic sparks shone in good schools and smooth highways that benefited everybody. But the machine operators for the most part did not prosper, and as industry succeeded they failed to win any but the barest reforms in their meager wages and sometimes hazardous conditions.

In the sense that the nation as a whole would flourish during the first quarter of the century, it was a make-or-break time for a state in a region which traditionally had resisted change. North Carolina counted 1,111 miles of macadamized roads in 1914, 592 of which were surfaced with gravel and 4,313 miles, with sand-clay. It takes but a glimpse at the map to see that this left the vast majority of the roads untreated. The federal government's push for the Rural Free Delivery mail system found farmers eager for the service, but handicapped by roads and bridges too poor to support improved communications. The offer of mail service was no small spur to the farmers' interest in better transportation routes. It also had cooled their hatred of taxes by the time the "good roads train" steamed through Winston, Asheville, and

"Stuck!" is the title for this 1909 picture, taken in rural Johnston County. The vehicle belongs to the "U.S. Office of Public Roads and American Highway Association." Courtesy, N.C. Division of Archives & History

Raleigh, stopping in each town for the construction of a few hundred feet of demonstration macadamized roadway.

Behind the train came Joseph Austin Holmes and Joseph Hyde Pratt, successive heads of the state Geological Survey who encouraged county bond issuers to finance roads. In November 1913 Governor Locke Craig proclaimed two holidays and asked the able bodied to spend them working on these new thoroughfares.

Leaving road-building to the counties proved a mistake, since politics often overruled practicality in location and maintenance was ne-

This boy joined the campaign for good roads during 1914, while marooned in the mud on Franklin Street across from the University of North Carolina. Courtesy, N.C. Collection, UNC Library, Chapel Hill

glected. By the time Cameron Morrison became governor in 1921—and devoted half his inaugural speech to roads—it was clear the state should take the lead.

This was an era of unbridled prosperity. Roads advocates weren't shy about begging bond issues as high as $200 million, but they settled for one-quarter of that amount. By 1929, 3,694 miles of paved, 2,205 miles of graded, and 868 miles of oil-treated roads constituted the state system, not counting those in the counties.

Besides the obvious farm-to-market improvement, the northeastern corner of the state (which

because of established transportation routes, had been more Virginian than North Carolinian) was brought into the fold. Tar Heels then were left to debate who truly was the "Good Roads Governor," Locke Craig for his moral support or Cam Morrison for his buildup of the Highway Commission.

Fewer and fewer of the roads led to textile mills: as the industry came of age, it began to centralize, particularly in Gaston, Alamance, and Guilford counties. The mill builders gravitated to the sources of hydro-electric power; success drew capital to an area, encouraging spinoff industries which supplied auxiliary raw materials and serviced machinery. When one mill became known for a particular product, others flocked to the locale—the manufacturing of denim flourished in Greensboro, damask in Roanoke Rapids, combed yarns in Gaston, towels in Kannapolis, underwear in Winston-Salem, hosiery in High Point. Industry was important to all those towns, and it even created some of them.

A Mecklenburg County farm boy, James William Cannon showed the kind of industriousness that led his parents to send him to Charlotte as a merchant's apprentice; he then

Prison labor did much of North Carolina's highway work and maintenance. Here a Wake County crew lined up outside of these mobile prisons in 1919. Courtesy, N.C. Division of Archives & History

went to his brother's business in Concord shortly after the Civil War. As the store's cotton buyer, Cannon sent raw material to the North for processing and noticed high shipping costs tacked onto the finished product when it came back. Like so many other textile pioneers, he figured he could do the whole job less expensively right at home.

What separated Cannon from many others was his eye for a product nobody else was manufacturing. After a few years of making cloth in the Cannon Manufacturing Company, which he started in 1888, he decided that the people who couldn't afford linen towels needed something to dry off with, too. Cannon began producing towels in 1894. He had mills in six towns by the early 1900s, but envisioned something bigger—a model textile city. Cannon commenced buying up wornout farmland some seven miles north of Concord, and between 1905 and 1910 he literally laid out a new town. From the wealth of textiles, Kannapolis—sometimes called Towel Town—grew like a weed. By the mid-1980s, it was one of the largest unincorporated towns in the country and the world's top producer of household textiles.

Moses and Caesar Cone grew up in their father's grocery store and later founded a cotton goods business in New York City. They, too, saw a gap in the market: durable work clothes. The brothers bought several hundred acres of land on the outskirts of Greensboro, and in 1895-96 built Proximity Mills—named for its proximity to the cotton fields. The business they founded became one of the world's largest makers of denim and corduroy, and the Cones' philanthropy spread throughout Greensboro, the state's second-largest city.

Although not at the hand of one individual, Gaston County grew mills as fast as other counties grew cotton. Like Cannon and the Cones, the builders were men who got started in the late nineteenth century but made their marks in the twentieth. R.L. Stowe, C.B. Armstrong, and A.C. Lineberger either constructed or headed some forty mills; in addition, they were bankers, merchants, and builders of Gastonia and Belmont. From thirty mills in 1904, Gaston counted

As the Labor Defender *declared in 1929, union leaders had high hopes of organizing workers to assert their power over textile bosses. Courtesy, N.C. Division of Archives & History*

ninety-seven in 1927—more factories and more active spindles than any other county in the nation.

In Winston-Salem, brothers John Wesley and P.H. Hanes made their name synonymous with women's hosiery and men's underwear. Two future giants got their start late in the period. After the discovery of the first man-made fiber, rayon, a Dutch group built the American Enka Corporation in 1928. They then proceeded to establish the unincorporated town of Enka near Asheville. In 1923 James Spencer Love adopted the name of the Alamance County town of Bur-

lington for his mill, which grew into the world's largest textile manufacturer, Burlington Industries.

In the years between the turn of the century and the Great Depression, accumulating capital was not the problem it previously had been, largely due to the success of the 1880-1900 mills. Capital also spun off the highly successful tobacco and furniture industries. When outside help was needed, northerners proved more willing to invest in the increasingly prosperous South. The movement of northern mills to North Carolina, however, is a more recent phenomenon: by the early 1930s, only 6 percent of the spindles and 3.7 percent of the looms in the state belonged to northern companies or southern branches of northern mills.

A trend toward larger plants increased efficiency: the average number of spindles per mill more than doubled between 1899 and 1927. The factories began finishing more of their own goods, rather than sending them to northern mills. They also started to make finer grades of yarns, and gradually displaced New England in the manufacture of high quality fabrics.

But other trends in the industry were disturbing. Increased demand for textiles during the World War I years led to big expansions, and the resulting overproduction created surpluses that cut into profits after the war. As the buying public grew more whimsical, styles changed so fast that many mills fluctuated wildly between overproduction and underproduction.

Lewis W. Hine traveled around North Carolina in 1908 documenting child labor with his camera. This publicity helped to get new restrictive laws passed. Typically, girls may have started working in the Gastonia mills as early as age eight. Courtesy, Lunn, Ltd., Washington, D.C.

And creeping over the horizon was the spectre of competition from Japan, Britain, and India.

By 1927 there were 579 textile mills in North Carolina and 170,000 people working in them. Factories became a formidable force in the life of the state, especially since many mill owners also were prominent town builders. These businessmen, as well as some outside the textile industry who skeptically looked upon their benevolence, waged a steady campaign to influence the public perception of the industry and the lives of its workers. In a textile-happy state, the owners usually prevailed.

Mill owners and managers literally proclaimed themselves saviors of a destitute people. When asked by a sociologist what his factory made, one owner said, "We make American citizens, and run a cotton mill to pay the expenses." Textile executives got unflinching support from the preachers to whom their intensely religious employees flocked. Another owner commented, "Belonging to a church, and attending it, make a man a better worker. It makes him more complacent—no, that's not the word. It makes him more resigned—that's not the word either, but you get the general idea . . . We think the churches are vital to our community and our mill."

If special editions of the *Charlotte Observer* in 1919, 1928, and 1930 were to be believed, the mills were a godsend and their employees, among the happiest and most thriving people on earth.

Much the same as it had done in 1895, the *Observer's* 1919 "Cotton Mill Progress" edition heaped praise on the owners for the "clean," "healthy," and "harmonious" conditions of the factory villages, in which some 70 percent of the state's textile workers lived. "Wherever a cotton mill has reared its walls to the heavens," the paper said, "there has come as quick accompaniment a good school and churches." That was quite true, and to the list could be added simple but rent-free or subsidized houses with garden plots; mill-provided seeds; heating fuel at cost; spacious recreational areas; hospitals; and even libraries.

Other things, too, could be and often were said about the workers. The jobs at which they toiled six long days a week were extremely monotonous, and their wages such that they had no choice but to spend their leisure time in mill facilities. For many who inhaled cotton dust hour after hour, shortness of breath was a way of life—very soon after 1900, health inspectors already were agreeing that mill workers were more susceptible to disease than the general population. In 1923 a government investigator described one plant this way:

. . . the lint was exceedingly bad. A blowpipe was used to clean the machines. The women also used it on themselves before going out to lunch. The hair of one woman who had no head covering was white with lint. Much coughing was necessary among the employees.

Besides cotton dust, the workers faced radical temperature and humidity changes between the factory and the outside. Poor lighting and constant noise also played havoc on the nervous system. The majority of the employees in the spinning and weaving rooms were women, and youth under sixteen comprised a large part of the work force before the advent of child labor laws.

Outside the mill in the villages, pleasant living does not appear to have been the status quo. Though many mill owners made an effort to improve the bad habits which their workers brought with them from the farms, sanitation generally was not good. In a 1926 survey of 322 villages, the devoted student of mill life, Harriet Herring, found fifteen with lights, baths, and sewerage; ninety-seven with lights, running water, and inside toilets; thirty-nine with lights and running water; ninety-five with lights but no other conveniences; and ten with no lights and no sanitary facilities.

The textile mills regularly employed children on long shifts at low wages. Parents and their offspring were forced to agree, according to one manufacturer, "to perform work in a faithful and satisfactory manner" and to do nothing "mean" or "insubordinate" unless they wanted to be discharged with a five-dollar fine for "damages." Courtesy, N.C. Division of Archives & History

Lewis W. Hine captures the mood of this young Lancaster, North Carolina worker. Courtesy, The Ackland Art Museum, UNC, Chapel Hill

Mill-provided schools proved much more the rule than the exception, but many managers were free to draft entire student bodies for labor during high-production periods. Dropout and absentee rates among factory children escalated above the norm, and many of these youngsters knew they were destined for lives in the mills.

Some owners were little more than slave drivers who justified their dictatorial methods by pointing to the good things the mills' wealth poured into their towns; on the other hand, many operators offered elaborate welfare departments which provided everything from plow-hands for the workers' garden plots to uniforms for their baseball teams. Whatever their attitudes, the owners took comfort in the fact that however squalid their employees' lifestyles, they were better off than they had been on the farm.

That was fine for the first generation of workers, who had never fathomed a weekly paycheck and didn't even know how to spend it, but their heirs were not as easily pacified. Their unhappiness with factory conditions found sympathy in the labor unions.

Efforts of the Knights of Labor had flickered and died in the state in the 1800s, and strikes promoted by the American Federation of Labor around 1900 failed similarly—the owners played on the unions' weaknesses by simply evicting and refusing to rehire striking workers. More successful strikes in Charlotte and Concord in 1919 boosted union membership in mills everywhere, but temporary concessions usually satisfied workers who still did not see unions as permanent solutions to their problems.

Wage and hour reductions after the 1920 business depression brought on more strikes, which sparked the career of one of the era's most incendiary anti-union voices, *Southern Textile Bulletin* editor David Clark. By repeatedly portraying labor organizers as communist parasites (in many cases they were openly affiliated with the Communist Party and appeared more interested in general violent overthrow than in the workers' problems), Clark helped whip up a frenzy that less than ten years later would explode in one of the most tragic labor episodes in the nation's history.

After 1923, while the southern mills continued to make money, New England textile manufacture started to fail. Anxiously avoiding the same fate (several who investigated the workers' conditions claimed the industry actually was teetering on the brink of failure), southern owners employed elaborate efficiency schemes that usually involved bigger workloads. During a time of major additions of spindles and looms, there emerged a phenomenon known as the "stretch-out," in which the same number of workers was responsible for more machines—an effort to speed up production.

In April of 1929, after two years of this frenzied pace, the Loray tire cord mill in Gastonia had reached the boiling point. Employees had run the conservative United Textile Workers Union out of the plant eight years before, but this time they were too fed up to say no to the National Textile Workers Union, despite its communist ties.

When five union organizers were fired, some 1,800 of their peers walked out. The owners imported replacements and reopened—they saw the strike as the incubator of a revolution. The *Gastonia Gazette,* which earlier had called for

The late twenties and thirties saw a lot of union organizing. In the midst of the Depression, leaders hoped that the workers would unite for better wages, hours, and conditions. Courtesy, N.C. Division of Archives & History

CAROLINA TEXTILE BOSSES GET IN THE WAY OF THE "AWAKENING GIANT" THE WORKING CLASS OF THE NEW SOUTH

The R.J. Reynolds Tobacco Company headquarters in downtown Winston-Salem served as a prototype for the Empire State Building. Courtesy, R.J. Reynolds Tobacco Company

mediation between owners and workers, began fanning the flames, warning that the "Russianized Reds" had no real interest in the workers' problems. State militia men were sent in and took a decidedly anti-striker position; tension and mob rule gripped the town for the next six months, although the strike itself had lasted little more than two weeks.

When it was over, Police Chief O.F. Aderholt had been shot dead in a police-striker confrontation and seven men served long prison sentences for his murder. In the hysteria that followed, striker Ella May Wiggins was similarly killed, but the seven men who were arrested went away unindicted and 14 others were acquitted by a grand jury.

This episode and a major strike in Marion inspired a surge in union organizing. However, the power of the owners and the workers' inability to coalesce behind this method of problem solving doomed the North Carolina labor movement to failure.

Not least among the owners' arsenal was a heavy hand in the state legislature. When the child labor issue first arose, the lawmakers proposed stiff new regulations but gave in to weaker industry compromises; finally hammering out tough restrictions, they neglected enforcement. At minimum, legislators laid the groundwork for later reform by establishing the Child Welfare Commission, the Workmen's Compensation Act, and the Industrial Commission. Yet, it was clear that the textile mill owner held as much sway politically as economically.

Tobacco manufacturers were on pedestals of their own, and when the U.S. Supreme Court finally chipped Buck Duke's empire out from under him, he was barely fazed.

The tobacco trust had folded its wings around the export market for smoking and chewing tobacco by the time Teddy Roosevelt initiated court action in 1907. At times it seemed the whole world was angry with the trust. Farmers blamed low prices on its dictatorial powers; middlemen were driven out when it started buying directly from farmers; the unions lamented its open shop practices; and competing manufacturers indicted it in their demise.

The trust did not, of course, spare the three firms that later would join Duke's American Tobacco Company as the prominent North Carolina (and national) manufacturers. P. Lorillard was bought out, but its founder was allowed to retain a separate corporate structure. Liggett and Myers became part of a sister organization to the trust, the Continental Tobacco Company. Reynolds was reorganized; however, R.J. stayed as independent as possible, sticking to his own brands and keeping trust people off his board of directors. He continually ruffled trust feathers, for example, with his introduction of the hugely successful Prince Albert smoking tobacco.

When the end finally came in 1911, Duke—wouldn't you know it—ironed out much of the breakup arrangement himself. Everybody from Roosevelt to the independent manufacturers called the settlement a sham: of sixteen successor companies, the four aforementioned still were perceived as big enough to control the business.

As an epilogue, Duke always insisted the trust was for the general good of the industry and that with his business sense, he would have pretty much controlled things even without it.

"I don't know that the combine was really of much advantage to us after all," he said. "We were doing well as we were; we were beating the other fellows in manufacturing and selling anyway."

After the breakup, Reynolds was left out of the cigarette business. Liggett and Myers, which incorporated in North Carolina in 1911, produced its famous Fatimas; American, its Omars; P. Lorillard (before locating in Greensboro in 1956), its Zubeldas. Then in 1913 Reynolds came on like a whirlwind with a blend of domestic and the increasingly popular Turkish tobaccos that made Camels (the cigarette and the advertising symbol) famous. And the imaginative competition continued—in the late 1920s a successor of Duke enraged the candy industry with his slogan for Lucky Strikes, "Reach for a Lucky instead of a Sweet"; Liggett and Myers dropped Chesterfields on potential South Carolina customers from an airplane in 1920.

Between 1900 and 1920, North Carolina rose from seventh to first in the manufacture of tobacco products. By 1923 she was producing half the country's cigarettes and about a third of its smoking tobacco. The industry's value shot from $14.6 million in 1899 to $259 million twenty years later.

In the furniture industry, High Point's takeoff during the last decade of the nineteenth century sparked a wildfire of manufacturing throughout the entire Piedmont. Three-fourths of the early plants were built in a "furniture corridor" between Durham and Asheville, and between 1900 and 1910 the number of factories in the state multiplied by five. Thomasville turned out 1,500 chairs a day by 1907; Lexington claimed five plants by 1903; and Winston had twelve by 1910.

With the lure of the great forests and the railroad's western push in the 1890s, some of the biggest operations sprouted in the foothills towns of Hickory, Lenoir, Morganton, and Drexel. And High Point didn't exactly hit a lull—thirty-three plants in 1900 had expanded to 107 by 1914.

But the rapid growth inevitably produced cutthroat competition, and soon after the turn of the century, the North Carolina industry faced the very real possibility of collapse in the face of more experienced northern and midwestern companies. One problem was the cheapness of the product. Manufacturers and salesmen outside the state ridiculed Tar Heel furniture producers for their $1.50-beds and fifty-cent tables. The *Southern Furniture Journal* leaped to the defense, saying that common folks needed furniture just as badly as the rich, and that because of the new southern manufacturers, the former had better-attired homes.

North Carolina plants began to look beyond the state's borders to a national market, and in the tradition of the tobacco peddlers, they turned to slogans like the "Blue Blazes Line,"

For many years the High Point area has been known for furniture manufacturing. The man pictured here hand-finished this bedstead. Courtesy, N.C. Division of Archives & History

Traditional tobacco cultivation required lots of hand la-
bor. Workers first harvested the most mature leaves from
the bottoms of the stalks. A mule patiently waited to haul

the load. Courtesy, N.C. Collection, UNC Library,
Chapel Hill

the "Red Hot Line," and the "Smokey Mountain
Line" of furniture. The industry also adopted
the practice of vending disassembled parts to
agents outside the state who then put them together and sold them.

A major change came in 1921 in High Point.
There had been some crude display marketing
of locally-made furniture in the factories themselves or downtown buildings—wherever the
producers could find vacant space. A successful
glass manufacturer and furniture salesman named
Charles Long had bigger dreams, and he convinced other southern manufacturers of High

Point's obvious advantages. In June 1921 the ten-
story Southern Furniture Exposition Building,
at the time the world's largest commercial structure devoted to furniture marketing, was ready
for business.

The very first national show lasted two weeks
and was a huge success. In succeeding years the
buyers and sellers turned down the offers of
bigger southern cities and continued to flock
four times a year to the center of the industry.
By 1925 the Durham-to-Asheville corridor was
the nation's biggest producer of wooden furniture.

Right through the hard times of the 1930s, North Carolina farmers maintained their tobacco production. Growers applied poison to keep off pests. Courtesy, N.C. Collection, UNC Library, Chapel Hill

North Carolina's wealth mounted as her industries thrived, but the prosperity did not extend to the thousands who made their living from the land. Despite the exodus to the towns and factories, 51 percent of the population in 1928 still consisted of farmers, and theirs was not a happy lot.

As prices fell, they railed against the tobacco trust. Farmers also continued to have trouble getting credit, which was so dear to their way of life. The people who ran the economy seemed insensitive to the bad things that happened to farmers when prices fluctuated. Like the mill workers, they became more militant—the North Carolina Farmers' Union grew from 1,000 members in 1908 to 25,000 three years later—but significant reforms only came with the New Deal.

The real tragedy of the period was tenancy, the natural result of the demise of the plantation system in poor rural areas. The number of farmers who were tenants hovered between 40 and 50 percent of the total farm population. A credit system in which they paid up to 22 percent more for supplies virtually ensured poverty; the size, and thus the efficiency, of farms decreased steadily; and whatever wealth they generated seemed to slip away.

Peanuts emerged to join tobacco, cotton, and hay as the major agricultural products of the early twentieth century. In 1920 the golden leaf surpassed cotton as the leading cash crop.

World War I did not have the far-reaching impact on the state that one might expect from such a global turning point, but it surely exerted influence around the factories. Production for the war effort, a sharp increase in cotton prices, and a rising domestic demand for cotton products that coincided with the military involvement accelerated the construction of new textile mills and the expansion of existing ones. Wartime significantly boosted the use of tobacco, as it always seems to do, by the boys overseas and those tending the home fires. The war helped break down the prejudices against smoking, and the disruption of trade with the Near East diminished the popularity of Turkish cigarettes and solidified the market for North Carolina blends. In April 1918 the government

Corporate officers met in 1911 at the home office of the North Carolina Mutual and Provident Association, forerunner of North Carolina Mutual Life Insurance Company. Seated around the desk, from left to right, were A.M. Moore, secretary-treasurer; John M. Avery, assistant manager; John Merrick, president; Ed Merrick, administrative assistant; and C.C. Spaulding, general manager. Courtesy, North Carolina Mutual Life Insurance Company

Carolina Power & Light, one of the state's major electrical suppliers, began its first operations at "Buckhorn," a Chatham County plant. Courtesy, N.C. Collection, UNC Library, Chapel Hill

bought all of the Bull Durham factory's output for shipment to the doughboys.

Other areas suffered as available money went to liberty bonds and available men went to battle—road building, for instance, came to a halt during the war.

The growth of manufacturing predictably meant a boom in banking. Numbers tell much of the story—in 1900 there were 129 banks with thirty-three million dollars in resources; twenty-eight years later there were 512 banks with $507 million available. Most powerful among financial institutions of the first quarter of the century were the First Union National of Charlotte and the Wachovia Bank and Trust Company of Winston. The latter was founded by textile magnate Francis Fries in 1879, and after a 1911 merger it adopted the name of the industrious Moravian settlement. Another major merger in 1930 left Wachovia the largest bank between Washington and Atlanta. All was not so rosy for the small-time banks during this period, however. For one thing, they faced the continuing dilemma of putting their resources into high-risk farm loans or alienating themselves from their communities by refusing to help the farmer. The laws made it easy to establish banks and many people started them just for personal profit, creating damaging competition. Of the 124 lending houses that failed during the period, almost all were in the smaller towns.

The insurance companies, which expanded with the growth of personal wealth, all had come from outside the state—all except one.

John Merrick worked as a brickyard laborer and a hod carrier. Later he became a bootblack for a Raleigh barber who encouraged Merrick to join him in a new shop in Durham. The former laborer went on to own five barber shops, and got himself heavily involved in community service.

Aaron Moore had farmed with his parents in Bladen and Columbus counties, and taught school even before he went to college. Necessity pulled him back to the farm, but he eventually studied medicine at Shaw University, finished second in his class on the 1888 state medical examiners' exam, and moved to Durham.

Even the repair truck ran on electricity, helping to promote the Carolina Power & Light Company's slogan, "Do It Electrically." Courtesy, N.C. Division of Archives & History

The two, along with others they had met through fraternal organizations, in 1898 formed the North Carolina Mutual and Provident Association to provide for "the relief of the widows and orphans, of the sick and those injured by accident, and the burial of the dead." Merrick, Moore, and the latter's nephew, Charles Clinton Spaulding, did not have the advantage of hiring experts to help them get started. They operated by the seats of their pants and the belief in their cause; during the first few months they paid $78.56 in claims from the $672.45 their fourteen part-time agents had collected in premiums.

The company's founders and its agents were black, and everywhere they went they faced the prevailing attitude that blacks couldn't make it in organized economic ventures. But before long they reached Merrick's goal of turning their fledgling firm into one of the South's strongest industrial insurance companies. Gradually the company grew as it expanded into other states and life got better for the clientele it sought. In 1966, seasoned by a citywide festival and a visit from Vice President Hubert Humphrey, the company unveiled an eight-story headquarters building that rubbed elbows with the tobacco factories and the big banks on the Durham skyline. By 1985, the North Carolina Mutual Life Insurance Company was the nation's largest black-owned financial institution, and 99 percent of its clients were black.

The champions of another North Carolina industry have always found the going tough, too. While others build successful companies from scratch, they start every single year that way; their challenges are the capricious sea and the whims of the fishes. Though their numbers were very few before the Civil War, the commercial fishermen were getting established in the first quarter of the twentieth century.

In foul weather they built their boats, mended their nets, and cleared their harbors; in fair, they mined the deep for shad, herring, mackerel, shrimp, crabs, and menhaden. By 1927, there were an estimated 15,000 North Carolinians making their livings from commercial fishing: nine menhaden processing plants flourished and the state's total catch that year was valued at $2.6 million. Still, fishing would not become a

Southern Bell telephone operators were part of a great leap forward in business communications. Courtesy, N.C. Division of Archives & History

Jumping with activity, Raleigh's Fayetteville Street reflected the changing forms of transportation before 1920. Courtesy, N.C. Division of Archives & History

full-fledged industry until after World War II.

The spread of electric power contributed immeasurably to the industrial progress of the state and the improving lifestyles of its people, and in the early 1900s the power companies became big industries themselves. The Southern Power Company was formed in 1904. From ten hydroelectric plants on the Catawba River, it grew to serve the Piedmont and the heavy factory sections, later becoming Duke Power Company in commemoration of its famous founder. Carolina Power and Light Company, meanwhile, was taking over failing local power plants and electrifying eastern North Carolina and the Asheville area.

One name stands out in the retail trade that catered to and thrived with the towns. In 1888 a Monroe merchant's apprentice named William Henry Belk scraped together money to open his own dry-goods store. By 1930 he had sixty-three department stores in five states; forty years later there would be 400 in eighteen states and Puerto Rico. The Belk stores were organized not as a chain, but in partnerships that gave each shop independent ownership.

By any count, commerce in North Carolina had come a long way in the thirty years after 1900, and the number of manufactures multiplied a dozen times. The wealth of the state grew even more. Tar Heel industry ascended to tops in the Southeast. And in the three enterprises which accounted for 75 percent of her wealth—textiles, tobacco, and furniture—she led the nation. If there was a celebration, however, not everybody felt up to it. The state still ranked among the nation's lowest in per capita wealth because the farmer and the factory worker couldn't partake of the feast. Yet those in rags were about to join the company of the rich: the Great Depression would yank the rug from under the state's improving economy.

4

FROM THE FARM
TO THE TOWN

Tobacco growing has long been lucrative for small North Carolina farmers. A postage-stamp yard between a rail fence and an old cabin was one family's crop in the 1930s. From the N.C. Collection, UNC Library, Chapel Hill

Crash! Like one of Henry Ford's shiny new cars running head-on into a concrete wall, the forward progress of nearly fifty years came to a grinding end with the fall of the stock market in 1929; other financial dominoes toppled behind it. North Carolinians who had expected to enjoy the fruits of bygone hard times instead were left to reassemble the broken pieces.

Crash! The people's growing faith in banks melted into fear of them. One by one the banks closed their doors—204 of them in four years. Crash! Cotton and tobacco prices fell down the open wells of overproduction and changing foreign markets. The mills retrenched, laying off already suffering workers.

Fortunately, North Carolina rested on the industrial base it had begun building in 1880—it was spared the utter devastation of a wholly agrarian state like Mississippi. But that was little solace to a hard-working man who had just removed the engine from his Model T to convert it to a horse-drawn "Hoover cart."

"My taxes this year is nine dollars, two more'n I made on my crop," said a Pleasant Hill farmer in 1939. His children became fond of telling their children things like that.

The experience of the Great Depression left a profound imprint on a generation of people who would be the modern-day builders of the South's industrial leader.

* * *

The shock waves from that dark day in October 1929 spread quickly and widely. Some of the banks' troubles owed to the people who had money but stopped spending it; they withdrew their savings at a rate that almost immediately dropped deposits in the state's banks by twelve million dollars. By 1933 the banks' resources had fallen a whopping 42 percent. Other problems for the banks resulted from their inability, in a weakened condition, to fight fires that had been building for some time: chronic bad management, wild land speculation in places like Asheville and Greensboro, and the automobile's role in the exodus from shaky small-town banks.

A run on deposits doomed the First National

Bank of New Bern; poor management closed the Home Savings Bank of Wilmington; the Farmers' Bank of Greenville fell to the general business slowdown. No failure was more dramatic than that of the mountain region's biggest bank, the Central Bank and Trust Company of Asheville. When the land speculation collapse rendered its promisory notes worthless, this institution collaborated with the city and county governments to keep the ensuing bankruptcy a secret for two years. The bank finally closed in 1930, setting off a chain reaction that struck down several other lending houses in the re-

gion. The mayor and the bank's president committed suicide.

Prices for all crops dropped drastically but, of course, cotton and tobacco declines were North Carolina's most acute concerns. Cotton was the victim of a worldwide oversupply, and American products were being pushed aside by better quality cotton from abroad. Also, the mills' turn to rayon and other synthetics pushed demand down. Tobacco farmers, too, simply had grown more leaf than the market could bear. More than half of the North Carolina tobacco was being shipped abroad, and these markets became extremely unreliable.

The farmers' problems didn't end there. When the big four cigarette companies all raised prices to fifteen cents a pack in 1931, the growers suspected price-fixing. Federal investigators never proved it to be the case, but they did confirm that the companies maintained suspiciously strong control over their suppliers. The purchasing prices offered by cigarette manufacturers were not only based on the crop's quality, but on the types of tobacco needed in a given year. This demand stemmed from the size and variety found in the previous seasons' stockpiles.

Succumbing to the low prices, one Yancey County man turned to carpentry, while his wife and daughters strung tobacco sacks for a Winston-Salem company: they received $1.40 for 9,000 sacks. The resignation in their words, expressed during a series of interviews in John Robinson's *Living Hard*, sounds like a summary of the era: "It just seems like us pore people can't get nowhere, no matter how hard we work ... I guess I've 'bout lived my life as far's this world goes. I've got nothin' to look forward to 'cept my children. I aim for them to have more'n I had."

It is not overstatement to say that the textile industry very nearly collapsed. Overproduction had been creeping up on the mill owners since the mid-1920s, and none of their efforts slowed it down. They didn't pay enough attention to conditions in the broader market; to keep their machines running full speed ahead was the only way they knew, even in the face of increasingly rapid changes. And the old, regressive paternalism still reared its head, as good-hearted owners, reluctant to lay off their workers, continued to operate long after they should have cut back production.

Half the mills ran at a deficit in 1929, and in 1932 three-fourths of them lost money. Stories of individual suffering on the part of the owners are few—perhaps they were too busy to complain, pinched between their own financial woes and the government's demand that they raise the wages and shorten the hours of their employees. One said the minimum wage law would up his labor costs 92 percent.

Oh, how the mill folks must have envied their neighbors in the tobacco factories! Since cigarettes were so cheap, the Depression did nothing but heighten demand for them. Inexpensive raw materials and manufacturing processes that remained fairly simple kept production costs to a minimum. Notwithstanding the dominance of the big four makers, North Carolina claimed at least one Depression-proof industry which continued to pile up profits throughout the period. In 1933, at the height of the misery, the chairman of the board of R.J. Reynolds proudly told stockholders that the company was in the best financial shape ever.

As might be imagined, new furniture was not a high-priority item for families struggling to eat. When demand for particular lines of furniture dropped, manufacturers closed all up and down the Piedmont's furniture corridor. The industry's value plumetted by one-half between 1929 and 1933.

In the slow, hopeless days of the 1930s, the

Getting the tobacco crop to market is still frequently a small family operation, just as it was when this photo was taken in 1939. From the N.C. Collection, UNC Library, Chapel Hill

Workers pack cigarettes at the R.J. Reynolds Tobacco Company. Courtesy, R.J. Reynolds Tobacco Company

cumulative effects of life on the ragged edge and the cotton mill owners' persistent use of the stretch-out pushed workers deeper into militancy. A major southern organizing drive by the American Federation of Labor in 1930 had failed miserably as the owners once again flexed their muscles, simply firing union participants and slashing wages as warnings to others who would join. Benjamin Greensboro's Cone Mills was known for calling in workers one by one, demanding that they denounce the union and dismissing them on the spot if they didn't.

Many were not intimidated. As one Cone worker told an interviewer for Tom E. Terrill's and Jerrold Hirsch's *Such As Us,*:

I came to the crossroads when I was eighteen and I took the road that led me to the mill. I came to the crossroads again when I was fifty-one and I took the road that caused me to be kicked out of the mill and onto the farm again. There's always been a question in my mind about the first choice. I've never had no doubt about the second one.

Not far down the road in High Point, temperatures in the 100s during the summer of 1932 cooked up a bizarre, spontaneous walkout. The instigators quite passively left their machines and toured the town's mills, shutting off electricity and enlisting their peers into the ranks. The movement spread to the plants of neighboring towns; by the end of one July day some 15,000 workers had effectively shut down 150 mills; the strikers partied in the streets that night.

Such parties were few and far between, however. In 1932 the textile mills and furniture factories were on two- and three-day weeks, and in the following year, the number of workers without full-time jobs approached 150,000—one fifth of the state's labor force. A fourth of the population depended on relief. Farmers and factory owners who had spent their whole lives cussing government controls now were begging for them.

The state did its part, thanks largely to a sensitive reformer who had moved into the governor's mansion in 1929. O. Max Gardner, a textile mill owner himself, was aware of the need for austerity and a redistribution of the wealth. He cut state appropriations, including its employees' salaries, and fought off the move for a sales tax by slightly raising income and corporate taxes. Through his efforts the state was able to meet its obligations.

Farmers applauded the Agricultural Adjustment Administration and the first government payments for production control. Finally they could adjust the supply of their tobacco crop to the market's demand, and begin climbing out of the grasp of the manufacturers. The government guaranteed them a minimum price, even helping them by acting as an agent for foreign buyers. And the New Deal left farmers with something for which they might otherwise have waited a long time: the Rural Electrification Authority lit up the homes of 30 percent of the farms by 1940, whereas only 3.5 percent had had power five years before.

Mill owners, too, welcomed controls, but they carefully straddled a line between out-and-out gratitude and their traditional, free enterprise conservatism. With regard to the National Industrial Recovery Act (NIRA) of 1933, they gen-

erally approved the minimum wage and hour restrictions which offered them production controls that they couldn't seem to impose on themselves. North Carolina industrialists also borrowed more than sixty million dollars from the Reconstruction Finance Corporation, ensuring business survival through disastrous 1933. (No banks in the state failed after that year.) They weren't as thrilled about the NIRA collective bargaining guarantees, and their heavy hand in the drafting of that legislation showed in the end product: little or no provision for enforcement.

Workers sensed their economic helplessness and United Textile Workers (UTW) member-

North Carolina's first Depression governor, O. Max Gardner (1882-1947), consolidated the University at Chapel Hill, State College in Raleigh, and Women's College in Greensboro. He also improved prisons and abolished chain gangs. Gardner was chairman of Sperry Corporation and later, in the 1940s, an advisor to the federal Office of War Mobilization and Reconversion. Courtesy, N.C. Division of Archives & History

Further diminishing the effects of the Depression was this Hamlet, North Carolina abattoir. Over 16,000 head of cattle arrived from the drought-stricken West to be fattened and slaughtered. Soon the bones piled up high under the scrub pines. Courtesy, N.C. Division of Archives & History

The North Carolina economic recovery program employed men to plant oyster beds near Southport, shoring up this coastal industry. Courtesy, N.C. Division of Archives & History

Burlington Industries' first plant opened in an Alamance County cornfield in 1924, before the construction was even completed. However, the pioneer employees initiated what became the nation's largest textile manufacturing operation. Courtesy, Burlington Industries, Inc.

ship suddenly shot up to 270,000 in 1934. A major strike that year almost crippled all of the state's large mills but, as usual, it was unsuccessful in the end due to poor organization and quickly-emptied union coffers. The UTW was sent packing.

In the final analysis, North Carolina was not much different structurally than it had been in the 1920s. Thankfulness for government intervention gave way to a feeling that the publicly-financed, New Deal spending spree was excessive, and business conservatism emerged wholly intact. With labor organizations in retreat, work-

ers seemed to return to a sort of pre-1929 docility.

There is nothing like a war to pump life into a slumping industrial economy. As the storm spreading over Europe began to blow in America's direction, it became evident that the massive factory conversion to the war effort—and the jobs it could provide—would be a generous complement to the New Deal.

The pre-war years found North Carolina manufacturers regrouping much faster than her farmers and mill hands, but industry still craved that final boost over the hurdle. Textile production was one of the first places Uncle Sam called.

North Carolina mills during the 1940s hummed as the whole country geared up for the war effort. This young Carrboro worker tended spindles in much the same manner as others had done four decades earlier. From the N.C. Collection, UNC Library, Chapel Hill

Facing page
The lady in the picture advertised snip-it slips, the petticoat which could be cut off at different lengths. Burlington could have used the same ad to market hosiery, another product manufactured by the company since the late 1930s. Courtesy, Burlington Industries, Inc.

Uniforms, blankets, bandages, parachutes, tents, and tire cord for the armies took up about 70 percent of the North Carolina mills' manufacturing efforts during the war years. Shipyards at Wilmington turned out 358 vessels, and, of course, G.I. Joe's ration kit was rarely without cigarettes.

The government spent about two million dollars in the state for finished war material and an estimated several billion more on goods sent to other states for finishing.

The furniture industry provides an example of how the war affected business at home, and the impact wasn't all positive. Factories didn't have to do much retooling to make gun stocks, cargo truck beds, ammo boxes, and airplane parts, but they suffered somewhat from a lumber shortage and a wearout of machinery that couldn't be replaced until peacetime. Beside losing manpower to the war, industrials saw their employees defect to the more lucrative trades which had vacancies because of America's military involvement. Boys just under the military service age replaced seasoned laborers, and they weren't as reliable. With steady incomes, the youthful workers suddenly had more money than they knew what to do with; they'd simply take time off to spend it.

The people turning the factory wheels were as passionately committed to the war as the soldiers in the field. They got upset if their companies didn't appear to be totally involved, as indicated in a 1942 memo from Burlington Mills chief J. Spencer Love to his supervisors: "Several have expressed disappointment that Burlington's direct part in the war and in defense production has so far seemed small." Love went on to assure them that the company was soliciting defense work in Washington.

It was clear long before the war was over that the Depression had run its course. The stage was set for another period of plenty, and business leaders were convinced North Carolina was in for a long run as the smash hit of the industrial South. None was better prepared than J. Spencer Love, and another memo, this one written in 1945, illustrates the feverish rush to peacetime conversion:

The Four Year Plan for expansion and modernization which has been laid out for some time will go into effect immediately. This plan calls for additional manufacturing facilities in every direction of the Company, several new lines and activities and improved building and equipment. Several million dollars' worth of equipment is already on order and several building additions are underway.

The Love story that began in 1923 is a tale of a man with the foresight of Tompkins and the panache of Cannon, an expansion-minded innovator who built the nation's largest and most diversified textile company.

After World War I, Love took a $120-a-month job as a payroll clerk in a Gastonia mill. Within a couple of years he had borrowed the money to buy the Gastonia Cotton Manufacturing Company, then quickly resold it and set his sights on Alamance County. There he adopted the gutsy habit he would use over and over again: convincing others to pool their resources and their confidence in him to build a mill.

Love was one of the first to recognize the promise of the wonder fiber of the time, rayon, and his mills multiplied as they refined the synthetic into a practical, low-cost product. His earliest factories each had one wooden wall, the easier to remove when expansion time came. By the dawn of World War II there were eighteen Burlington rayon mills, and the company was the country's largest rayon weaver.

During the war years Love saw his chance: rayon's uses were growing steadily, nylon's introduction in 1938 had ignited the hosiery market, and Depression-failed mills were available for the taking. By 1950 Burlington had spread to twenty-one communities and was making 40 percent of America's hosiery. Yet, Love's crystal ball said the price of rayon would drop. He then slashed the tags on his products, setting off an industry-wide price-cutting war that forced many smaller competitors out of business. In 1962 Greensboro-based Burlington Industries was a worldwide manufacturing firm, with fifty-seven plants and 65,000 employees in North Carolina.

Spencer Love had smelled the great wave of the future—the coming of synthetics. Though cotton and wool production continued, by the late 1940s almost all textile expansion was in hosiery and finishing plants. The manufacturers' vocabulary took on a chemical twang—Dacron, Orlon, Dynel—and outsiders like Dupont (Kinston) and Union Carbide (Eden) built large factories to work with the new fibers. Meanwhile a home-grown company, Glen Raven Mills of Alamance, introduced the world to pantyhose.

While the workrooms converted to synthetics, the front offices of mills underwent some radical changes, too. In the hectic years between the war and 1960, few weeks elapsed without headlines like "Merger Proposed By Textile Firms," followed soon afterward by "Textile Merger Given Approval." Actually, the merger movement had started much earlier, when the ties between southern mills and northern commission houses matured in the 1920s. Beset by financial trouble, individual mills proved susceptible to

merger offers from large northern firms; later, when the northern mills were hit with the same problems, they were attracted south by the better labor atmosphere.

There was no better example than J.P. Stevens and Company. Founded in 1813 in New England, Stevens branched into fragmented arms run by different members of the family. As World War II approached, they all had consolidated into one corporation, centered on an extensive textile commission business in New York. Stevens reorganized in 1946 to take advantage of post-war conditions which made a combination of manufacturing and merchandising operations lucrative indeed.

A lot of southern mills depended on Stevens to market their wares, and for some time the corporation had planned to move into the production end of that regional industry. The fact that many of their northern mills had unionized during the war strengthened the reason for heading south. Reorganization gave Stevens immediate control of nineteen southern factories, and two years later the majority of its stockholders were from the region.

Though most of the mills acquired during the first round were in South Carolina, Stevens soon owned some in Greensboro, Shelby, Gastonia, Rockingham, Roanoke Rapids, Wallace, and Stanley. The company boasted forty factories by 1955, all but eight of them in the South. In 1963, Stevens claimed fifty-five Southern mills.

The Stevens pattern, repeated on a smaller scale by other large companies which relocated to North Carolina, was succinct: make use of the machinery in worn-out or unionized northern mills by moving it south and expand into new production fields by buying up existing southern mills.

There were several other important developments in North Carolina textiles between 1930 and 1960. As paternalism declined, as wages and lifestyles improved, and as it became less financially practical to maintain houses for workers, the mill village often became a thing of the past. In the 1930s and more frequently in the 1940s, owners offered the houses for sale, with the tenants almost always getting first option;

many more were sold when mills changed hands and the new owners declined to buy the villages. Surprisingly, perhaps, this turned out to be a happy chapter in the workers' story. The dreary subsistence of tenancy often dissolved into proud ownership, a feeling of living more in a democracy than under the owners' authoritarian control, and a better integration of work and recreational aspects of the community.

One of the most significant milestones in the labor movement came with the 1947 passage of the state's right-to-work law, which succeeded at encouraging a union-free environment for prospective industries. The North Carolina Department of Labor happily reported in 1960 that less than half a percent of the work time had been lost to stoppages, the lowest rate in the South and second lowest in the nation.

By the end of the 1950s the threat of textile imports hung over the nation's industries like a pall. American mills felt the pinch almost immediately after duties on Japanese textiles were cut in half in 1955. Japanese imports quadrupled within three years and U.S. exports hit a modern-day low. North Carolina industry leaders and congressmen howled in Washington, but to little avail.

Textile manufacturers showed little or no interest in diversifying their corporate holdings, an option chosen by tobacco companies and other industries to protect themselves against the uncertainties of their markets. An Erwin Mills spokesman said, "We're fully occupied with our textile operations and have confidence in the future of the textile industry within itself."

By the late 1950s North Carolina had some 1,100 mills with a value of $2.8 billion; there were more spindles in a fifty-mile radius of Charlotte than in all of New England. True, other types of industry were making their way into the state, but not at the expense of textiles: 55 percent of North Carolinians employed in manufacturing worked in the mills.

Seldom could a discouraging word be heard from the fat and happy tobacco industry. Nervous in the foxholes and restless on the home-front, smokers compounded their habits during

The Depression started a trend which would accelerate during the post-war years: migration from rural to urban areas. This Wilkes County family displays the signs of economic hardship which compelled others to leave their homes. Courtesy, N.C. Collection, UNC Library, Chapel Hill

the war, and the increase proved to be not a temporary fling but a trend—between 1950 and 1960 cigarette production rose 53 percent. Chesterfields, Lucky Strikes, Camels, Philip Morrises, and Old Golds poured out of the state's factories; with P. Lorillard's move to Greensboro in 1956, all of the big four were in North Carolina. There was no reason to believe the Tar Heel hold on this industry wasn't permanent.

Retaining a solid grip on wooden furniture manufacturing, the growing centers from High Point west branched into upholstery, opening a new opportunity for the area and a new outlet for the textile industry. Promotional methods changed, too. For many years High Point's sales approach invited drop-ins, but lacked a formal structure. Fortunately, the tradition of spring and fall buying trips already took advantage of closeout bargains and focused the spotlight on

next year's lines. To the great unhappiness of other furniture centers, particularly Chicago, this practice continued after the war. Once the semi-annual shows were formalized in 1955 with official dates and more exhibit space, the January and July markets migrated south from Chicago, too. In 1923, 772 people attended one of the first High Point sales events; in 1950 more than 5,000 came to town.

North Carolina's tickets to the modern commercial era were not cheap. Contrary to popular belief, northern companies did not simply fly south with the birds—attracting outside industry proved hard work, and the state was lucky to have people like Luther Hodges who were equal to the challenge. Economic progress, too, demanded compromise. State farms continued to decline as, one by one, rural families reluctantly gave in to the factory magnet that had been tugging at them for nearly a century. Even the cities didn't offer enough hope to the cast-aside blacks, and thousands of them sought their better lives in New York, Washington, and Chicago.

The drain of the countryside into the towns picked up speed after the war; in 1960, 40 percent of the population was urban, and just 18 percent fell under the "rural farm" classification. In the late 1950s the number of farms began a rapid decline as the invasion of tractors, combines, and cultivators made large-scale growing more practical. Another factor was the sharp drop in tenancy that had started around 1940. This trend might have been a sign that rural people were bettering themselves, but the labor vacuum it created gave rise to a new social problem—migrancy.

By 1960 thousands of migrant farm workers were coming into the state each year. They arrived with nothing and led a hand-to-mouth existence, obtaining no higher status than that of slaves. These migrant workers comprised a whole new class of forgotten people whose health and welfare the state only now has begun to address.

The farm-to-factory trend shows clearly in a 1947 survey of Gaston and Davidson counties. In those jurisdictions nearly 40 percent of the families reported some members earning money away from the fields, causing farm income to drop. Local residents couldn't argue—the more work being done off the farm, the larger the family's income. For those who remained, tobacco became very firmly entrenched as the state's most important crop, while cotton disappeared steadily.

At least to some degree, the state held on to the farmers; the same could not be said for blacks, rural and urban, who took valuable skills with them when they began giving up on North Carolina in the 1940s and 1950s. The numbers are incredible: in the 1940s some 164,000 blacks, 15.6 percent of the black population, left the state, and in the 1950s 207,000, or 19.2 percent, fled. Ten counties lost more than 27 percent of their non-white populations during the latter decade.

Those who moved characteristically left some

family ties here, and many remained torn between the good qualities of both "homes." Said an eight-year-old boy who had lived four years in Columbus County and four in Boston, "I'm half-and-half from here and from back home." Back home were his beloved grandparents, and, his father said, white folks who don't like us.

The out-migrants passed a few industrialists heading in the opposite direction. To say they all were running from labor unions, desperate for the shelter of a solid right-to-work state, is to oversimplify. Other reasons entered the picture: the South's population growth and economic coming-of-age created hordes of new customers for nationwide and worldwide businesses. It simply made dollars and sense to be closer to largely untapped markets. Water (power) was cheaper and other natural resources—like trees for the pulp and paper industries—proved more abundant in the unspoiled region. A better climate gave the South a milk-and-honey aura, and what finer location to settle than the top manufacturing state?

But it is hard to refute labor resources as the strongest attraction, especially in North Carolina, where the textile and apparel industries showed no signs of relinquishing their dominant roles. Not only did the state's wage rates rank near the bottom nationally (her per capita income only fared better than those of Alabama, Arkansas, Mississippi, and South Carolina), but industry recruiters bragged that Tar Heel workers were among the least likely to agitate for improvement.

Although the state had a few industries completely unrelated to the traditional patterns by 1960, they were scattered and showed little evidence of a trend toward diversification. A possible exception was the electrical and electronics products industry, boasting fifty-four firms and 24,800 employees in the urban counties.

Those two factors—the forty-fourth per capita income rank and the lack of diversified industry—surprised and irritated Luther Hodges when he became governor in 1954. A textile man himself, he wondered how long the state could continue to grow around the same industrial base it had known since the 1880s. More-

Luther Hartwell Hodges (1898-1974), who had a long career with the Marshall Field Company, became the "businessman's governor" in 1954. He began one of the first vocational schools, helped establish Research Triangle Park, and took numerous trips abroad to bring new industry to North Carolina. Courtesy, N.C. Division of Archives & History

over, half of the jobs and 54 percent of the industrial wages rested in just ten counties. Fending off criticism, Hodges rushed a tax break into law: the 6 percent tax would be levied only on the portion of income traceable to North Carolina operations and property—not on business conducted outside of the state.

But what good were incentives if nobody heard about them? Besides being an astute businessman, Hodges was a born huckster. In fact, he had a hunch that his real calling was in door-to-door sales. During the fall of 1957 Hodges and some seventy-five North Carolina businessmen hit New York City like a cyclone, swarming through the corporate offices of firms that might be persuaded south. The governor wrangled television and radio appearances and forced himself to the podium wherever industrialists gathered. His product was North Carolina, and extras like tax incentives, long-term loans, and local concessions (cut-rate building sites and water, for example) were negotiable. The tour continued to Chicago, Philadelphia, and later, Western Europe. "Hodges' Raiders," as one newspaper called them, had other, more tangible things to offer. The state's banking system, which doubled its branch offices in the 1940s and 1950s to bring large institutions to more people, was back on sound footing. Financial resources climbed with commercial growth—77 percent between 1950 and 1960—and two of the state's banks, Wachovia and First Union, joined the nation's top ranks through a series of mergers.

The coastline that had so hampered progress during North Carolina's infancy finally got some serious attention. Until after the war's end, Wilmington and Morehead City had taken purely independent strides in improving their ports and attracting shippers. However, in 1949 the state legislature released $7.5 million for harbor development; three years later both ports

noted a booming business in everything from tobacco to wild animals, and the venture showed profits five years ahead of schedule. At last a solid link between the seacoast and the interior existed, calming fears that Charleston and Norfolk were bleeding commerce from the Tar Heel State.

Shortly after 1958, the North Carolina boosters also celebrated the beginnings of a fifty-eight-campus community college system that would put industrial training within a reasonable driving distance of just about everybody.

Hodges was the first governor to pursue industrial recruitment seriously. The campaign could not be expected to show overnight results, and it did not. North Carolina still lacked a key ingredient to a better balanced and more sophisticated economy: the means to attract large numbers of professionals and technicians and a pool of skilled labor.

That's what Hodges dreamed about while he was out selling: he took the job of best man at the marriage of the state's three prominent universities to the worldscale businesses he had courted.

5

BASKING IN THE SUNBELT

Headquartered in the city of Greensboro, Burlington Industries opened in 1971. This structure was cited for numerous awards, but was torn down in 2005. Courtesy, Burlington Industries, Inc.

One was a dreamer, one a brainstormer, one a champion salesman.

As head of the University of North Carolina's Institute for Research in Social Science, Howard Odum had devoted his life to a better South, and everything he knew about the region and its people pointed to a crying need for sophisticated economic development—something to pull southerners out of the farm-and-mill mire that, in the 1950s, strongly suggested they had once again become complacent while the rest of the country moved ahead. Odum was one of the very first to ponder the possibilities for three thriving, prestigious universities which harbored, within twenty-five miles of each other, some of America's best minds.

Romeo Guest was a construction man. Ever since his days at Massachusetts Institute of Technology, ever since he saw what could happen when scientists and industrialists cohabited in a park near Boston, he envisioned something bigger than his family's specialty, textile mills.

We already know how Luther Hodges could make the earth move for North Carolina. When Guest gave the name "Research Triangle" to the ideas of people like Odum, the governor's eyes lit up and he launched into the biggest and most crucial selling job of his career.

Though the Research Triangle Park was just one 5,000-acre plot far from the Appalachian hills and the sandy coastal flats, in the 1960s and 70s it became a symbol of North Carolina's future; a solid piece of evidence that the state could be among the industrial leaders not only of the South, but of the nation. Yet, while the Research Triangle was gathering up more Ph.D.s than any other place in the country, the Tar Heel State remained saddled with the lowest manufacturing wage in the nation—a constant reminder that true economic maturity was a long way off.

* * *

If Howard Odum had a fault, it was that his dream was too broad. He made the connection between university research and high-technology manufacturing, but he envisioned it happening

Part of North Carolina State University's mission has been to educate and promote research beneficial to the textile industry. One of the school's laboratories (above) and its textile building (left) appear in these 1931 photos. Courtesy, N.C. Division of Archives & History

Above
Artist John Clymer depicts the hustle and bustle of early nineteenth-century commerce surrounding the pioneer Schenck-Warlick cotton factory, located in Lincoln County. Reproduced with permission of American Cyanamid Company. Courtesy, North Carolina Collection, University of North Carolina UNC Library, Chapel Hill

Below
The port of Wilmington has played an active part in North Carolina commerce since colonial days. Artist Samuel D. Bissette captures the scenic waterfront as it appears during the twentieth century. Courtesy, Samuel D. Bissette

Left
In the North Carolina Mountains, traditional crafts still flourish and many people take pride in the work of their hands. Courtesy, N.C. Division of Tourism, Film, and Sports Development

Below
A doctoral institution, The University of North Carolina at Charlotte focuses on teaching with a strong emphasis on applied research to find innovative solutions to business challenges. Internationally respected experts in the College of Information Technology protect Internet security and privacy, visualize massive amounts of complex data, investigate Web intelligence, and create virtual environments. Courtesy, Wade Bruton

Above
The water-powered Old Mill of Guilford is still operating over 200 years after it was first put into service. Courtesy, Greensboro Area Convention and Visitors Bureau

Right
Everything within Old Salem has been adapted to recreate an authentic 18th century atmosphere. Gardens, streets, and residents all display traditional adornments. Courtesy, N.C. Division of Tourism, Film, and Sports Development

Old Salem provides many educational opportunities for families and school groups. Courtesy, Old Salem

Above
The Capitol Building in Raleigh, built 1833–1840, is a neoclassic building that has been painstakingly restored. Courtesy, N.C. Division of Tourism, Film, and Sports Development

Opposite page bottom
Shelton Vineyards was established in 1999 by two brothers with a love for wineries. It is now the largest family-owned winery in the state. Courtesy, N.C. Division of Tourism, Film, and Sports Development

Right
The military impact of Fort Bragg on Fayetteville is undeniable. The town is proud of the husbands and wives, mothers and fathers who work daily to protect our country. Courtesy, Fayetteville Area Convention & Visitors Bureau

Each summer the authentic stern wheel riverboat
Henrietta II *carries Wilmington visitors along the Cape*
Fear river. Courtesy, Joe Swift

all over the South—he didn't hone his ideas down to something workable, and as a result, several of his proposals for academic-industrial cooperation during the 1950s failed to get moral and financial support.

Romeo Guest had the narrower vision of a man looking for something to build. He is credited with first sketching on a map a triangle whose corners were the University of North Carolina at Chapel Hill, Duke University at Durham, and North Carolina State College at Raleigh. In addition, Guest suggested that the pine-covered land in between could be home to a world-class research park which would draw on the talents of the three schools to attract the country's most progressive companies. If those companies located their research and development facilities in such a park, it logically followed

The Research Triangle Institute meeting of November 5, 1969, brought together an illustrious group of state economic boosters. From left to right, George Herbert, president; Watts Hill, Sr., chairman of the board; and governors Luther Hodges, Dan K. Moore, Robert W. Scott, and Terry Sanford. Courtesy, N.C. Division of Archives & History

that they might bring their manufacturing divisions to other parts of the state, sharing a slice of the cheap-labor, weak-union, good-southern-life pie on which northeastern textile firms had been feasting for years.

John Scott, one of the park's earlier planners, recalled that:

North Carolina was highly industrialized, but it was heavily labor-intensive and dominated by

textiles, tobacco, furniture, and agriculture-related industries. It was a vision that we had a rare set of circumstances with three major research universities situated in a triangle. It was known that to be successful, there had to be a wedding of university research and government research and private research._

It didn't take long to sell this notion to the governor. Hodges and Guest rounded up others like themselves—former state treasurer Brandon Hodges of Asheville, bankers Archie Davis and

Facing page and below
While mechanization has come to the fields of Northampton County, some workers still work by hand under the often oppressive sun. Photos by Roger Manley

Robert Hanes of Winston-Salem, and banker George Watts Hill of Durham—and set about raising $1.5 million to develop the park. Retired textile magnate Karl Robbins swept in from New York to engineer the land purchase.

With the money raised, the toughest task awaited: How do you persuade the world's corporate giants to invest in a dream down on Tobacco Road? George Simpson, a sociologist on loan from the University of North Carolina to head up the research end of the park's genesis, knew how. You go recruiting, and you take with you academic scientists who can wow the corporate executives by suggesting solutions to some of their problems. Simpson, himself, used this method when courting the Kimberly-Clark Company; a North Carolina State professor

tagged along, showing the company how to lick the problem of bark removal. Kimberly-Clark made the connection between good business and the availability of good research.

The big companies started trickling in. One of the first was Chemstrand, a chemical fiber leader, whose May 1959 announcement illustrated a significant point about the park. It was commencement time, and finally North Carolina could offer to its college graduates a solid inducement to stay at home rather than "exporting" their intelligence elsewhere as their predecessors had done.

The Research Triangle Park was off and running. Hodges, who had become the state's secretary of commerce after his governorship ended, took a dollar-a-year job as head of the park's development foundation in 1963. The park had some checkered days in the early 1960s—actually turning away some industries deemed inappropriate, yet lacking the one or two big attractions to catapult it into the world prominence which it sought.

The breakthrough came in 1965 when the crème de la crème of high-technology industry, the computer giant IBM, announced plans for a major research and production complex which not only anchored the park, but enticed several other major companies to settle there. IBM executives came to Raleigh April 13, 1965, one hundred years to the day after Sherman's army invaded the city. Research Triangle business people consider the former no less significant than the latter.

As Luther Hodges wrote, "Where there is research, there is industry." As George Herbert, director of the Research Triangle Institute, said of the apparent change in the state's attitude, "We're building for twenty and twenty-five years from now, not for tomorrow or next week."

While the park was reeling in well-educated, highly-paid scientists and executives, that kind of milk and honey remained a vague dream for much of the rest of the state.

In the 1960s North Carolina came to bask in the Sunbelt phenomenon—a mass migration of people and jobs to the South resulting from the

realization that living conditions in the urban Northeast and Midwest had deteriorated. This major, new demographic change got a big lift from the continuing mechanization of agriculture, which exacerbated the trend toward consolidation into larger and fewer farms and spurred the decline of small family operations. The trend was particularly pronounced in North Carolina, where the average farm was eighty-four acres, one-third the national average size.

As consolidation turned more and more people away from agriculture, they looked to the factory, as previous generations of Tar Heel farmers had been forced to do. This new rural industrial labor supply encouraged what the state's industrial recruiters had been begging for—the spread of big business beyond the cities to the countryside and smaller towns.

But the industries for whom those people went to work were primarily textile, apparel, and furniture manufacturers. These three enterprises still made up 60 percent of the state's manufacturing at the close of the 1970s, and wages (and the quality of life they could buy) stayed low. In 1983 the state still ranked fiftieth in industrial wage—the average worker earned $6.35 per hour. Textile workers averaged somewhat less. North Carolina also ranked forty-fourth nationally in percentage of its workers having high school educations.

Added to the low-wage mire was the fact that two of these three industries were particularly vulnerable to foreign competition, keeping the state's overall economy on shaky ground. As one economist said, "If ever a textbook case existed for economic diversification, we have it here in North Carolina."

Conspiring against diversification and the opening of the predominantly rural counties to

Rows upon rows of cigarettes move along the conveyors above workers' heads at the Whitaker Park manufacturing facility, R.J. Reynolds Tobacco Company, Winston-Salem. Courtesy, R.J. Reynolds Tobacco Company

progressive industry were other factors like union fears and the so-called "Black Belt Phenomenon." In the 1960s and 70s, when out-of-state firms were exploring suburban North Carolina, local chambers of commerce ran subtle but vigorous anti-union campaigns, discouraging industries which were likely to bring unions with them.

In 1983 North Carolina still was the nation's second least unionized state. Wilbur Hobby, who headed the state's AFL-CIO and became somewhat of a workingman's hero—one time run-ning a spirited, non-traditional campaign for

George W. Hall established the Hickory Furniture Company in 1901 as a home industry. Furniture continues to be an important industry in the state. Courtesy, Hickory Chair

Two workers oversee sock-making operations in Scotland Neck. Photo by Roger Manley

governor and later reclaiming his job on the assembly line—cited several reasons for the continuing failure of organized labor: the agrarian nature of the workforce and the general distrust of unions harbored by these people; organized opposition in a public school system which never taught the pros and cons of unions; and little or no help for state unions from the national labor organizations.

Whatever the success statewide in attracting new industry, eastern North Carolina's Black Belt—part of the South where blacks comprised large percentages of the population—never saw the fruits. Industries shied away from these counties for fear that blacks were more prone to union activity; new businesses seeking skilled workers knew they couldn't find them as easily in the areas where education levels were pitifully low; and, particularly in the textile regions, business leaders did little to encourage newcomers who might upset the prevailing wage scales. However, one civil rights activist took advantage of a 1968 federal act which made loans and grants available for the creation of new towns, and aided by federal funds, launched a bold venture. Unlike most fledgling communities formed on the rims of big cities, Floyd McKissick started Soul City in the middle of nowhere—in rural, poor, predominantly black Warren County.

The flambouyant McKissick insisted that Soul City was not exclusively for blacks and cast about everywhere for industries wishing to utilize a ready labor pool. His ideas came to hold the kind of promise that interested even the county's white establishment. But in 1981, with only thirty-one lots sold (McKissick had predicted a population of 2,000 by 1978) and only one industry—a poultry processing plant—Soul City looked more like a microcosm of the unhappy plight of rural North Carolina counties.

The low wage ranking was by no means the only thorn pinching the state's economy at the close of the 1970s. In contrast to the great promise of high technology and the Research Triangle Park, stood the deepening foreign import threat to the textile industry and the pall of the anti-smoking campaign, hanging over the heads

A sliver operator's head appears above the machines which take long strips of carded cotton and twist them into threads. Photo by Roger Manley

of tobacco manufacturers and farmers.

The Surgeon General of the United States in 1964 verified in no uncertain terms what tobacco skeptics had been talking about for 100 years: good times for the cigarette industry—the "Depression-proof" industry, which had regaled in such unbridled prosperity for such a long, uninterrupted span of years—were over. The health warnings of the 1960s and the out-and-out anti-smoking campaign of the 1970s brought nothing new, really. As early as the 1890s, moralists had tried to keep educational institutions and churches from accepting Buck Duke's money, and elsewhere, 1920s crusaders like Lucy Gaston Page habitually berated smokers in public, occasionally snatching the "coffin nails" from their mouths.

But the government's report was serious business. It pulled together some 6,000 studies which rather conclusively showed what the tobacco industry feared most: smoking was related to lung cancer, contributed greatly to chronic bronchitis, and significantly increased the rise of heart disease.

These were not comforting words in a state where, as late as 1979, nearly 65,000 people made their livings directly off the golden leaf and where the economies of whole towns and counties swayed with its fortunes. That year, for instance, North Carolina tobacco paid $394 million in federal, state, and local taxes. In short, the Tar Heel State was as dependent on tobacco as a two-pack-a-day smoker.

The medical reports gave rise to a federal ban on broadcast advertising of cigarettes, and in the 1980s it became socially acceptable to ask strangers not to smoke in public places. Friends, too, were requested to temporarily dispense with the habit when in others' homes.

North Carolina—whose farmers grew two-thirds of the country's flue-cured tobacco and where Reynolds and Philip Morris made two-thirds of America's cigarettes—never had faced a dilemma like this. Cigar-puffing Agriculture Secretary Jim Graham pushed tobacco leaf lapel pins on visitors to his office, but admitted that he would discourage his grandchildren from smoking. On the question of whether to discuss

A warper tender wears his mask as protection against cotton dust. Photo by Roger Manley

the hazards of smoking in the public schools, a state public health consultant said this: "We're still debating this a great deal. Where do you put the limit when you're talking about education and economics? It's hard to go into a rural area and tell children not to smoke when Daddy is growing tobacco to put food on the table."

Farmers and politicians took to wearing caps decorated with tobacco leaves and a thumbs-up logo, begging "Pride in Tobacco." The Tobacco Institute, which became one of Washington's most powerful lobbies, hired its own doctors to counter the Surgeon General's reports.

But, starting in 1977, cigarette sales began to drop, and diversification suddenly was a necessity for the big manufacturers. Reynolds got into everything from vodka to Chinese food, with fantastic results—it became the South's largest corporation, climbing the Fortune 500's top thirty list of the nation's biggest companies. Philip Morris bought soft drink companies and a brewery. Liggett and Myers diversified into all imaginable areas, and in the late 1970s, pondered getting out of cigarettes altogether. A move to cigarettes with fewer of the harmful ingredients was introduced by one of the costliest advertising campaigns in marketing history.

The future of the tobacco farmer remained much less certain. State politicians abandoned their scrutiny of the health studies as a lost cause, and turned to defending the fifty-year-old price support system as a bastion of the family farm. But when Senator Robert Morgan called tobacco farming "one of the last islands of traditional rural life," he was talking to a growing number of tobacco critics in Congress—those who just plain didn't like smoking and saw the price support system as increasingly impractical. In the 1980s, that system, upon which the farmers had depended for so long as insulation from the whims of the big manufacturers, was becoming an economic burden. Hundreds of millions of pounds of leaf lay unsold in warehouses, with competition from cheaper foreign tobacco on the rise. North Carolina leaders still were managing to keep the wolf away from their door, but nobody could say for sure what would happen to the price system.

The state's textile industry remained tops in the country through the 1960s and 70s, counting over 1,300 mills and some 250,000 workers at the end of the period. Yet the industry had its own troubles, and not from the other forty-nine states.

Like the auto makers in Detroit, the fabric and apparel manufacturers cringed as more and more of their markets were absorbed by competitors from across the seas. Japan, Taiwan, Korea, and China—the traditional low-wage countries—led an invasion that grew from 1.5 billion square yards of fabric and clothing in 1964 to 7.4 billion square yards twenty years later. By 1983 imports accounted for about 18 percent of the U.S. textile market. The number of North Carolina textile workers dropped by 60,000 in the ten years after 1972, and most of that was blamed on plant closings and cutbacks which translated into layoffs.

The industry's traditional vulnerability to wildly unpredictable markets got worse as clothing styles changed faster and faster. What tobacco-dominated areas just started to worry about already was a reality for some textile towns, as the entire industry's woes gushed out of the

people who ran the mills and the looms.

"It's not the company's fault. It's those senators and congressmen letting other countries import stuff here," said a fifty-nine-year-old worker as he and 319 others walked away from Raleigh's Pilot Mills for the last time in 1982. The company's vice president gave other reasons why the ninety-four-year-old plant shut down: "Corduroy has fallen out of favor as a jean fabric ... Because of the age and size and physical layout of the building, it would be impractical to modernize it ... I think it's probably rather typical of the industry at this moment. I don't know anyone who's doing really well."

Raleigh could survive on government and the Research Triangle's attractions. Not so the small town of Hillsborough, which suffered considerable economic hardship in 1983 when the Cone Mills' Eno Plant closed. "We just couldn't produce anything there was a significant demand for, to produce it at a profit," a company executive said as 550 workers braced for the eighty-six-year-old factory's demise.

The Eno shutdown gave politicians one more occasion to bark at Congress for not controlling imports. In spite of heavy lobbying against foreign trade by state officials, mill owners, and textile labor unions, this rather unholy alliance realized by the 1980s that it was making little progress.

For those few who hit the right combination, hard times were unheard of. Greensboro's Blue Bell, for instance, became the world leader in feeding an insatiable demand—from cowboys to hippies to Madison Avenue execs—for blue jeans. The company's profits bulged from $5.3 million in 1967 to $70 million a decade later. While other firms endured the growth of imports, Blue Bell presided over a wide-open world market, enjoying its position by watching visiting Russian athletes fill their empty suitcases with the prized denim pants.

There were three other major developments in the North Carolina textile industry after 1960. First, thousands of workers who had worked amid flying cotton dust for years found out why they were having so much trouble breathing. In perhaps the saddest chapter of the mill workers'

Working amid the dust and noise of cotton machinery, an old-timer checks a power loom. Photo by Roger Manley

story, byssinosis, or brown lung disease, was exposed as a serious health hazard. Estimates indicated that as many as a fourth of those who regularly worked around cotton dust had some degree of the disease.

Exposure to cotton dust first was recognized as a health hazard in British mills during the 1930s, and a North Carolina doctor said in 1936 that he had treated about twenty-five workers with the same symptoms. In 1967, health officials tested 500 workers in an Eden factory, finding sixty-three of them afflicted with the disease; after studies in other mills, the state in 1971 finally added byssinosis to its list of illnesses whose victims were eligible for workmen's compensation.

A Salisbury woman who had been employed in the mills for thirty-five years was in the habit of keeping her work clothes separate from other dresses, in order to confine the cotton dust. But she hadn't made the connection between the lint and her breathing problems: "Of course,"

Research Triangle Park struck gold when it lured computer giant International Business Machines (IBM) to North Carolina in 1965. Within a decade, over 6,000 people were employed at the facility, working on the development and manufacture of communications and telecommunications products and programs. Courtesy, Research Triangle Foundation of N.C.

she said, "nobody told me I was endangering my health."

It was several years after recognition of the problem that the state made any serious attempts to clean up the work places and to compensate the victims. The companies balked at government cleanup requirements, yet the state inspected 210 mills between 1974 and 1980 and found 128 of them in violation of dust control standards, many three times above the limits.

The state, too, was to blame. It took a sheepish attitude toward the mills, leveling only token fines, bargaining with management over modifications of the cleanup orders, and extending deadlines for compliance. As to the textile companies, the reality of cotton dust cleanup hit like a ton of bricks—so ingrained were they in doing business with little or no regard for protection of their workers, that some practically had to rebuild their mills to meet the new standards.

In the 1980s, workers also continued to have trouble with medical claims, primarily due to the continuing debate among doctors as to the exact relationship between cotton dust and byssinosis. But it was clear that many thousands had suffered without compensation during a century of neglect. And the most significant exposé of brown lung came in 1980 from the same newspaper—*The Charlotte Observer*—which for so long had coddled the industry.

By the 1980s, labor unions had made few inroads in the North Carolina mills or in Tar Heel industry in general. Union membership as a percentage of the non-agricultural work force was 25 percent nationally; in the South it was 13.5 percent, in North Carolina, 6.9 percent.

One breakthrough came in the J.P. Stevens mills in and near Roanoke Rapids in 1974, when employees of seven mills voted for representation by the Textile Workers Union of America. Stevens for ten years had been summarily firing pro-union workers, threatening plant shutdowns (i.e. loss of jobs) if the unions came in. The courts repeatedly had branded the giant textile manufacturer a corporate outlaw. After the unions finally moved in, the judge who conducted seventeen days of hearings for the National Labor Relations Board in 1977 said of the company: "The record as a whole indicates that (Stevens) approached these negotiations with all the tractability and openmindedness of Sherman on the outskirts of Atlanta." Not until 1980 did the union achieve its first contract with the Roanoke Rapids plants, and not until three years later did labor officials praise the company for a conciliatory attitude.

While the cigarette and textile industries struggled against unstable markets, furniture manufacturers enjoyed better days during the 1960s and 70s. High Point had wrested the semi-annual market from Chicago, and in the 1970s it confronted and fought off a strong challenge from Dallas to steal the market away. Though the more regional winter and summer shows gradually evaporated due to the extremely high promotional costs, the fall and spring national markets got even stronger. In the 1980s some of the major companies which had formed a satellite trade center around Hickory to the west began to drift to High Point to be nearer to their competitors.

With 1,300 of the some 5,000 American manufacturers displaying their wares in the Southern Furniture Market, this semi-annual event came to draw more than 38,000 people to High Point and the surrounding area, making it North Carolina's biggest single economic activity each year. High Point's downtown became one huge showroom, and in the 1980s the arrival of decorators (wishing to conduct business with traditional furniture buyers and sellers) raised the possibility that the market was evolving into more of a year-round affair.

On the production end, an industry which had grown up in cabinet makers' shops and small, family-run factories gradually joined the general business trend of consolidation into fewer—but larger and more powerful—conglomerates. By the late 1970s there were over 600 manufacturers in the state, and the industry, growing faster than tobacco or textiles, counted some 80,000 workers. North Carolina still made 60 percent of the nation's wood furniture and 28 percent of its upholstered furniture. Maybe society wasn't too happy with an out-of-control divorce rate, but to the furniture business, it meant one-third more people living alone, needing things upon which to sit, lie, and set their dinner plates.

North Carolina came by southern industrial prominence through the exploitation of its cotton, its tobacco, and its trees. Its people watched proudly as those exploits brought the state regional greatness, yet they grew anxious as national industrial leaders stayed far ahead on the strengths of more predictable economic foundations. In the 1960s and 70s, North Carolinians went looking for a piece of the action.

Luther Hodges' contribution to the state's economic development should not be measured so much in direct results, but in the spirit he ignited. Every governor since Hodges has made industrial recruitment a priority. It has been said that during Jim Hunt's first two terms, 1977-1985, the governor spent a fourth of his time courting industry.

Those governors and an increasingly sophisticated Department of Commerce have sold North Carolina as both a center for fine universities and a haven for non-union manufacturing bliss. They have stretched a lot of mileage out of the

The state acquired the Reed Gold Mine property in 1971 and has restored it as a state historic site where the public can explore old tunnels and pan for gold. Courtesy, N.C. Division of Tourism, Film, and Sports Development

state's climate, small town southern charm, and cultural amenities, which give it a leg up on much of the Sunbelt. Its tradition of low wages also heightens the sales pitch.

The state opened a western European recruitment office in the mid-1970s and a Tokyo branch during the 1980s. Among the results from the former were a Dutch cobalt processing plant in Laurinburg, an English automobile parts plant in Sanford, and a German abrasives manufacturer in Hickory. For many decades, the recruitment movement has typified the southern habit of rolling out red carpets and treating the big cornpanies in a better way than do other states. As Hunt once told the townspeople at a potential industrial site, he would "move Heaven and Earth" to bring the plant in.

In 1965, a Raleigh businessman got a phone call from a person identifying himself only as "John." The caller instructed the surprised local executive to look for a prematurely gray man in a hotel lobby at a specified time. After requesting to be shown around the budding Research Triangle, the visitor disappeared. He returned some time later, identifying himself as a representative of IBM and proclaiming that a major North Carolina installation would be opened contingent on construction of a four-lane highway between the Research Triangle Park and Raleigh. Without even revealing the name of the company, the Raleigh businessman-turned-intermediary obtained Governor Dan Moore's promise to build such a highway.

The state legislature was similarly swept off its feet in 1981 when Hunt saw what he called a once-in-a-lifetime chance to pull in the lucrative microelectronics industry. Hunt ramrodded a twenty-four-million-dollar appropriation for an elaborate research center which would act as a magnet for the industry. One senator later said, "Who the hell knows anything about microelectronics? In my opinion the legislators just accepted what they considered fact from the governor." Licking their chops, of course, over the economic prospects.

Industrial recruitment produced solid results in the 1960s and 70s, and during the next decade, the outlook proved even more promising. The state claimed 275 electronics and other high-technology firms alone in 1983, almost all of them relatively recent acquisitions. Though these companies clustered together in the urban areas, they were located in sixty-five of the one hundred counties, including some of the most remote ones.

There was also growing evidence of diversification. Between 1978 and 1983, more than a third of the investment in new or expanded industry focused on the chemical industrial equipment, and instrumentation fields.

In 1983 North Carolina led the country in new companies; a survey of the 1,000 largest U.S. corporations found it to be the second most likely state to be chosen for a new industrial plant and it ranked second on Fortune magazine's list of most probable sites for new research and development facilities.

The Research Triangle Foundation had been on the skids in 1965. It was surviving on the dreams and little else, with just a couple of kinds of the major research firms it had hoped to attract.

In the 1980s, after dozens and dozens of areas throughout the United States had failed to turn their high-tech, research and development fever into a concrete plan, the Research Triangle Park had only two peers—California's Silicon Valley and Boston's Route 128. Some 22,500 people in the park were paid an average annual salary of $25,000. In the nearest bedroom community, Cary, the average family income was more than $29,000.

The park housed the best and the brightest: IBM, Burroughs Wellcome, Becton, Dickinson and Company, the Environmental Protection Agency's largest research lab, the National Institute of Environmental Health Sciences, and the Chemical Industry Institute of Toxicology. And one of General Electric's biggest facilities was on the way.

Research Triangle Park also boasted the National Humanities Center, and in the works, it had a microelectronics research center on which the state pinned hopes of attracting *the* industry of the future. Though difficult to gauge, North Carolina's economic development experts generally agreed that, just as industries had followed IBM to the Research Triangle Park, they filled this technological center to derive benefits from North Carolina at large.

A few miles from the park, Raleigh's last textile mill closed in 1982. A few miles in the opposite direction, the rich aroma of downtown Durham's cigarette tobacco appealed to fewer and fewer people. To all the world, North Carolina appeared on the verge of transition akin to what happened when Michael Schenck and Absolom Warlick started spinning yarn on the Catawba River.

6
PRESERVATION AND INNOVATION

The Mint Museum of Craft + Design in Charlotte explores the evolution of craft from its rural beginnings to the contemporary art of today. Courtesy, Visit Charlotte

Soon after the turn of the century, the exodus started—young people slinging a few belongings across their backs and fleeing the rural, isolated North Carolina mountains for cities where they could find work. To one so enamored of mountain life as John Campbell, it was a needless loss, and he thought much of the blame rested with schools that didn't prepare a young person to make a living at home in the southern Appalachians.

Campbell died before he could consummate his dream of a folk school to guide the formation of farm cooperatives, to combine the old mountain customs and the fruits of the hills into small industries, and to encourage mountain people to believe in their own heritage. The dream did not die.

In the tiny community of Brasstown, at the far western corner of the state, Campbell's wife and a companion in 1925 founded a school committed to preserving mountain ways. Among other accomplishments, Olive Dame Campbell and Marguerite Butler rounded up aimless whittlers and molded them into the beginnings of one of this country's foremost woodcarving centers. Sixty years later, their school was very little changed. Tucked in the remote hills on 365 acres of land, modern-day mountaineers and big-city escapees studied homesteading, blacksmithing, weaving, and woodworking, oblivious to the hectic pace of a full-speed-ahead state.

It is a long way indeed from the John C. Campbell Folk School to the North Carolina Biotechnology Center, where the pine forest stood aside for white-coated scientists whose tools were test tubes and microscopes.

The research center coordinated the work of universities and industries which brought together one of the largest concentrations of geneticists in the country. One lab probed the intricacies of gene cloning; a second took biotech into the field to explore the elements that created different tobacco flavors. Meanwhile, state legislators mulled over what another ten-million-dollar allocation to the center would mean in terms of the state's industrial future.

North Carolina stubbornly refused to change the

Here mountain farmer W.J. Martin turned a piece of wood into art. Such indigenous crafts are fostered and preserved at the Campbell Folk School, Brasstown. Photo by Doris Ulmann. Courtesy, N.C. Division of Archives & History

An autumn ritual, preparing apple butter guarantees a sweet winter treat as well as a little extra income for mountain folk who sell to tourists. This 1909 picture shows a couple cooking their spicy preserves in a brass kettle over an outdoor fire. Courtesy, N.C. Division of Archives & History

old . . . and resolutely refused to miss out on the new.

* * *

The Great Smoky Mountains region has been called "the land of do without." Because its population was so scattered and its land so rugged, only one significant retail center developed in the North Carolina mountains, and Asheville proved to be an inconvenient distance away from many of the hilltop hamlets. This factor created a need for self-sufficient living that persisted long after the flatlanders had built roads, airports, seaports, and stores at every stop.

Hard-core mountaineers as early as the 1920s complained that too many people had foresaken the old ways for cheap, store-bought clothes and tools. Yet the fact is that for people throughout the region, a fierce pride in their heritage has kept alive the old ways and preserved the make-your-own spirit for others who are several generations removed from it. This fierce pride exists, of course, with the realization that mountain craftsmanship is good business.

One woman in Marble, Cherokee County, re-

*In the 1920s Jacques and Juliana Busbee encouraged a re-
vival of the potting craft, which had fallen on hard times
due to Prohibition (a much smaller demand for "little
brown jugs"). Using traditional methods, including a
mule-driven clay grinder, artisans like Charlie Teague and*

*Ben Owen made Moore County pottery a prized posses-
sion—even in New York City. Courtesy, N.C. Division of
Archives & History*

calls her idea to make a blanket for her cow to
wear on its back. A traveler then spotted the
blanketed cow. Never mind that the flatlanders
wanted to hang the things on their walls—a
cottage industry was born!

The Brasstown Carvers proved on a small scale
that outsiders were attracted to the delicate arts
of the mountaineers, and in the 1920s Olive
Dame Campbell helped to organize the Southern
Highland Handicraft Guild. The guild grew to
national prominence, with more than 600 members from nine states in the 1980s; its festival-like
shows and sales operations moved into modern

convention centers, but the carved dulcimers,
elaborate quilts, and gourd figurines remained the
same.

The flatlanders were not without their contributions to the functional folk arts. Historians
have argued over whether the famous potters of
the Piedmont came from England, Virginia, or
Pennsylvania, but Salem's industrious Moravians
apparently had a hand in establishing North
Carolina as one of the country's premier ceram-
ics centers in the eighteenth and nineteenth
centuries.

Moore County became a haven for a small

industry whose craftsmen bequeathed their art from generation to generation. The pottery was sold by itinerant wagoneers, much the same as was tobacco, and the industry grew in no small part from the illegal whiskey business' demand for "little brown jugs." In the 1920s, the negligence of more recent generations let this craft nearly slip into obscurity, but two Raleigh artists, Jacques and Juliana Busbee, moved to Moore and revived it. Jugtown pottery was once again a hot item.

On the coast, Harker's Island developed a reputation for first-class wooden fishing boats that stretched up and down the eastern seaboard. Six or eight Harker's Island builders survived into the 1980s, paying no attention to the advent of fiberglass and swearing that there was no substitute for carefully-sanded juniper plants shaped into solid fifty- and sixty-foot vessels. Some of these craftsmen worked in the same sawdusty sheds where their grandfathers had toiled, and their wooden boats still lined the North Carolina harbor villages.

Preservation came naturally for the continuing industries; in places like Edenton and Salem, and at isolated sites all over the state, it took more of a museum-like approach, requiring support from business leaders and foundations established by the families of the state's industrial pioneers. A Winston-Salem grocer named Howard Gaines became an unlikely contributor to historic preservation in 1947, when he announced plans for a new store on the site of a house built by Moravian settlers almost two centuries earlier. With the descendants of R.J. Reynolds at the forefront, the fight against the grocery store was the rallying point for a massive crusade—which ultimately preserved more than sixty eighteenth- and nineteenth-century buildings and gardens in the village constructed by people whose industriousness was an inspiration for the whole region.

The coastal town of Edenton was one of the foundations of the state's early mercantile economy, but the coming of the railroads, which made other places more accessible, sent it into decline by the mid-1800s. The change proved a blessing in disguise to the state's heritage: as the

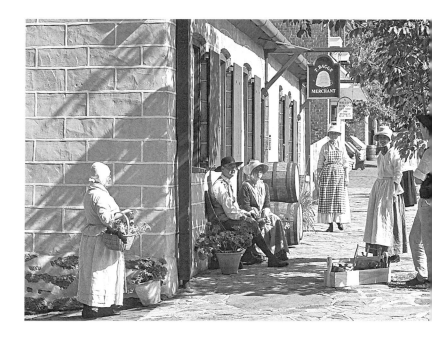

An 18th century Moravian town has been reconstructed as the living history village, Old Salem, situated within the modern city of Winston-Salem. Courtesy, N.C. Division of Tourism, Film, and Sports Development

The Busbees' cabin at Jugtown became a display center for local arts and pottery. Today their showroom is run by a non-profit corporation which continues to support traditional craftspeople and sell their work. Courtesy, N.C. Division of Archives & History

industrial revolution bypassed the town, no one disturbed its Victorian homes and magnificent Georgian courthouse. Edenton became an ideal place to preserve a bygone way of life.

History books and even the tales of oldtimers pale next to the sight of heirloom buildings. By 1980, North Carolina had more historic districts than any state in the Southeast and was spending more private money on preservation than all of those states combined.

Some sites took on new business roles. One of Julian Carr's cotton mills, built beside the Chapel Hill railroad depot in 1899, was converted in the 1980s to a shopping and office mall that gave an economic boost to a depressed area. Not far away, the 1854 Falls-Neuse Manufacturing Company, a paper plant-turned-cotton mill and the state's last remaining stone industrial building, became a housing outlet for the Research Triangle Park's population boom.

Other historic structures were just for looking: remains of the 1799 Reed Gold Mine in Cabarrus County, believed to be the site of the country's earliest discovery of gold; the 1875 Bull Durham factory, the state's first successful tobacco plant; an 1884 factory of the Duke brothers in Durham; and Glencoe, an entire Alamance County mill village constructed during 1882.

Old buildings and restored villages are the ties that bind the state to its past, but perhaps nothing unifies North Carolinians like their churches. Although the land might have been uppermost with the farmer and the hum of the machinery the lifeblood of the mill worker, faith rested in religion. Whatever social lives citizens had revolved around the "meetin'" house in the state that has been called the buckle of the Bible Belt. North Carolina was overwhelmingly Protestant, and the preachers were not likely to

have had any formal ministerial training. Those who felt they had received "the call" gravitated to the pulpits, but many of them were circuit riders who alternated between churches too poor to pay their own preachers.

From the earliest days North Carolinians came by their religious fervor with some government help. In 1715 the colonial legislature set

The Mill Villages in Roanoke Rapids represent typical mill town architecture where only gardens, awnings or shutters distinguish one company-built home from the next. Photo by Roger Manley

a harsh tone for life on the Sabbath by forbidding any work, hunting, fishing, or organized recreation. A colonist might have been spared a penalty for shooting game on the Lord's day to feed his family, yet some businesses were not treated so leniently in later years. "Blue laws" that continued into the twenty-first century in some parts of the state prohibited the sale not only of alcoholic drink but of any item which church leaders thought could be denied until Monday. In other cases, businesses were not even allowed to be open on Sunday.

By the 1920s the churches claimed half the state's population as members and generally stuck to local and personal influence. But on occasion, such as the Darwinism controversy surrounding the 1925 Scopes trial, they jumped into an organized statewide crusade. When reporting the Mecklenburg school board's ban on the teaching of evolution, *The Charlotte Observer* said eloquently, "Mecklenburg County youthful brains are not to be inveighed by any study likely to bring into question the truth of the Bible ..." Several anti-evolution bills, mostly aimed at the "wayward" University of North Carolina, eventually failed. The churches, nevertheless, had served notice of their moral authority.

For those who worked in the textile plants, religion often was a not-so-subtle extension of the industrialists' influence on their employees' lives. The mill and the church complemented each other: many owners contributed heavily to the church building funds, or built houses of worship outright. Industrialists also recruited and paid the ministers, a valuable service since clergy were hard to find. In return they expected, and got, a high degree of loyalty.

Seldom were labor unions blessed from company-supported pulpits. The church sanctioned the mill, and in many towns this insulated the

Duke Chapel, the neo-gothic centerpiece of Duke University's West Campus, features a 5,200-pipe Flentrop organ, 210-foot tower housing a 50-bell carillon, and intricate stained-glass windows. Courtesy, 1994 Durham Convention & Visitors Bureau

factories from criticism and helped them avoid government regulation that might hold back their growth. The control in some places was such that ministers referred to churches as either "industrial churches" or "independent churches"; a Gaston County clergyman complained that in one instance, "the preacher has to ask the mill owner when he can pray."

More than a few churches in and out of mill towns got their impetus from the intense fervor that swelled inside dusty circus tents on muggy summer evenings. The evangelistic revival, a sometimes week-long extravaganza of hymn singing and passionate, hellfire-and-brimstone preaching, was a staple of rural North Carolina religion. Revivals proved most popular in factory-dominated areas, often giving rise to general community festivals, and always ending with the preacher beseeching all to come forward and give their lives to the Lord.

One who answered the altar call as a sixteen-year-old boy was destined to devote his life to global evangelism. Billy Graham started out witnessing on street corners and warning ordinary sinners to repent, but with his captivating oratory and air of sincerity, the Charlotte native rose quickly to the top of his field. In the 1980s, after enduring heavy criticism for supporting an unpopular war in Vietnam, after serving as religious adviser to presidents (one of whom, Richard Nixon, disappointed him and left him severely disillusioned), after watching 12,000 people turn out for a hometown party in his honor—Graham was one of the world's best known and most revered people.

Billy Graham did not join hands with another national religious figure of the 1970s and 1980s from North Carolina. The fact that Jim Bakker, a Michigan native who conducted his first crusades in Tar Heel mill towns, settled on Charlotte as the site for his multimillion-dollar television evangelism center may say something about religion as a force in the state. Bakker's following was unquestionable. By the mid-1970s he was raising hell against sin on a daily television show and raising more than one million dollars every week from his viewers nationwide. Drawing constant criticism for an extravagant

A college started by blacks for blacks at the end of the nineteenth century, St. Augustine's in Raleigh continues to pursue its educational goals. Three of the campus landmarks viewed in this 1899 photo are, from left to right: Taylor Library, the chapel, and the Lyman Building. Courtesy, N.C. Division of Archives & History

lifestyle which included a $350,000 house and a stable of fancy cars, Bakker also was chastised for asking God for air conditioners and motor homes for his flock.

All of the flash was a bit much for a more basic man like Graham, but in a sense Bakker's operations illustrated how the Bible Belt arrived at its position during the 1980s. Prayers and faith that ordinary people would overcome illness and other worries to lead worthwhile lives were the same as always, but religion had become big business, with quaint country churches giving way to massive, suburban evangelistic temples with fleets of buses to bring in the faithful.

If North Carolina has been an innovator in education, the credit is due to its university and community college systems. From colonial days through the 1970s, the state's public schools have struggled to keep up with the rest of the nation, and much of the reason is the comparatively slow pace of economic development.

Most of the larger cities have run even with the national norm for schooling, but farmers traditionally have put the chores first and the books second. The small, family-operated farm usually required all hands on deck in the spring and early fall, as well as the summer. In an attempt to win favor for a lengthening of the academic year in 1909, the superintendent of the Durham County schools wrote:

Again, we have noticed that those farmers who put their children in school in September when our schools open and keep them there regularly until the next April or May when our schools close, harvest better crops, make more money, and are more prosperous in every way than those who apparently have the same opportunity in life, but send their children to school irregularly for only a part of the school year.

It is difficult to understand his reasoning, but the writer clearly knew he had to appeal to the farmers to successfully sell his idea.

In the mill towns, too, work almost always came first, and if the parents weren't feeling the pressure to have the kids help out with the family's income, the mill owner might be demanding their help in speed-up periods. Often mills provided schools where, in the surrounding communities, the state or county did not. Owners had many reasons for their interest in education—school discipline made more reliable mill workers, and, theoretically at least, better educated people would help the southern plants to overcome the idea that they were limited to manufacturing coarse yarns while their northern counterparts did the weaving and finishing. However, the fact remained that, whether related

to the quality of their schools or to their socio-economic position in life, mill children were not as well educated as the general population.

There were no public schools in colonial North Carolina. Big landowners organized private academies for their children, while farm children went to the same School of Hard Knocks their parents had attended. Prior to 1771, the few North Carolinians who attended college went out of state.

The University of North Carolina (UNC) at Chapel Hill still beams with pride at having been the first state university to open its doors, but it, too, suffered an inauspicious beginning as the legislature neglected to fund it. The university finally accepted students six years after it was chartered.

The legislature followed this pattern of charter-but-no-money with the academies it set up in the early 1800s. Most of them failed, leaving behind a state that became known for its ignorance. As part of his exposé of the state's Rip Van Winkle reputation, Archibald Murphey calmed a blind fear of what education in the hands of common people would do, and prodded North Carolina into setting up a system of public schools. With blacks and girls excluded, it was far from perfect even for its time, but in 1817 it was a start.

Educators claim the state had one of the best antebellum school systems in the country, a fact that tends to get obscured, they say, by the destruction suffered during and after the Civil War. With the 1870 census showing illiteracy among half the population over age ten, however, it's difficult to see how they arrived at their claim.

A lifelong rivalry between the universities in Chapel Hill and Raleigh started with the latter's founding. The first funds for college-level agricultural and mechanical schooling went to the University of North Carolina, and it took three years of railing by *The Progressive Farmer* to convince the legislature that those programs needed a separate campus. The forerunner of North Carolina State University opened in 1889.

The post-Civil War struggle for new freedom

Duke University is an internationally renowned research university. Courtesy, N.C. Division of Tourism, Film, and Sports Development

and basic civil rights was personified in about a dozen colleges built by blacks for blacks before the turn of the century. Several of them survived, notably St. Augustine's and Shaw in Raleigh; Johnson C. Smith in Charlotte; and colleges in Durham, Greensboro, Winston-Salem, Fayetteville, and Elizabeth City, which later joined the University of North Carolina system.

While the University of North Carolina-Chapel Hill and North Carolina State flourished, smaller, private educational institutions fought money problems throughout the twentieth century. In 1920 the state had thirty-one colleges, but with a total cache of fourteen million dollars, one writer described their finances as "almost exactly the wealth we produce by our sweet potato crop alone in a single year." Private

colleges consequently were turning away one-fifth as many students as they had enrolled.

Until the late 1920s, the state didn't seem to be able to decide what kind of public school system it wanted. Then, with the passage of a series of laws, the course shifted from a scattershot network of county-run, county-built schools to a more unified design by which the state assumed funding for academic programs and teachers' salaries. The legislature also mandated a six-month—and later eight-month—school term. In a new, clearer division of responsibilities, the counties were left with the duties of constructing and maintaining school buildings.

But the rich county/poor county differences that had nagged the state since its earliest days persisted in the schools—the "haves" could supplement state money handsomely and the "have-nots" scraped by with the minimum.

The modern North Carolina school system paid its teachers miserably less than the national average and spent substantially lower amounts on each student. When, in 1983, the state admitted to itself that it mirrored a declining and decaying national school system, the problems eerily echoed the words written by the Durham superintendent at the beginning of the century: "There seems to be but one solution to the problem. Put more money into the schools, lengthen the school term, and employ trained teachers. In answer to these propositions many will say that we are too poor to do these things; but in truth we are too poor not to educate our children."

Alongside the frustrated public schools, some of the brightest lights in education anywhere—namely the community colleges, the universities of the Research Triangle, and two special schools—shone in the 1980s. The industrial push of the late 1950s brought with it a commitment to technical training that grew to twenty-three community and thirty-five technical colleges, the nation's third largest system. Hardly any North Carolinian was more than a short drive from one of the schools, and in 1980 over 14 percent of the adult population took at least one of their courses. As the state began embracing high-technology, its technical schools boned

Combining craftsmanship with the need for subsistence, this elderly Roanoke Rapids man restores cane seats on chairs. It is impossible to discover the total wealth of home-grown North Carolina talent. Photo by Roger Manley

up on the needs of each individual company and geared up to train workers for them.

From the beacon of learning at Chapel Hill, William Friday rose over the course of a brilliant twenty-eight-year career as the University of North Carolina's president to join the likes of Archibald Murphey in educational prominence. Under Friday's leadership, the Chapel Hill program became peerless among liberal arts universities in the Southeast, and North Carolina State blossomed from a quality agricultural school to one of the premier scientific and technical research centers. In 1971 Friday engineered the assimilation of twelve colleges around the state into the then four-campus University of North Carolina system, creating a mammoth state-supported university network which by the 1980s served 120,000 students.

A kindly, soft-spoken and deep-thinking man, Friday nevertheless could turn into a fierce fighter who made legislators cower when it came to the matter of money for his schools. For those who wondered why he didn't run for governor, there was a standard answer: "Why would he want to take a step down?"

In the 1970s it was clear that North Carolina's young whiz kids—those whose academic striving outstripped not only their fellow students, but their teachers—were languishing in the public schools. Battling criticism that the state was pouring precious dollars into an elitist crusade at the expense of the masses, Governor Jim Hunt picked up from academics the idea of a special residential high school and rolled it through a skeptical legislature. The result was the North Carolina School of Science and Mathematics in Durham, a rigorous regimen for kids who never had been challenged in their local schools—the country's first state-supported residential program for the gifted.

Another first-and-only school put down roots not far from the cigarette factories in Winston-Salem. The North Carolina School of the Arts, part of the University of North Carolina system, came to be no less a treasure to the state than the golden leaf, attracting dancers, actors, and musicians from around the world and developing a reputation as one of the best art programs.

As unlikely as it might have seemed just a few years before, North Carolina in the second half of the twentieth century was becoming known as a top-notch, cultural state. Throughout its development, it had the strong tradition of visual arts—Outer Banks painters and Smoky Mountains craftsmen—but it was better typified by farmers and mill hands who had little notion of or time for such frivolities as theatre and dance. Even the amazing talents of mountain musicians never went beyond their own region.

Seemingly unrelated to anything else that was going on in the state after the turn of the century—save perhaps the philanthropy from the huge fortunes of industrialists like Duke and Reynolds—fine art began pushing folk art for equal time. In this area, North Carolina has an extraordinary list of firsts: the first state-supported theater devoted to American drama, Playmakers at the University of North Carolina; the first outdoor drama in the country, Paul Green's "The Lost Colony," which essentially introduced a new art form; and the nation's first cabinet-level agency for support of the cultures. North Carolina similarly was an innovator in allocating public money for an art collection, setting up a state agency for support of professional drama, and establishing the country's oldest local arts council, housed in Winston-Salem.

There were, however, hints of reluctance on the part of politicians who expressed more concern with the basic necessities. The "horn tootin'" bill which created the North Carolina Symphony in 1943 and the "toe dancin'" bill for the School of the Arts twenty years later followed lively and sarcastic debates.

To such skepticism, Governor Terry Sanford took an aside from his education and industry-recruiting campaigns to say; "There may be toe dancing, but if there is, I want to be in the audience." Perhaps no one at that time saw the connection between Sanford's quiet tip of the hat and the creation of the North Carolina Arts Council, which during the 1980s attracted more than six million dollars annually.

Private support, too, has been important, and money and elbow grease for the arts sprang

Charlotte is home to multiple performing arts companies as well as several theaters that host touring artists and performances throughout the year. Courtesy, Visit Charlotte

straight from the same industrial fortunes that built the factories, railroads, and cities. R.J. Reynolds handsomely shared his tobacco success with the arts: the diversified company which bears his name is a big part of the reason why Winston-Salem became a national model for grass-roots cultural support. This spirit has caught on among banks, textile companies, and other businesses. As one executive said, "It's almost expected of you."

In the 1980s, the flower of North Carolina arts was in full blossom. Charlotte's Spirit Square was a maze of studios, performance centers, and

exhibit halls located in a 1909 downtown church. Formerly a textile mill, car dealer's showroom, and parking lot in downtown Winston-Salem, Winston Square resounded the heartbeat of that city's deep cultural commitment. The North Carolina Museum of Art, too, began to receive national attention when it moved into a striking new building in Raleigh.

Durham's American Dance Festival, Greensboro's Eastern Music Festival, and the Brevard Music Festival in the mountains annually at-tracted some of the best students and professionals. Paul Green's idea spawned several other

outdoor theaters, while the North Carolina Shakespeare Festival found a home among the furniture factories and showrooms in High Point.

* * *

Only in recent years have they had anything nice to say about Thomas Wolfe in Asheville. For quite a while after the 1929 publication of his novel, *Look Homeward Angel,* folks had been more than a little affronted by this local boy-made-good who chose to expose his hometown not as the placid, green and scenic place they knew it to be, but as a seamy, money-hungry town the pleasantness of which had been lost in a knuckling-under to the tourist and timber trades—a warning that not even the isolated mountains were immune to exploitation that went by the name of "progress."

In a state that has been characterized among the most slovenly and among the most industrious, the men and women of Wolfe's day straddled the fence between preservation and innovation. North Carolinians still do—guarding the writer's boyhood home as a treasure, yet shadowing it with a tall, modern hotel.

How would Wolfe have reacted to a 1984 study which rated Asheville the third best place to live in the country? (The Greensboro-Winston-Salem-High Point metropolitan area tied for first, Raleigh was fifth.) Would he better understand the balance between preservation and innovation?

Although ostracized in his native Asheville for Look Homeward Angel, *Thomas Wolfe's birthplace is now a state historic site, preserved as it was when the author grew up. The change of attitude toward Wolfe perhaps confirms the dual commitment to preservation and innovation. Courtesy, N.C. Travel & Tourism*

7

"THE GOODLIEST LAND"

The natural beauty of the Outer Banks attracts many summer visitors seeking unspoiled, sunny beaches. Courtesy, Outer Banks Visitors Bureau

You have to crouch in the lowest deck of a seventy-foot, sixteenth-century sailing bark to really appreciate what our forebears went through to get us here. Forget the hostile Indians, the frigid winters, the paucity of food. Ponder two to three months on the Atlantic, packed into a juniper-walled cubbyhole with fifty or so other people, a few farm animals, and the rest of the cargo of a new civilization.

America passed her 200th birthday in 1976 with a fitting year-long, nationwide celebration; eight years later came the less-noticed 400th anniversary of the real beginning of English-speaking settlement of the country. The party was held at the same place where those first settlers stepped off their boats—twenty-two years before Jamestown and forty-five years before Plymouth Rock—on Roanoke Island, North Carolina. The centerpiece was a stunningly authentic recreation of one of the ships that sailed in 1584, when the business of the first North Carolinians was just getting here and surviving.

This rugged little vessel, with its elaborate rigging and spartan quarters, docked at Manteo for all to see and explore, serves as an example that when North Carolina perceives an opportunity to show off, nothing is too expensive or takes too long to prepare.

One of those earliest English explorers had called this first chunk of the New World "the goodliest land under the cope of Heaven," and by the 1980s, its leasing to visitors—some of the last unspoiled beaches on the East Coast and some of the country's oldest and most scenic mountains, with dozens of attractions in between—was big, big business. Tourism joined textiles and tobacco as the state's Big Three industries.

Other things, too, were happening in a land which at times had been a sleeper, things which held bright but challenging possibilities for new economic trends. The first wave of high-income, well-pensioned senior citizens, raised during the Depression and looking to relax in paradise, made the state the fastest-growing retirement haven, just as the older segment of the nation's population was mushrooming. A major industry that had started in the California town of Holly-

wood also took notice of North Carolina's variety of natural beauty and started leaving a few calling cards.

* * *

Charleston has always been a showplace of the South, from its heyday as a mercantile seaport where immeasurable numbers of men got incredibly rich and spent most of their money at home, to the well-preserved splendor that feeds the dreams of modern-day visitors from everywhere. But in summer, Charleston is and always has been hot and muggy.

As early as the mid-1800s, the same roads over which the wagon trains imported Charleston's bounty to the more isolated parts of the South also bore human caravans of summertime escapees. They apparently settled in the first place they felt cool breezes: the area around Flat Rock in the Blue Ridge Mountains south of Asheville, beyond the Saluda Gap and up the Buncombe Turnpike from the South Carolina heat, became a summer resort of stately manors built by Charleston families.

In a vastly different setting in the southeast-

ern corner of the state's Piedmont, an area known in the late 1800s as the Pine Barrens was home to acres and acres of longleaf pines, one of the few things that would grow in the sandy soil. Although the Indians shunned the area and farmers subsequently cussed its infertility, it gained notice by those who observed that the dread disease of tuberculosis did not flourish there.

A man appointed by the governor to speed the state's post-Civil War recovery in 1881 began advertising as a health resort the new town of Southern Pines, and northerners flocked in numbers beyond anybody's expectations. Meanwhile, a Boston millionaire named James Walker Tufts was looking for a place to establish a warm-climate vacation community. Tufts chose an area but a stone's throw from Southern Pines and carved out a New England-style village of cottages with ornate landscaping, a hotel, streets, utilities, and vast undeveloped fields where men and women of leisure could play a curious game little-known to Americans—golf. Conceived as a rest and recuperation spot for people of small means but eventually priced out of their reach, this paradise became known as Pinehurst.

Back in the mountains, tourist traffic from Charleston, Northeastern cities, and even the Midwest soon bestowed economic benefits on the area surrounding Asheville. The famous, like Henry Ford, Thomas Edison, Woodrow Wilson, and Franklin Roosevelt, and the not-so-famous, who came simply to relax and breathe the peaceful and healthful mountain air, called

Above
Showing her ribs, the Elizabeth II *took shape on the shores of North Carolina at Manteo. The vessel was built to commemorate the 400th anniversary of the first settlement, Roanoke Island. Courtesy, N.C. Division of Archives & History*

Right
Here a crew member raises the ship's mast. Courtesy, N.C. Division of Archives & History

Millionaire George W. Vanderbilt would have been welcomed anywhere, but chose Asheville as his haven. Vanderbilt commissioned architect Frederick Law Olmsted to design the breathtaking gardens surrounding his estate. Courtesy, N.C. Division of Archives & History

Asheville "Little Switzerland." Millionaire George Vanderbilt ended his quest for the most beautiful place on earth for a mansion site, buying thousands of acres just south of the city at the turn of the century. F. Scott Fitzgerald, too, fell in love with the place and mentioned it in most of his novels. By 1920 Asheville was a boomtown built on the tourist trade.

While putting together a series of guidebooks to the states, author Irvin Cobb in 1924 noticed that thousands of people who ran from undesirable weather—the heat of Florida and the cold of the Northeast—passed through North Caroli-

na. Trouble was, they were asleep in their train cars. Cobb suggested that somebody stop the trains, rouse the passengers, and show them what they were missing.

Cobb titled his North Carolina edition "North Carolina—All She Needs is a Press Agent." In 1937 she finally got a promoter when the state set up the Division of State Advertising to coordinate local tourist attractions into an organized public relations campaign. Within a short time, the resorts weren't just for the rich anymore.

As the advertising campaign progressed, the beaches—with a longer warm season and smaller crowds than those farther north—turned from strictly weekend escapes for eastern North Carolinians to tourist magnets for states from Virginia through the Northeast and Midwest. Visitors started coming to the mountains not just for relaxation but for recreation—camping and hiking on the ridges and fishing and canoeing in the streams that cut between them. And in the middle, promoters pushed old plantations, state parks, historic districts, and increasingly prestigious music and arts festivals.

By the 1980s the state's "Variety Vacationland" had a full-time staff of "press agents." The industry's growth even made the mills and factories envious: tourists—72 percent of them non-North Carolinians—spent $3.4 billion in the Tar Heel State during 1983, a dollar figure which had risen 10 percent from the previous year and 16 percent from the year before that.

For a steadily growing Sunbelt state, North Carolina was doing a remarkable job of preserving its attractiveness, rather than manufacturing playgrounds. The same treacherous coastal waters and shoreline that had inhibited economic growth in the formative years now impeded land development and kept the Outer Banks pristine—at the very time when beaches elsewhere were overrun with buildings and people. In the western parts of the state, some counties gave up more than half of their taxable property so that the government could maintain unspoiled mountain forests.

North Carolina's appeal was not lost on a fast-growing group, retired people from all over the country with the desire and the incomes to leave their homes and spend their golden years

Vying for Asheville's booming tourist trade, the Manor Hotel used this picture to spread the word about its services. The "chimes" mentioned in the advertisement summoned hotel guests to meals. Courtesy, the N.C. Collection, UNC, Chapel Hill

The beach cottages at Nags Head on the Outer Banks have provided a retreat for generations of North Carolinians. Within a few miles are Jockey's Ridge, the largest sand dune in the East, and Kitty Hawk, where the Wright brothers made their historic flight. This scene captures the slow, relaxing days of 1915. Courtesy, Postcard Collection, William R. Perkins Library, Duke University

in more peaceful and comfortable surroundings. By the mid-1980s this migration signalled profound economic changes to many parts of the state.

The retirees, often from the Northeast where they had wearied of commuting, crowds, and crime, traditionally had moved to warm-weather resorts in Florida and Arizona. But as the nation's older population grew rapidly, those areas began to take on some of the characteristics of the places from which the retirees had escaped. One result: North Carolina, ranking seventeenth in popularity as a retirement haven in 1970, leaped to seventh a decade later to become the fastest-growing retirement state.

The reasons paralleled the tourist recruiters' sales pitch. People who shivered in the Northeast and Midwest or sweltered in Florida, were, in the words of one New Hampshire native, "drunk on the climate" of North Carolina. The retirees typically were affluent and well-educated and, except for those in their later years, quite active. What they liked to do they could afford to do, and they came for picturesque mountain trout streams, the golf courses around Pinehurst so numerous that promoters lost count, and arts and cultural attractions offered in the bigger cities. With increasing worries about health problems, they were comfortable living near prestigious Durham, Chapel Hill, and Winston-Salem hospitals.

At the conclusion of hectic working lives in fast-paced cities and suburbs, they craved small town-ness. Thus, one of the state's most charming—but economically debilitating—aspects became the serum for a financial shot in the arm. A college professor who retired to Chapel Hill from New York said, "One thing that impressed me about this town was when I drove down the main street, I just liked the feel of it—the way the university and the town complemented each other." Others came to get away from it all. Said a woman who with her husband left New Jersey for rural Transylvania County to raise rhododendron in a secluded mountain cove, "I can't think of any place in the world I'd rather live."

Along with their appreciation of the good life, the retirees brought their checkbooks. Between 1970 and 1980, the state's retirement income rose from $819 million to $3.7 billion—from 5.3 percent to 8 percent of the total personal income. One estimate held that the average migrant retiree would bring a quarter of a million dollars to North Carolina during his or her lifetime, a boost that no industry could come close to matching. Enhancing the potential economic impact of the retirees was the fact that they made few demands on schools, law enforcement, and other public facilities.

Houses they did need. Asheville began to experience a new boom in construction of houses and apartments. Real estate became big business in mountain hamlets like Brevard, which had suffered an absence of tax revenue since a national park enveloped 60 percent of the land in its county. The Pinehurst area saw a sudden upsurge in the construction of $100,000-plus homes. In Tarboro, a large apartment-nursing complex for retirees anchored the revitalization of a depressed and blighted downtown; the creation of "life-care centers" like this one represented an entirely new enterprise that spread quickly across the state.

The new North Carolinians added to the quality of life in other ways. Restaurants and retail outlets were upgraded to fit more cosmopol-

Vacationers still flock to the Morehead City area for sunshine and the fresh sea breeze. No doubt visitors who stayed at the Atlantic Hotel in 1908 would find today's beach resort attire a bit shocking. Courtesy, Postcard Collection, William R. Perkins Library, Duke University

Recycling techniques have been employed to accommodate Asheville's growing retirement community. The George Vanderbilt Hotel, constructed in 1924 by a group of local businessmen, now serves as a senior citizens' apartment building. Courtesy, the Ewart Ball Collection, Southern Highlands Research Center, UNC, Asheville

itan lifestyles, and the retirees proved to be some of the biggest supporters of local arts programs. Also, they invariably gave a lift to volunteer projects.

Despite these developments—and the concerns among retirees and the people serving them that some rural areas were growing too fast and that new institutions like life-care centers were blossoming without the proper regulation—the state Department of Commerce was slow to recognize migrant retirement as an industry. It continued to focus instead on the traditional recruitment of the industries more directly tied to new jobs, leaving the retirement business to an unencumbered private sector.

The state was not quite so shy with a restless motion picture industry. At various times starting in the 1950s, Hollywood had found certain aspects of North Carolina attractive on the few occasions when producers ventured out of the big California studios for location filming. The house and grounds of Vanderbilt's photogenic Biltmore estate, for example, drew several moviemakers.

By the late 1970s, the technical end of the industry had matured to the point at which location filming was as much the rule as the exception, and a studio executive told state recruiters that most of it took place in the South. At about the same time, the production at Biltmore of a major feature film was pumping some two million dollars directly into Asheville's economy. These were the sparks that ignited a serious effort to recruit the film industry to the state.

As usual, the red carpet rolled forth. Hollywood had started taking the industry for granted, and was sometimes grudging in the use of city streets and other facilities for out-of-studio filming. In North Carolina, if a film producer wanted the run of a state park, if he wanted to close off Asheville streets to traffic or take over an old Wilmington neighborhood for a day, he just said the word. And, of course, at a time when unions and high wages for support personnel had become a tremendous problem in Hollywood, movie producers shared with other industrialists knowledge about the state's labor policies.

The early results were quite encouraging. Between 1980 and 1984, thirty feature films were made in North Carolina. The old, established companies showed few signs of leaving Hollywood—they generally were believed to have too much invested there—but major production firms not affiliated with the studios nibbled at the lines, and one big one bit.

After one of his associates discovered that the restored Orton Plantation near Wilmington provided the exact setting for which he was looking, international producer Dino De Laurentiis made a major thriller film there in 1983. De Laurentiis, who previously had produced almost all of his hundreds of films overseas, liked his experience in North Carolina. After a lively competition between Wilmington and Charleston for the location of his first American studio, he chose Wilmington.

The producer's right-hand man explained a decisive factor which held a key to the industry's future in the state: "There aren't many geographical locations in the world where you can find as many location advantages. You can find any geographical setting for location filming you want in Carolina except the desert. Then I was informed Fort Bragg has some wonderful drop zones that look like deserts."

De Laurentiis began building some ten sound stages, immediately announced plans to make five films at Wilmington, and started hiring local people and spending money—lots of money—in the town. During the plantation filming, for example, the company spent $78,000 on lumber and fixtures at local stores. They employed 500 local people for acting or service jobs. A Chamber of Commerce executive conser-

vatively estimated that for the first film made at the studio, five million dollars flowed into the city's economy.

Considering the films produced before 1984 and the financial contributions from a budding television commercial business in Charlotte, the state Department of Commerce calculated that $355 million had found its way into the state during four and a half years. The movie people went first class, they often combined work with onsite vacations, and they attracted ancillary business like the camera company, which moved into Wilmington to serve De Laurentiis.

In the mid-1980s, the jury still was out on the North Carolina-Hollywood connection, but, as with the computer and the electronics industries before it, the state had firmly planted a foot in the door. And, as with the well-established tourism trade and the burgeoning business of retirement migration, North Carolina had summoned its seemingly limitless natural beauty for its economic advantage.

The port of Wilmington has played an active part in
North Carolina commerce since colonial days. Courtesy,
N.C. Division of Tourism, Film, and Sports Development

Facing page
The North Carolina Studio used this four-story Chinatown
set for the 1985 film Year of the Dragon. Courtesy, North
Carolina Film Corporation.

8

A TIME
OF CHANGE

Not yet home to the tallest building in the Southeast, downtown Charlotte in the mid 1980s was on the verge of a building boom. Courtesy, N.C. Travel & Tourism.

Change never really felt welcome in North Carolina. The folks from the bustling cities in other colonies were fond of telling stories about the slothful lot they had encountered down south: content to scratch around when they had to on their little farms, or to whittle away the days and fiddle away the nights on the mountainsides. One wag said it was the plenteousness of the land: the fields, forests, and streams were so abundant with what people needed to subsist, and the climate so agreeable, that basic living was easy; with the population so small and so scattered (and so scantily schooled), no incentive existed for doing much more than merely getting by.

Later on, there was a moral reluctance to foresake the farm life, however tenuous economically, for the close quarters of a mill village and the impersonal, shut-in factory job. (And what modern economists call venture capital also was lacking.) It took a devastating war that changed a way of life to alter such habits.

A hand-to-mouth economy perpetuated itself: tobacco farmers and textile mill owners alike were slow to automate, because their businesses naturally operated on such low profit margins that they didn't have the cash for improvements.

Gradually, strong-willed men—with more than a little help from a picture-postcard landscape, an alluring small-town charm, and that agreeable climate—coaxed the state down the path of industrial diversification. One could call that the turning point. One also could put the turning point a bit later—at a time in the mid-1980s when there seemed to be more questions than answers, when the old foundations of the industrial leader of the Southeast were quaking, and when the new foundations barely had thrust past their infancy.

What was in store for a textile industry greatly threatened by developing countries whose manufacturers could produce goods so much less expensively? Would the flow of new positions in new industries continue to keep up with the loss of mill jobs to automation? What of the tobacco farmer and the industry which he fed, now that even the Baptist Church railed

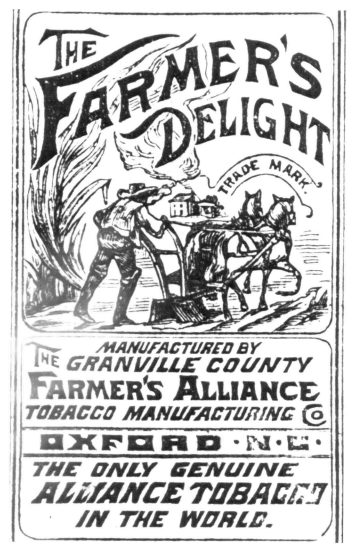

Once the farmer's delight, tobacco growing is no longer certain to bring big profits. Courtesy, N.C. Division of Archives & History

against him? Did the state have the money and the will to bring its schools up to the standards modern businesses would demand? And was conversion as simple as saying, "We did it with textiles, we can do it with microchips"?

Turpentine, trees, and tobacco had sufficed at one time. In the waning years of the twentieth century, however, it was clear that North Carolina would have to rely less on what it had at home and more on its industrial panache in an increasingly competitive nation and world. Change—rapid change—was banging on the door, and couldn't be kept waiting.

* * *

Benny Keith, of northern Wake County, was riding the tobacco sleds when he was knee-high to the mules and knew less about the business than they did. But by 1971 (maybe it was '72, he said), his father had had enough—he planted his last crop of leaf. The neighbors who provided the labor all had gone their separate ways, and for Benny's father, it was a choice of either investing money he didn't have in automation, or getting out. Benny was an accountant. Because his family held onto its land and because he loved to farm, the Wake County native raised cattle in his spare time.

Down in Rocky Mount, where the Tar River swings north briefly before heading to the sea, is a stately monument to the textile industry's past. In the mid 1980s, Rocky Mount Mills still manufactured cotton and synthetic yarns on some of the very foundations upon which Joel Battle built the state's second mill in 1818. The company owned a good-sized village, though with seventy houses it was only half as big as it once was.

In the 150-year-old house built by one of Joel's sons, Thomas Battle, a sixth-generation descendant of the mill's founder, surrounded himself with textile artifacts. But Battle had little time to dwell on the past. The mill was running three shifts five and six days a week; Battle installed a lot of German-made machines and some computer-operated equipment. But, he was understandably cautious: "We're such an up-and-down business. You go through lean times,

In this 1980s era photo, logs at Brown's Agricultural Basket Company in Woodland are turned into baskets for holding apples, peaches, sweet potatoes, and other kinds of produce. These crops continue to play a bigger role in the state's economy, as tobacco's share dwindles. Photo by Roger Manley.

and you have to cut back...."

Electronics were in; textiles—well, sometimes the politicians crowing about industrial development forgot to mention textiles.

Between 1978 and 1982, the number of farms in the state declined from 81,706 to 72,799. That was a 12.2 percent drop, a figure that was not offset by the small increase in the average size of farms. The number of farms had fallen since the

mid-1940s, but until the mid-1970s the decline had been very slow.

Tobacco acreage and production dropped similarly and, as industry diversified, so did farmers. Tobacco produced half of all farm income in the 1950s, and by the 1980s it accounted for less than a third; poultry, hogs, fruit, and vegetables took bigger shares. The decline in farm employment was much more dramatic—far

Above
A cotton industry worker services a jacquard loom. Jacquards were the first digitally-controlled machines capable of weaving complex, multi-colored designs. Photo by Roger Manley

Left
At Occonechee Neck, Northampton County, small farming operations still require the full participation of family members. Photo by Roger Manley

Rows of carding machines smooth and straighten fibers as they are spun into yarn. At one time people carried out this task at home, using pairs of bristled boards. Photo by Roger Manley

too much to be explained away by automation—while jobs in manufacturing and most other categories swung the other way.

To Benny Keith, who longed to farm full-time, the reasons for the exodus seemed simple enough. The price for cattle never rose between 1969, when he went off to college, and the early 1980s. The cost of fertilizer doubled or tripled, and the price of barbed wire to keep the cows at home went up fivefold. "If there was any way to make a living in farming, I'd rather do it than anything else," he said. "If I could make it work."

When Keith left the office, he often faced several more hours of work on the farm. He loved to walk around the pastures and count the cows: "Being a farmer is sort of like an athlete with an inborn ability, it just gets in your system and you can't get it out." But he sometimes wondered if it was worth his efforts. "When you stop making money it takes all the fun out of it."

By the mid-'80s, others in northern Wake stopped wondering. Very little tobacco was being grown there, and many of the families who held their land for generations sold out to satisfy Raleigh's spreading housing demand. "It's gotten to the point you don't know half the people who live up here," Keith said. "You used to know everybody who owned every foot of land in the area."

One thing was certain: when the land was sold, it stopped being a farm. "There's no way for somebody who isn't in [farming] to buy into it. To buy the equipment, you'd have to pay more on the interest than you could ever hope to make on the farm."

If there was any doubt that tobacco was on shaky ground, much of it disappeared in 1984. It was then revealed that the unsold tobacco in the warehouses of the Flue-Cured Tobacco Cooperative Stabilization Corp., the guardian of the price support system which buys the golden leaf with borrowed federal funds and waits for a better market than the farmers could get, had ballooned to 756 million pounds. The group put the tobacco up for sale at bargain prices, and experts feared that this move would cost the government some $250 million—and mean the loss of many friends in Congress who would

Commercial fishing in North Carolina is a multi-million
dollar industry. Courtesy, Outer Banks Visitors Bureau

begin to see the program as a subsidy.

Not even the Baptist Church could be counted
as a friend anymore. The Southern Baptist Convention voted in 1984 to condemn the use of
tobacco products, calling for an end to any
subsidies and suggesting that more farmers find
something else to grow. (North Carolina's Baptist
Organization quickly distinguished itself from the
national group by encouraging Tar Heel Baptists
to weigh the economic considerations along with
the moral and ethical questions.)

Tobacco, however, had not lost its most
important ally. People just weren't going to stop

smoking altogether, a fact Philip Morris recognized when it opened a massive new cigarette
plant in Cabarrus County in 1983.

Textile manufacturers have never faced
such a moral outcry, save perhaps from nudist
colonies. But for them, the profound change—
which began when foreigners started mass-
producing fabric and when the government
came down on dirty work environments—has
not abated. While textiles still dominated
the state's manufacturing in 1984, the loss of
jobs to plant closings and to automation in
the 1970s contributed to the urgency of

One could buy fresh seafood off the dock or sit down to a plate of oysters at all hours at the New Bern fish market in 1906. Courtesy, N.C. Division of Archives & History

bringing in other types of manufacturing. Consequently, textiles were put on a back burner.

Although Thomas Battle's family twice endured having their mill burned to the ground, he probably spoke for them all when he said, "We're proud of it, and we've enjoyed it all." But Battle admitted that textiles' kingship was on the wane.

"I would see it declining. The effort to attract industry certainly isn't in attracting textiles. The new plants around here all are high-profit industries," and, he said, are formidable competition in the labor market. "'We don't compete with a pharmaceutical company or a lock company or a glass company." During World War II, Rocky Mount Mills employed 850 people, but automation reduced that to 425 by 1984. "Everything we do," Battle stated, "is oriented to one less job."

Frustration over foreign competition was mounting. "We've got a tremendous problem with imports," Battle noted.

They say, well, why don't you just compete with them. We can't compete with them. How do you compete with a wage scale that's half what your is, with production processes that get tremendous subsidies? I don't have any great hope that, with the [Reagan] administration taking the view of free trade, there will be any great relief in the curbing of imports.

At least one other significant industry faced an uncertain future. Since the days when the state's population was concentrated in the coastal towns, men have spent very rich days and very lean ones on the rivers, sounds, and the Atlantic Ocean. In 1982 North Carolina ranked seventh nationally in the volume of its fishermen's catch and tenth in the value of the catch; among localities, Beaufort-Morehead City ranked seventh and sixteenth, respectively, and the tiny communities of Wanchese, Oriental, and Vanderriere also were in the top fifty.

Fishing, however, remained the same as it always was—a great gamble. In the words of one trawler crewman, "Every time you throw the lines off the dock it's like going to Las Vegas." The industry had its second best year in 1982, when fishermen harvested $63.8 million; a year later, the catch was down 13 percent and the take was only $57.4 million.

Development of processing plants in the state would have added to the value of the catches, but there was very little movement in this direction. Two problems apparently stood in the way of big-time processing: too little demand for seafood and fish at home, which made it more lucrative to simply box and ship the catch to Northeastern cities; and seasonal facts of life which have given Tar Heel fishermen only a few months each year (as opposed to year-round seasons farther north) to go after the popular fish.

Despite an estimated $325 million-a-year contribution to the coastal economy, a 1979 state report questioned whether the term "industry" applied to fishing and showed how little this pursuit had changed over the years:

Many North Carolina fishermen and commercial dealers appear to operate out of their pockets on a cash basis. Among the smaller ones there is little planning, virtually no organization, uncoordinated employment and supervisory policies, and no established controls. Cooperation among dealers and fishermen is generally minimal while competition is keen. Fierce, prideful independence characterizes the commercial fisherman.

By the mid 1980s, the furniture industry had slipped some in the state's manufacturing rankings, giving way to tourism and electronics. But it was no less a source of pride, as people from all over the country continued to associate North Carolina with fine furniture. Manufacturers here also had reason for one of the brightest outlooks as the baby boom came of age: the thirty to forty age bracket made good money and was intent on living in high style.

The business of finance, not to be outdone in the rising tide of change, was verging on a possible rearrangement, as Charlotte flexed its muscles to become a Southeastern banking center. Three North Carolina lending institutions—North Carolina National Bank, Wachovia, and First Union—were among the top fifty banks in the country with regard to resources. They also stood to add to their stature under new rules of

(continued on page 161)

As the capital of North Carolina, Raleigh is the seat of state government and a center for international business and higher education. Courtesy, Greater Raleigh CVB

Today cereal boxes feature coupons or little "gifts," but in the early years of this century the trading cards found in tobacco products were hot promotional items. W. Duke Sons & Company distributed these "costume ball" cards, undoubtedly a sensation with hat fanciers. Courtesy, Tobacco Collection, William R. Perkins Library, Duke University

W.T. Blackwell's "Bull Durham" tobacco became known
all over the country, not just from ads like this, but from
paintings on the sides of buildings. Courtesy, Tobacco
Collection, William R. Perkins Library, Duke University

When it came to advertising Honest Long Cut Tobacco, W. Duke Sons & Company used a series of demure but curvaceous ladies to catch the customer's attention. Courtesy, Tobacco Collection, William R. Perkins Library, Duke University

Another series of W. Duke Sons & Company tobacco trading cards, "Shadows" amazingly transformed the profiles of comic characters into animal images. The goal, of course, was to collect a complete set. Courtesy, Tobacco Collection, William R. Perkins Library, Duke University

The Hazards of Automobile Travel. *North Carolina's first roads evolved from trails and wagon roads. As the first automobiles came on the scene, use of the existing roadways was perilous indeed. Courtesy, Samuel D. Bissette*

Below
Dismal Swamp Canal At South Mills. *Completed in 1812 north of Elizabeth City, the twenty-two-mile Dismal Swamp Canal opened up water commerce from the Chesapeake Bay to North Carolina's Albemarle Sound. It is now part of the Intracoastal Waterway. Courtesy, Samuel D. Bissette*

Above
Schooners At Elizabeth City. *Sailing ships were a part of the state's history from the very beginning up to the early twentieth century. These ships varied from the small sound freighters to the large five-masters that came into Wilmington. Courtesy, Samuel D. Bissette*

Left
Mount Airy Street Scene *With changing times, the old and the new were thrown together dramatically. Here covered wagons share the street with overhead electric wires. At the left, just out of the picture, is the Mount Airy Saloon—soon to be a victim of state-wide prohibition in 1909. Courtesy, Samuel D. Bissette*

Below
Ferry Over The Yadkin River. *For the larger rivers, cable ferries were the practical solution for those wishing to cross. This ferry was later replaced in 1922 by the Swift Island bridge connecting Stanly and Montgomery counties. Courtesy, Samuel D. Bissette*

The Cape Hatteras Lighthouse was built in 1879. In 1999 it was moved 1,300 feet inland to protect it from beach erosion. Courtesy, N. C. Division of Tourism, Film, and Sports Development

North Carolina's third and present Executive Mansion was primarily constructed by convict labor using many in-state materials. Completed in 1891, it is one of the state's best examples of Queen Anne architecture. Courtesy, N.C. Division of Tourism, Film, and Sports Development

Above
Charlotte's hands-on children's science museum, *Discovery Place*, includes a three-story rainforest, a planetarium, and an OMNI-MAX theater. *Courtesy, N.C. Division of Tourism, Film, and Sports Development*

Below
The North Carolina Museum of Art features a selection of works spanning 5,000 years, from ancient Egypt to the present. The museum's paintings include internationally recognized Renaissance, Baroque, British eighteenth-century, and American nineteenth-century pieces. *Courtesy, Greater Raleigh CVB*

Each summer the renowned American Dance Festival takes over the campus of Duke University in Durham. The festival, begun in Bennington, Vermont by Martha Graham, moved to North Carolina in 1978. Courtesy, N.C. Division of Tourism, Film, and Sports Development

In 2004 renovations began on the Pine Knoll Shores Aquarium. The facility will triple in size and include a 306,000 gallon ocean tank. Courtesy, N.C. Division of Tourism, Film, and Sports Development

Wool E. Bull is the mascot of the world-famous Durham Bulls Baseball Club. The Triple-A Bulls are the International League affiliate of the Tampa Bay Devil Rays. Courtesy, 1997 Durham Convention & Visitors Bureau

The 73,000 seat Bank of America Stadium is home to the Carolina Panthers. Located on the edge of downtown Charlotte, it is a striking addition to the city's skyline. Courtesy, Visit Charlotte

*Approximately 700,000 people attend the State Fair each
year, making it the largest annual event in North
Carolina. Held each year during mid-October, the ten-day
fair features livestock, agricultural arts, and cultural
exhibitions, an amusement midway and nightly
nationally-acclaimed musical performances. Courtesy,
Greater Raleigh CVB*

Above
Lowe's Motor Speedway attracts crowds of 150,000 to the various NASCAR events held each year. Courtesy, N.C. Division of Tourism, Film, and Sports Development

Below
North Carolina ski resorts, such as Sugar Mountain, draw thousands of visitors annually. Courtesy, N.C. Division of Tourism, Film, and Sports Development

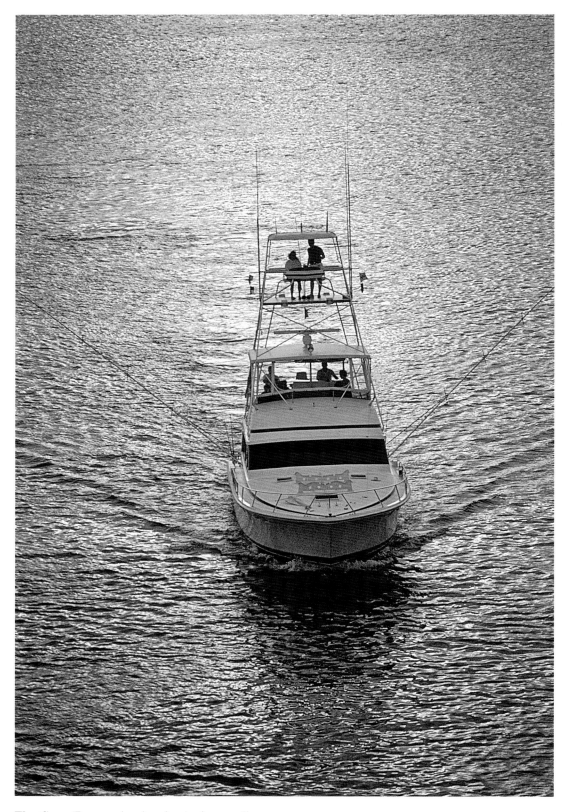

The Cape Fear region is a boater's paradise.
Courtesy, N.C. Division of Tourism/ Bill Russ

"Unto These Hills Outdoor Drama" in Cherokee, portrays the history of the Cherokee Indians from 1540 until the tragic "Trail of Tears" in 1839. Courtesy, N.C. Division of Tourism, Film, and Sports Development

One of the world's finest natural habitat zoos is located in Asheboro. The North Carolina zoo is home to over 1,100 animals from a variety of continents. Courtesy, N.C. Division of Tourism, Film, and Sports Development

A nationally prominent gathering of Scottish clans is held each year during the Highland Games on Grandfather Mountain. Courtesy, N.C. Division of Tourism, Film, and Sports Development

The Biltmore Estate, located in Asheville, includes the largest private residence in America, lovely formal and informal gardens, and a winery. Courtesy, N.C. Division of Tourism, Film, and Sports Development

The N.C. Maritime Museum preserves this state's rich maritime heritage with cultural and educational programs. Courtesy, N. C. Division of Tourism, Film, and Sports Development

Southern Pines has developed a reputation not only as a golf destination, but also as an equestrian center. Courtesy, N. C. Division of Tourism, Film, and Sports Development

Above
Hikes to the summit of Chimney Rock Park are rewarded by astounding views of Hickory Nut Falls, which was displayed dramatically in the feature film Last of the Mohicans. *Courtesy, N.C. Division of Tourism, Film, and Sports Development*

Below
Twin Falls near Brevard is one of 250 waterfalls in Transylvania County. Courtesy, N.C. Division of Tourism, Film, and Sports Development

a game to which several states in the region agreed. The hitherto forbidden practice of regional interstate banking had begun to flourish, allowing lending houses in some states to merge with other banks across state lines. Passage of the legislation prompted executives to study which smaller banks they could take over to their advantage, which larger institutions might want to swallow them, and with which comparably sized lending houses they might merge in order to shore up their assets and ward off a takeover by one of the giants.

The move was a prelude to national interstate banking. By allowing the bigger Southeastern banks to absorb others and grow, regional legislators hoped to make them formidable entries into a much larger game.

Such a broadening of the merger privilege seemed to suggest the demise of the personable, small-town banks on which North Carolina farmers and small business people depended for so long. Yet nobody was certain how widespread the new trend would be. In the end, such a change boosted economic development for the state as a whole, allowing several banks already prominent in their region to grow stronger.

On another front, business people continued to bemoan the state's inventory tax as a monkey on the backs of the industrial recruiters. In the mid-1980s manufacturers, retailers, and wholesalers paid some $205 million annually on their business inventories. Despite strong opposition from local governments, the inventory tax was finally repealed in 1987.

More often than not, business gets what it wants and needs from state government. Relations seldom were better than in the period that began in 1977, when Governor Jim Hunt and Commerce Secretary Lauch Faircloth brought industry recruiting into the Commerce Department and formalized a process that previously had relied on piecemeal efforts by the governors who followed Luther Hodges.

With a strong shove from business people, the governor and the legislature in 1984 turned their attention to the state's schools. In the industrial push of the mid-twentieth century,

good schools had become a priority not only of North Carolinians, but of the people who considered moving businesses here. They sought employees who could operate sophisticated machines and who were responsible, informed citizens. Also, they wanted to be able to ensure the well-educated executives who they brought with them that their children would get the best in their new home.

As industries sailed into the state, the public schools seemed to be foundering; the bottom dropped out in 1983 with the release of a series of reports on the deplorable condition of public education nationwide. Test scores were dropping, teachers expressed discontent with their jobs, the schools had drifted away from the basic preparatory skills, and—most importantly perhaps—the children in the rising foreign industrial powers were believed to be better trained. Because it was in the process of recruiting first rate industries and because its schools always had been below the national norm, North Carolina couldn't ignore the indictment.

"A lot of folks have asked about catching up with the Japanese, catching up with the Germans. I think it's left the rhetoric stage," observed state schools Superintendent Craig Phillips. "Industry used to want to know just what kind of tax breaks they were going to get. Now they want to know about the people."

The legislature in 1984 responded to the crisis and to the report of the North Carolina Commission on Education for Economic Growth by pouring an unprecedented $272 million into the schools. "That's nice, Phillips commented, but it still leaves the state well short of the national average per-pupil expenditure"—a problem which he believed would call for business to really put its money where its mouth was.

"One of the things we need to keep on probing is how we translate what is really surface interest into what is business really willing to invest in every child." A $50,000 grant to a local school system or a one-year executive loan to the schools may help out, he said, but they prove to be very small tokens in the overall scheme.

"I don't want to appear ungrateful, because these are great gestures, but it's different from them coming over to the legislature and saying, 'We want to double our corporate taxes so you can spend twice as much per kid.'"

Phillips also worried about complacency after the legislature's bold, $272-million move. "There's a real danger that some very responsible people will say, 'We've taken care of them' ... and there's still a long way to go." More and more, the industries will be watching.

The community college system, which has always focused its efforts on training for both old and new industries, enjoyed nothing but praise as one of the country's best, and it has been seldom overlooked in a corporate executive's list of compliments. But the system's director, former Governor Bob Scott, was also wary of complacency. He knew his history.

North Carolina State University was started when it was apparent the University of North Carolina wasn't going to teach farming and manufacturing skills. Similarly, the community colleges got their impetus in the post-World War II economy, which found universities delinquent in

North Carolina's biggest resource remains its people. Over the next few decades, increasing educational opportunities and a new wave of businesses will change the nature of the Tar Heel workforce. Photo by Roger Manley

meeting the training needs of the new industries that Luther Hodges was rounding up. "If we in the community college system do not stay alert," Scott said, "another vacuum will be created, and another type system will come along and fill it."

That meant paying teachers enough to stop their exodus to the payrolls of the industries for which they were training their students. It also meant coaxing the money to outfit some schools with expensive microelectronic, computer, and robotics equipment. And finally, it meant maintaining the delicate balance between vocational training and academics.

"There's always those who want us to become academic," Scott said. "We don't want ivy growing up around our windows to the point we can't see what's going on out there. On the other side of the coin, the high number of functional illiterates in the state is a drag on the economy, and certainly hampers our ability to train the workforce. Our emphasis now is going to be on the ability to adapt to changes quickly."

* * *

One could apply that statement to the bigger picture of North Carolina's economic development in the last decades of the twentieth century.

By any account, the quality of life in the state was very, very good and the prospects for the future, bright enough to draw the envy of any state in any other region. It epitomized the positive characteristics of the Sunbelt—close to the top of every expert's list of the best places for businesses to migrate and grow (the AFL-CIO's excepted).

North Carolina's even mix of rural farmland, small towns, and almost-big cities was touted as the future population distribution arrangement for many industrialized parts of the country. In the words of one person who compared this gradual, dispersed growth with the traditional pattern of concentration around one gigantic metropolis, "The state has passed from rural to industrial without becoming urban."

Still, the North Carolina of the 1980s was short enough on experience, close enough to the earlier stages of growth, and uncertain enough of its place in the

A cardboard manufacturing machine at the Halifax Paper Board Company helps turn forest resources into another North Carolina product. Photo by Roger Manley

national economic community to leave a lot of doubts unsettled.

A report from the Commission on the Future of North Carolina, for instance, suggested that the advantages of the Sunbelt phenomenon were very slowly but very steadily evaporating, creating an urgency about acquiring the right type of industrial base. The report pointed out many other critical issues: that areas of the original industrial heartland, such as Pennsylvania and Maryland, were catching up with the southern states in incentives like price breaks for land, lower cost financing for buildings and machinery, and relaxed tax burdens and zoning restrictions; that the era of surplus labor was declining as the baby boom leveled off; that the loss of federal funds in the 1980s budget cutting—money which the Sunbelt states had used to improve infrastructure—threw local governments back into the old dilemma of either keeping taxes low to avoid scaring industry off or raising taxes to enhance their attractiveness. The report also postulated a cooling off of industry's honeymoon with rural areas, since the number and types of businesses which can do without the sophisticated climate of a metropolitan setting are limited.

That offered an "I told you so" opportunity to the critics of Governor Hunt's Balanced Growth Policy—the name given to the battle plan drawn up when he formed an industrial recruitment army in the Commerce Department. The blueprint called for improving the state's national position by attracting high-wage, non-traditional industries, and by channeling them to rural and small-town areas. This would give a lift to the places which needed it most, while ensuring needy job seekers that a commute to the bigger cities would be unnecessary.

Those who looked a little deeper saw a contradiction: the really sophisticated industries would shy away from rural areas and the types willing to locate in those quarters would simply perpetuate the low-skill, low-wage tradition. Others charged that the policy was nothing more than good ribbon-cutting rhetoric designed to mask the simple effort of bringing in any industry which could compensate for the loss of textile jobs. Critics further presumed it ludicrous to try to influence any corporation's choice of location.

Opposition to "balanced growth," nevertheless, was akin to ranting against motherhood and democracy. The criticism was, to say the least, muted and the results, by whatever name, were hardly questionable in a state that so badly needed to diversify.

"High tech" probably is the most overused term in the industrial lexicon; as former Commerce Secretary Faircloth said, every industry is high-tech these days. But by the standard definition, the emphasis on categories like electronic components, communications equipment, and computer services netted North Carolina more than its share of the benefits.

Then there was microelectronics. Hunt and his army were dazzled early in 1980 by the possibility that General Electric would build a $100-million microelectronics research, development, and production complex in the state. The governor called together the presidents of the University of North Carolina, Duke, and the community college system, and they agreed that if the state could put forth highly visible evidence of an education and research program in microelec-

tronics, it could snare a significant slice of one of the most sought-after industries. Hunt warned that a year's wait would be too long. With the legislature's blessing and a sizable allowance from its wallet, the Microelectronics Center of North Carolina (MCNC) was born.

Owned cooperatively by five universities and the Research Triangle Institute, MCNC was engaged in finding ways to get more and more onto a computer chip, and to merge its discoveries with those of other fledgling technologies. A lab for students and faculties of the universities, it also served as a clearinghouse for industries (including its neighbors in the Research Triangle Park) which fueled its research with money and shared in the results.

By 1985, the state had put $43 million into MCNC. In return, it expected nothing less than a flagship for the U.S. computer industry in its battle with foreign competitors. Closer to home, a few more plums like General Electric, which decided it liked MCNC's neighborhood, would be nice.

MCNC was also the focus of hundreds of questions. Will microchips indeed be the goose that lays the golden egg? Will the state successfully attract and develop its own nucleus of highly-skilled technicians and innovators, becoming a haven for industrial pioneers, or will it simply be home to the low-wage, assembly-line arms of companies in other states?

Up until the mid 1980s, North Carolina had made only the most elementary moves in encouraging small-time enterprises with big-time ideas. Hunt spoke for many forward-thinking business people when he said, "We need seed capital, so our entrepreneurs and innovators can finish developing their products, and then we need a lot more venture capital to mass produce it or sell it broadly. As I look at what we need to do in the near future, that is probably the most important."

High-tech companies multiplied and grew like weeds. The air was thick with idea people of limited means: between 1970 and 1980 in the state, the number of high-tech businesses employing less than twenty people rose by 96 percent. The legislature gave the first tip-of-the-hat to such ventures, with an entr-

In 2001, the U.S. Environmental Protection Agency, built a $272 million facility with over 1,000,000 square feet of lab space in Research Triangle Park. Courtesy, Research Triangle Foundation of N.C.

preneurial grants fund of almost a half-million dollars. "We have all these electronics and microelectronics companies, but we have not had enough people come out of them and start their own firms," Hunt said.

How well the state knew its former self, and the histories of other industrial magnets, was critically important.

* * *

In 1984, North Carolina no longer had to struggle against the label "an agricultural state on the verge of industrialization." It had graduated to a bigger challenge: a wary watch over the impact of successes on its coveted way of life.

The rushing Tar River still cranked some of the wheels which turned out yarn in the Rocky Mount Mills. Good Nash County people continued to file in and out of the red-bricked buildings where they ran the machines, and up the highway to Battleboro, their friends and neighbors made glass and locks and medical supplies and other things.

Benny Keith remembered the people who used to help with the tobacco on his family's Wake County farm and what had become of them— one a dentist, one an electrical engineer, one an airline mechanic, one an optician, one a civil engineer, several in manufacturing, and one grading grain for the state.

A bulldozer cleared away some more of the Research Triangle Park's pine trees. A moving van from New York followed a biochemist and her family to their warmer, greener new home. And a computer whiz kid from a small North Carolina town walked out of a North Carolina university with plans for a North Carolina career.

9

MOVING FORWARD

City Market, with its cobblestone streets and tile-roofed buildings, is a focal point of Raleigh's downtown revitalization. This 1911 Spanish-style market is now the location of numerous specialty shops, an antique mall, several restaurants and pubs, and a comedy club. Courtesy, Greater Raleigh Convention and Visitors Bureau

North Carolina became one of America's fastest growing states by the beginning of the twenty-first century. Agriculture and low-tech manufacturing dominated the economy for many years, but at the dawn of the new millennium the state began a successful transition to the Third Industrial Revolution, characterized by high-technology and information-based commerce. Thanks in part to air conditioning and improved race relations, the New South arrived in the 1980s, and northern and foreign companies continued to flock to North Carolina.

State leaders emphasized public education as the key to the future, but struggled to solve the twin challenges of race and growth. Not content to rest on their laurels, the state's colleges and universities teamed up with many businesses to produce cutting edge research and future researchers. Politics in North Carolina since 1985 has seen the continuation of the trend away from the "solid" Democratic South and toward a more competitive scene, with the edge going to the Republican Party in the new century. As for religion, the state remains a part of the "Bible Belt," with evangelical Christianity an important part of every community. But the newcomers of the 1980s and 1990s introduced real religious diversity throughout the state. Indeed, greater diversity and tolerance aptly describe other changes in the last decades of the twentieth century. Ruled by Jim Crow throughout much of the century, North Carolinians broke free in the 1960s and continue to battle its harmful effects. Out-migrants a century ago, African Americans now move into the state in large numbers, lured largely by economic opportunities, but also by a number of draws, including history. Sports and tourism also attract thousands of visitors every year. Loyalties run deep throughout this state that has become increasingly sports crazy. Thousands of tourists flock to North Carolina's beautiful and diverse beaches, mountains, and cities, and some never leave!

Once known as the "Rip Van Winkle State" for its poor economic prospects, North Carolina has become a desirable place to live and do business. The state's population grew 35 percent from 1980 to 2000. Its largest city, Charlotte, which anchors

Nine of the country's top banks operate out of Charlotte and the growing skyline is testimony to the power of banking. The tallest building in the city, and in the entire southeast, is Bank of America Corporate Center. Courtesy, Visit Charlotte

the nation's fifth largest urban region, has emerged as a financial, distribution, and transportation center for the Southeast. North Carolina's smaller cities and towns have garnered dozens of accolades, including several "Best Small Towns in America," "Top College Towns," and "Best Places to Live." For example, *Forbes* magazine ranked Raleigh-Durham in the nation's top three places for business in 2003 and 2004. The character of North Carolina's communities is a predominant factor in business relocations. In 2002 a Harris Poll ranked North Carolina one of the top five states for desired relocation, and *World Trade* magazine named North Carolina one of the "Top Ten Places to do Business." Since the turn of the twenty-first century, *Site Selection* magazine has

repeatedly chosen the state as number one for business climate.

State government incentives have been a large part of North Carolina's positive business climate. Tax credits, industrial revenue bonds and industrial development grants have spurred economic growth. The incentives seem to be working. During 1990–2000, the Gross State Product (GSP) increased over 100 percent. The Job Development Investment Grant alone brought in 6,000 jobs in 2003–2004. In 2005, fourteen Fortune 500 companies were headquartered in the state, with a combined revenue of $142 billion.

North Carolina's highest growth industry has been finance. Banking deregulation in the 1990s and the Interstate Banking Act of 1994 encouraged interstate banking. Several North Carolina banks, especially those in Charlotte, took advantage of these opportunities. With its banks controlling over $1.3 trillion in assets, the Queen City is the second largest banking center in the U.S, and headquarters to five of the nation's top financial institutions. Although the finance industry is only the seventh largest employer in the state, it contributes 19 percent of North Carolina's GSP. Growth in the banking industry has also promoted small business growth. Seven of the nation's top ten small business lenders have offices in the state.

The state's banking behemoth—Bank of America (BOA)—grew up in Charlotte. Assuming the presidency of NCNB Corporation in 1982, Hugh McColl took it from a one state bank with only 172 offices, to America's largest financial institution, before the end of the century. McColl arranged a merger with C&S/Sovran to form NationsBank in 1991, then the nation's third largest bank. In 1998, he trumped that move by merging with San Francisco-based BankAmerica to form Bank of America, headquartered in Charlotte. Today, BOA serves one in every four households, and has 6,000 banking centers in twenty-nine states and offices in thirty-five countries. It also boasts the tallest building in the southeast, Bank of America Corporate Center, or, as local wags dubbed it, the "Taj McColl."

In the shadow of the BOA tower, One Wachovia Center was built by First Union National Bank during its heyday. President Ed Crutchfield took over at First Union in 1973 and grew the bank from a $5 billion institution in 1984 to one worth over $250 billion when he retired in 2000. A year later, First Union merged with Wachovia Corporation (formerly of Winston Salem) to become the nation's fourth largest financial institution with $492 billion in assets. Although BOA and Wachovia now dominate the Charlotte skyline, Winston Salem-based BB&T is the state's third financial institution in the Fortune 500.

The rapid growth of high-tech companies has also been a bright spot in the state. Strong support from corporations and academic institutions has attracted enough technology facilities to create high-tech products wholly made in state. North Carolina ranked among the top seven fastest growing information technology states during 1996–2005, and IT revenue almost doubled from 2000–2002 alone. Over 4,000 IT firms are located in the state, including the

headquarters of IBM Global Services and significant divisions of Microsoft and Cisco. North Carolina is also home to over 156 biotechnology and 210 life science companies that provide over $9.5 billion in annual revenues. With industry leaders GlaxoSmithKline and Merck headquartered in the state, the North Carolina's biotechnology industry is growing 15 percent each year.

Cisco Systems is Research Triangle Park's fourth largest employer, with over 2,500 workers onsite. Courtesy, Research Triangle Foundation of N.C.

North Carolina has several important research parks that continue to attract new companies and industries. Strategically located near Duke University, North Carolina State University, and the University of North Carolina at Chapel Hill, Research Triangle Park (RTP) has grown from a 1950s dream into the largest research park in the nation, currently employing 38,000. With its R&D component doubling since 1985, the 7,000 acre park is an international research and development center and home to IBM, GlaxoSmithKline, Nortel Networks, and other high-tech heavyweights. Also located in RTP are the North Carolina Biotechnology Center (a nonprofit source for biotech research grants), and the National Institute of Environmental Health Sciences (a division of the National Institutes of Health that focuses on biomedical research, prevention and intervention).

An up-and-coming technology destination is the Piedmont Triad Research Park (PTR),

While the movie industry hasn't vacated Hollywood for North Carolina shores, the Tar Heel state claims its own filming sophistication. Here, the popular WB television series, Dawson's Creek, *is being filmed at UNCW. Courtesy, N.C. Film Commission*

affiliated with Wake Forest University and located near Greensboro, Winston-Salem, and High Point. Attracted by PTR's potential as well as tax credits and a job development grant, Dell Corporation broke ground in 2005 on a $115 million plant located in the Triad region. The University of North Carolina at Charlotte's Charlotte Research Institute (CRI) is a collaboration between industry, government, and academia that will positively impact the state's economy. Within CRI, the Center for eBusiness Technology Institute is working with Bank of America and Wachovia, and also expanding into Homeland Security. The Center for Optoelectronics & Optical Communications designs and fabricates optical circuitry and optical imaging

devices. And the Center for Precision Metrology manufactures mechanical parts within a nanometer. A $50 million Motorsports Testing and Research Complex is planned to strengthen North Carolina's role as a major motor sports destination. In February 2006, construction began on a biotechnology research center on the former site of Cannon Mills in Kannapolis. The North Carolina Research Campus is a joint venture between businessman David H. Murdock and the sixteen-campus UNC system.

The film industry has also surged in recent decades. Geographic locations, historic sites, metropolitan areas, and a growing number of support companies make North Carolina a top film destination. Since the early 1980s when Dino De Laurentiis built a studio in Wilmington, North Carolina has ranked behind only California and New York in annual film revenues. Now owned by EUE Screen Gems and expanded into a nine studio complex on thirty-two acres, the Wilmington facility is the largest movie production facility east of California. More than 1,500 film professionals employed by 400 production and support companies reside in the state. Between 1980 and 2004, over 700 features, thirteen television series, and numerous commercials were filmed in North Carolina, generating a total of $6 billion in revenue.

North Carolina's shining stars may be finance, technology, and film, but the backbone of the state remains the historically dominant industries of furniture and textiles. Sixty percent of all furniture made in the U.S. is manufactured within the Piedmont Triad. Each year, High Point hosts the Home Furnishings Market in April and October, while nearby Hickory is home to a nationally known furniture outlet. In 2004, the furniture industry employed over 60,000 workers and had $2.8 billion in revenue, but those numbers represent a 21 percent decline since 1998. Environmental regulations and cheap labor overseas, resulting in increased imports, have forced plant closings and layoffs. Over 17,000 furniture jobs have been lost to foreign competition in the past decade.

North Carolina is the top textile manufacturing state in the U.S., but as with furniture, textile companies have fallen on hard times recently. NAFTA and global competition have forced change on the industry. Greensboro-based Burlington Industries declared bankruptcy in 2001, but a 2003 acquisition by WL Ross & Co. led to reorganization through the development of international partner mills. Now Burlington—still one of America's largest textile producers—has operations in Mexico and India as well as a strong base in Hong Kong. But when large textile manufacturers cut costs through international expansion, domestic plant consolidations, and automation, the results hurt North Carolina's workers. Between 1993 and 2003, 30 percent of the state's textile plants closed, and 160,000 jobs were lost, mostly in the apparel and decorative industries. Fortunately, the technical textile industry is growing. Aerospace, medical, military, and industrial businesses, among others, have a growing need for textiles with specific technical capabilities. North Carolina, with its long textile history and strong technical base, is

In The University of North Carolina at Charlotte's metrology center, engineers, physicists, chemists and computer scientists collaborate with corporate colleagues to put quality control into manufacturing processes. Courtesy, University of North Carolina, Charlotte. Photo by Wade Bruton

poised to infiltrate this market. For example, non-woven fabric and fabric coating mills witnessed 30 percent growth during 1993–2003. Responding to challenges, North Carolina is able to adapt.

Home of new technology and traditional manufacturing, North Carolina continues to develop an impressive transportation system to move its products and people across the state and around the world. The North Carolina Department of Transportation oversees the second largest state maintained roadway system, and plans to bring a four-lane expressway within ten miles of 96 percent of the population. The recent addition of the North Carolina Turnpike Authority will expedite highway construction and create toll roads to keep the traffic moving. Public transportation systems in the state carry over 40 million passengers each year, and that number promises to increase substantially in the near future. New projects include light rail in Charlotte and commuter rail or bus rapid transit in the Triangle and Triad regions.

First in flight, North Carolina has 125 public airports and over 300 private airports, but the majority of traffic flows through the Raleigh-Durham and Charlotte Douglas International

Agriculture is the backbone of North Carolina's economy. Local farmer's markets can be found throughout the state. Courtesy. N.C. Division of Tourism, Film, and Sports Development

Airports. Nine major airlines and fifteen regional airlines fly into rapidly-growing Raleigh-Durham. The largest hub of US Airways, Charlotte Douglas connects to 155 cities and numerous international locations. Other North Carolina airports help move travelers and goods throughout the country. Cargo giant, Federal Express, is investing $300 million for a sorting and distribution hub at the Piedmont Triad International Airport.

Trains and ships also move products and passengers through the state. Charlotte is at the center of the largest consolidated rail system in the country. Taking advantage of the state's 3,379 freight rail miles, 25 percent of the top North Carolina manufacturers ship by rail. Interstate passenger service links Charlotte to Raleigh and Rocky Mount, and the Charlotte-Raleigh corridor is expected to be upgraded to high-speed service. Expanded Amtrak service routes extend to New York, New Orleans, and Miami. The major deep deepwater ports at Wilmington and Morehead City boast competitive pricing and many advantages for shippers. With the expected doubling of international trade by 2020, North Carolina's ports will play an increasingly important role in moving products and crops overseas.

Once the state's major industry, agriculture is still an important part of the economy, employing 18 percent of the work force and contributing $59.1 billion annually to the GSP. North Carolina is one of the country's top poultry producers and the seventh largest apple producer in the U.S. Other main crops include tobacco, corn, blueberries, cotton, peanuts, and Christmas trees. But hog farming dominates the state's agricultural sector. Hog farming grew in popularity as tobacco farming declined, due to the need to find diverse uses for the land. Changes in environmental regulations allowed for large companies to invest in the state, and in 1992, Smithfield Inc. built the world's largest meat processing plant in Bladen County. Four years later, the state was producing 9 to 10 million hogs annually, making it the second largest hog producing state. The growth of hog farming slowed after 1997 when the General Assembly, concerned with the environmental impact of hog waste, passed the Clean Water Responsibility Act. Since then, industry and government have been working together to solve the waste problem.

The state's agricultural sector faced an enormous challenge in September 1999 when Hurricane Floyd brought massive flooding that tainted water supplies with hog waste, pesticides, and dead farm animals. The storm caused hundreds of millions of dollars of damage to crops, livestock, and farming facilities. One of the hardest industries hit was tobacco, with over 80,000 acres destroyed. But it takes more than a hurricane to topple big tobacco. Despite declining sales of

American grown tobacco, North Carolina is the number one tobacco producing state in the nation, supplying 40 percent of all U.S. tobacco. The crop remains the fourth biggest agricultural product in the state, producing $587 million in income in 2004.

Still, North Carolina's tobacco farmers have faced huge challenges due to foreign competition and waning demand for tobacco products. To-bacco production has declined precipitously in recent years, and many growers have been look-ing to diversify their farms. Various organizations in the state are providing help. Created from proceeds of the 1998 Master Settlement Agreement with cigarette manufacturers, the Golden Leaf Foundation provides grants to retrain tobacco-industry workers and revitalize tobacco-dependent communities. From 2001–2004, it awarded 270 grants worth over $105 million. The North Carolina Tobacco Trust Fund Commission has sponsored alternative crop programs and has granted over $50 million in its first few years. With the help of grants, farmers have been able to grow alternatives like strawberries, peas, and beans. But the profits on these crops are not nearly as large as tobacco. Enter the grape.

Large-scale grape cultivation in North Carolina is a recent phenomenon. Seeking to encourage the industry, lawmakers passed a law in 1972 reducing taxes on wines produced from locally grown grapes. One of the first vineyard-wineries opened at Asheville's Biltmore Estate in 1978. Despite ideal grape growing conditions, however, the industry grew slowly until 1986 when the North Carolina Grape Council was established. With the Grape Council leading marketing, research, and educational efforts, the number of wineries grew to eleven by 1997. In the late 1990s, Charlie and Ed Shelton donated $50,000 to Surry Community College to develop a grape cultivation program, and opened Shelton Winery on 160 acres just outside of Dobson. Soon, other wineries followed. Today, the nationally desig-nated Yadkin Valley is the main wine growing locale in the state. Close to forty wineries were operating in North Carolina in 2005. Some are large, opulent facilities like the newly opened Childress Winery near Lexington. Others are

Westbend Vineyards is located on sixty acres of rolling land along the banks of the Yadkin river. New vineyards are popping up in the nationally designated Yadkin Valley at the rate of four to six per year. Courtesy, N.C. Division of Tourism, Film, and Sports Development

simpler affairs, such as the Old North State Winegrowers Cooperative Association in Mount Airy, where thirty-eight small growers work together to produce the Carolina Harvest label. Wineries are only a recent example of North Carolina's ability to grow, diversify, and adapt to the changing national and international economic climate.

Growing, diversifying, and adapting are part of the modern learning process. Not since the 1850s under Calvin H. Wiley, the founding father of state-funded education, has North Carolina undergone a period of change in public education as revolutionary as that of the past three decades. After years of segregation and token integration, federal courts forced the state to get serious about school integration in the late 1960s. Since then, residential segregation and the end of the busing era have continued to challenge the state's cities and rural areas. In the twenty-first century, choice plans, charter schools, and economic-based programs hold promise as school boards attack the lingering effects of Jim Crow. Test scores continue to rise, despite the strains of increasing immigration and decreasing budget flexibility. And the state's high ranking institutions of higher education continue to respond to the needs of teachers and businesses within the state.

Racial integration was the dominant issue in

education during the second half of the twentieth century, nowhere more so than in Charlotte Mecklenburg Schools (CMS), the state's largest and the nation's twenty-third largest school district at almost 120,000 students. In 1997, a lawsuit reopened the historic Swann case. Closed since 1975, Swann had forced school boards across the nation to aggressively integrate schools, even those in residentially segregated cities like Charlotte. The new lawsuit argued that race should not be used as the basis for school assignments because courts had ruled the district fully desegregated. Praising neighborhood schools and condemning busing, some black and white parents welcomed the new action. Others warned of resegregation of schools and reversing progress in residential integration. In 1999, the CMS school board was ordered to stop using race as a factor in student assignments, and after two years of appeals, it let busing die. To combat re-segregation, the school board developed a complicated "choice" plan, but by 2004 it was clear that this plan was flawed. Many suburban schools saw enrollment swell at the expense of inner city schools, and population growth in the county further complicated the issue. Despite the fact that the number of black students testing at grade level doubled between 1995 and 2001, the issue of racial inequalities remained a contentious one among parents in Charlotte-Mecklenburg.

The danger of re-segregation in North Carolina remains real. Between 1994 and 2001, the number of North Carolina's mostly minority schools—those with 80 percent or more minority enrollments—has doubled. Many other schools are approaching minority ratios that often produce white flight. Some school districts throughout the state are looking for more creative approaches to the issue of diversity. Sharing similar population pressures as Charlotte, Wake County, which includes state capital Raleigh, has begun to provide school assignments based on economic diversity rather than race. Stemming from research that shows a strong correlation between concentrated poverty and low achievement, this promising new approach seeks to achieve economic integration by mixing poor with middle-or upper-class children. No school can have more than 40

percent of its students eligible for reduced price lunches. Wake's creation of a system of middle-class schools has resulted in racially diverse schools where test scores are on the rise.

The state's public school systems face other obstacles, as well. Several North Carolina counties have been among the nation's fastest growing in recent years, straining local school resources. For example, Union County grew by 24 percent between 2000 and 2004, overwhelming its schools. The sight of dozens of portable classroom trailers crowding school parking lots has provoked parental dissent. School boards, such as booming Wake County's, have had to think outside the box by building modular schools and creatively shuffling student assignments. The increasing rate of Hispanic/Latino immigration has also strained local budgets because many of the new students require English as a Second Language (ESL) programs.

Despite these challenges, North Carolina's schools are steadily improving, and the state is rising in national rankings. One reason for the success is that creative new programs are flourishing. The Charter Schools Act of 1996 allowed for more parental choice by creating publicly funded schools that were independent from local school boards. These alternatives to traditional schools were typically theme based, featuring math and science schools, or schools for the academically gifted. Operating in 2004 with 52 percent white and 48 percent minority students, charter schools seem to be popular with black and white parents, and demand continues to rise. Another innovative program, the publicly and privately funded Smart Start program, has been providing better early childhood services since 1993. The program has been a resounding success, garnering national awards and serving as a model for other states. Most importantly, North Carolina's children are entering kindergarten prepared for school.

The state's universities and colleges have joined the public education crusade. North Carolina's Community College System is the third largest in the country, operates fifty-nine campuses statewide, and reaches about a sixth of the population. In 1999, the community colleges began training primary and secondary school

teachers to use the new LEARN North Carolina internet site developed at the University of North Carolina at Chapel Hill. This use of modern technology allows teachers in poor, rural districts with limited resources to offer Advanced Placement level courses to high school students via online classes. Besides training teachers, the nationally ranked Community College System works with new and expanding businesses to develop specialized training programs.

With a variety of public and private institutions of higher education, including the sixteen campus University of North Carolina System, the state's colleges and universities are also responding to business needs. North Carolina-based companies, especially in the financial industry, recruit a large number of in-state graduates. With the emergence of more biotechnology and pharmaceutical programs, the state's universities are filling the needs of the booming tech sector. Business leaders know that North Carolina is home to a variety of top quality colleges and universities. *U.S. News & World Report* ranked Duke University the fifth best national university in 2005. Wake Forest University and UNC-Chapel Hill placed in the top thirty, and North Carolina State University ranked number eighty-seven. Davidson College was the eighth best liberal arts college in America. The state was also home to twelve of the top fifty southern comprehensive colleges.

For many North Carolinians, religion remains at the core of education and everyday life. The

Charlotte native Billy Graham has preached the Gospel in over 185 countries. Today, he is the most recognized Christian evangelist in the world. Courtesy, Billy Graham Evangelistic Association

"Bible Belt" state that once strongly supported the anti-Darwinism crusades of the 1920s remains predominantly Protestant. Since the early nineteenth century, the leading Protestant sects in the state have been Baptists (currently almost 50 percent of the state's population), Methodists (13 percent) and Presbyterians (4 percent). But with the flood of new businesses and workers starting in the 1980s, the state's religious demographics have begun to shift. Jewish and Muslim numbers are increasing. Most significantly, the rapidly growing cities of Charlotte, Raleigh-Durham, and Greensboro have witnessed a surge in Catholicism. Statewide, the official number of Catholics has more than quadrupled since 1970, and the pace seems to be accelerating, especially with large numbers of Hispanics and Latinos entering the state. While greater religious diversity appears to characterize the state's future, most Americans still equate religion in North Carolina with two Protestant evangelists, Billy Graham and Jim Bakker.

Since first appearing on Gallup's "Ten Most Admired Men in the World" in 1948, Graham has made the list a record forty-seven times. An inspiring leader to millions throughout the world and an advisor to several U.S. presidents, the Charlotte native received the Congressional Gold Medal in 1996, the highest honor the U.S. Congress can bestow upon a citizen, and was awarded an honorary British knighthood in 2001. His 1997 autobiography *Just As I Am* was listed

on three best-sellers lists simultaneously. In 2003, the Billy Graham Evangelistic Association announced the move of their headquarters from Minneapolis to Charlotte. At the official dedication ceremony in April 2005, the aging evangelist announced plans for a Billy Graham Library on the grounds. With estimates of over 200,000 visitors per year, it promises to become a major attraction in the region. As Billy Graham edges towards retirement, his son Franklin is assuming more of a leadership role in his father's organizations. Actively involved in the family ministry since 1989, the younger Graham's "Samaritan's Purse," headquartered in Boone, provides Christian relief and aid to individuals worldwide.

While the Graham family ministry continues into its second generation, the Bakker family evangelical enterprise proved to be less enduring. Jim and Tammy Faye Bakker's Praise the Lord (PTL) Ministries prospered throughout the 1980s, gaining a loyal following and millions in donations. PTL owned a broadcasting network, opened a religious theme park, and doled out large bonuses to their gregarious leaders. As Jim and Tammy Faye increasingly led a lavish lifestyle, skeptics began to question how this nonprofit organization, which they dubbed "Pass the Loot" Club, used its incoming millions. After a sex scandal and fraud trial, Jim Bakker went to prison in 1989, the Bakkers divorced, and PTL disintegrated. New marriages, books, and TV shows have restored Jim and Tammy Faye's finances, but televangelism remains tarnished in the wake of the PTL fiasco.

Athletics have historically been popular in North Carolina. In the early twentieth century, teams from textile mills and colleges gave residents opportunities to cheer, but over the past few decades, sports, both amateur and professional, have become big business, drawing large crowds and having a strong economic and promotional impact on the state.

Since 1990, North Carolina has hosted over 100 major sporting events. Just three of those events, the U.S. Women's Open Golf Championship, and men's and women's Atlantic Coast Conference Basketball Tournaments had a combined economic impact of $77 million. Other events, such as the 1994 Final Four in Charlotte and the 1999 and 2005 U.S. Opens at Pinehurst, drew national attention and tourism to the state. College and other amateur events continue to fuel the passion of loyal fans within the state, but the arrival of major professional teams since the 1980s has had the biggest impact on North Carolina.

When the NBA announced an expansion team for Charlotte in 1988, support for the state's first major professional team swelled throughout North Carolina, and the Hornets' logo became a best-selling souvenir nationally. Little did Lord Charles Cornwallis know when he labeled the area a "veritable nest of hornets" in 1780 how far his metaphor would travel! Fans attended in record numbers during the first Hornets' decade, especially when native son Michael Jordan came to town. The Hornets gained a sister team, the WNBA Charlotte Sting, in 1997. Despite off and on seasons, strong support of the Hornets continued until public disgust with owner George Shinn led to the Hornets' move to New Orleans. Undeterred, the city's strong fan base led the NBA in 2003 to announce that its first team with African American majority ownership would play in Charlotte. Robert Johnson's Bobcats moved into the new Charlotte Arena in 2005.

North Carolina received its next professional franchise in 1993 when the NFL selected Jerry Richardson's Carolina Panthers. The popularity of professional sports had not waned during the Hornets' trials, and football fans flocked to Charlotte's Bank of America Stadium. The Panthers played their first game in 1995, and by 2004, the team played in its first Super Bowl.

But Charlotte didn't have a monopoly on professional sports in North Carolina. The NHL's Hartford Whalers moved to the state in 1997 and became the Carolina Hurricanes. Playing their first two years in Greensboro, the Hurricanes moved into Raleigh's RBC Center in 1999. When the team brought the Stanley Cup finals to the state in 2002, it lost to Detroit but won the hearts of the state's hockey fans.

The first professional team for the Research Triangle area, the NHL's Carolina Hurricanes are headquartered in Raleigh and play at the RBC Center, which opened in 1999. Courtesy, Greater Raleigh CVB

Each season, devoted Blue Devil basketball fans set up tents outside Cameron Indoor Stadium in the hopes of obtaining preferential seating at the next Duke home game. 2002. Courtesy, Duke University Photography and Durham Convention & Visitors Bureau

While professional teams, including twelve minor league baseball teams and six minor league soccer teams, made inroads after the 1980s, college sports—especially ACC men's basketball—remain at the center of the state's sports universe. "Tobacco Road" is synonymous with college hoops. The great rivalry between Duke University's Blue Devils and the Tar Heels of UNC-Chapel Hill is legendary, and the two teams have won seven national championships. North Carolina State University's Wolfpack earned their second national championship in 1983, and Wake Forest is a perennial threat in games with its in-state rivals. Fright wigs, body paint, long lines, tents, team logos, and screaming fans ("fanatics") remain a staple of ACC competition within the state.

Another "team" sport associated with the state, stock car racing, witnessed a surge in popularity during the closing decades of the twentieth century. NASCAR was born in Florida, but its heart and most of its racing teams reside in North Carolina. NASCAR drivers such as former Huntersville resident Jeff Gordon became celeb-

Lowe's Motor Speedway has come a long way since it was built in 1959. The modern facility hosts several major racing events annually, including the NEXTEL and Busch series. Courtesy, Visit Charlotte

rities during the 1990s, and the 2001 death of Kannapolis native and Mooresville resident, NASCAR legend, Dale Earnhardt, unleashed a national outpouring of grief. Lowe's Motor Speedway, located just outside of Charlotte hosts three Nextel Cup and two Busch Series races annually. Several motion pictures have been filmed at the speedway and Charlotte business leaders secured the city as the location of the NASCAR Hall of Fame in 2006. With dozens of teams located in North Carolina, NASCAR and the motor sports industry have a $5 billion impact on the economy. UNC Charlotte's Charlotte Research Institute has developed a $50 million Motorsports Testing and Research Complex, further testimony to the strong future anticipated for the fastest growing sport in America.

Each year in early July more than sixty-five performing acts, like Chuck Davis and the African American Dance Ensemble, perform at Durham's Annual Festival For the Eno, a major arts and crafts benefit to purchase park and preservation lands along the Eno River. 1993. Courtesy, Durham Convention & Visitors Bureau

North Carolina's cultural arts are also racing ahead. Nonprofit arts generate annual earnings of $723 million, and the number of organizations grew over 60 percent in the past decade. Almost 2,500 such organizations now exist. For-profit arts have an even greater economic impact, with 6,100 craft artists alone generating over $538 million.

Attendance at cultural events is also on the rise. *Smithsonian* magazine named North Carolina to the Top 10 for cultural and heritage tourism in 2003. Both performing and visual arts are experiencing renewal. Raleigh is home to the North Carolina Museum of Art, the North Carolina Symphony, and North Carolina Museum of Natural Sciences. Charlotte has the Mint Museum of Craft + Design, the Blumenthal Performing Arts Center, and the Levine Museum of the New South. Smaller towns, such as Brevard and Flat Rock, are musical and dramatic destinations of their own, and they take pride in local craftsmanship and folk art.

The surge in professional sports and cultural events since 1985 has raised North Carolina's regional and national profile as a vacation and tourist destination. At $12.5 billion, tourism is one of the top industries in North Carolina.

Citing friendly people and natural beauty as the top draws, the state's 49 million annual visitors are attracted by three distinctly different settings for vacations—beach, mountains, and everything in between!

Three hundred miles of shoreline draw visitors from all over—especially those from the Mid-Atlantic and Northeast—to enjoy North Carolina's beaches, resorts, fishing, and historic sites. History and beaches make an especially attractive duo along the coast. Edenton, Bath, New Bern, Beaufort, and Wilmington are just a few of the coastal towns riddled with history.

The new North Carolina Museum of Natural Sciences is the largest of its kind in the Southeast and features four floors of hands-on exhibits, dioramas of the state's natural habitats and the Acrocanthosaurus, also known as the "Terror of the South." Courtesy, Greater Raleigh CVB

With the highest peaks east of the Rockies, North Carolina's portion of the Appalachian Mountains provides quite a contrast to the Outer Banks. Hiking, skiing, climbing, mountain biking, canoeing, camping, white water rafting, and even llama treks are among the many activities available for adventurers. Walking trails, the Blue Ridge Parkway, over 300 waterfalls, and countless mountain vistas allow the semi-adventurous to enjoy the mountains as well. Boone is a classic college town, Blowing Rock is for art lovers, and Asheville shares the best of both and more. Built in 1913, Asheville's Grove Park Inn added a $42 million spa complex in 2001 and solidified its reputation as one of the state's luxury vacation

Visitors can tour Tryon Palace in New Bern, which was the residence of the colonial and state governor in the eighteenth century. Courtesy, N.C. Division of Tourism, Film, and Sports Development

The historic Grove Park Inn Resort in Asheville has recently undergone a renovation and expansion, including the addition of a luxurious 40,000-square-foot spa. Courtesy, N.C. Division of Tourism, Film, and Sports Development

Built for one of North Carolina's least favorite governors, New Bern's Tryon Palace has been a tourist destination since 1770. The state's lighthouses remain popular for those exploring the Outer Banks. After an amazing journey a half mile inland, courtesy of the National Park Service, the state's most famous lighthouse, the Cape Hatteras, attracted thousands to its 1999 relighting ceremony. Four years later, thousands of visitors traveled to sandy Kitty Hawk to honor Orville and Wilbur Wright at the "100 Years of Flight" celebration. And of course, North Carolina's beaches remain some of America's most beautiful.

Originally built in 1970, Charlotte's Southpark Mall has recently undergone a transformation into an upscale shopping destination with such high-end retailers as Tiffany, Neiman Marcus, and Nordstrom. Courtesy, Visit Charlotte

destinations. Not to be outdone, their elegant neighbor, the Biltmore Estate, constructed a four star, four diamond hotel the same year. Well aware that the house, gardens, and winery draw an affluent crowd, Biltmore now gives visitors one more reason to extend their stay. For the hopefully affluent, the 1997 opening of the Harrah's Cherokee Casino has provided gambling thrills at the entrance of Smoky Mountain National Park. After only five years, the Casino, owned and operated by the Eastern Band of the Cherokee Indians, has become the state's largest tourist destination with 3.3 million visitors annually.

Between the coast and the mountains, North Carolina offers its visitors big cities, Civil War sites, wonderful zoos, amusement parks, and golf resorts, among other attractions. Charlotte is the state's largest city, but Greensboro, Raleigh,

Paramount's Carowinds is a large theme park that straddles the North Carolina/South Carolina border. With rides that range from gentle boat trips to exhilarating roller coasters, the park draws large crowds each year. Courtesy, Visit Charlotte

Durham, and Winston-Salem also feature the urban edge many tourists crave. Carowinds offers amusement ride thrills, while Old Salem is a restored eighteenth century Moravian settlement. North Carolina has joined the Civil War Trails project, and Bentonville Battlefield—the state's largest and site of the last major battle of the war—is a must for Civil War buffs. The North Carolina Zoo, located in Asheboro, was the first state-supported zoo in America. Designed to simulate the animals' natural habitat, the zoo has become one of the nation's best. For those in search of birdies and eagles, the state boasts over 600 golf courses and a moderate climate condu-

cive to year round golf. A golf mecca for over a century, Pinehurst is perhaps the finest of the state's many golf resorts.

Visitors and natives have witnessed unprecedented and positive change for North Carolina during the past few decades. The New South has arrived in most urban areas in the state in the guise of growth, jobs, traffic jams, and affluence. Banking and a variety of high-tech industries hold great promise for white collar workers. Rural areas still dependent on the old economy continue to struggle with declines in textiles, furniture, and tobacco. Educational progress, whether at the primary, secondary, college, or university levels, has been for the most part, stunning, and the future looks bright as business and education leaders continue to work together. Church leaders also see no decline in religious commitment throughout the state. Sports on the professional and collegiate levels has never been more popular. Bumper stickers with the Panthers' logo, Tar Heel basketball, or a favorite NASCAR driver's number can be seen on every highway and country road. North Carolina's reputation for beach, golf, or mountain vacations has been buttressed by exposure in movies, sports competitions, and bank commercials.

No longer the "Rip Van Winkle" state, North Carolina is wide awake, flexing its muscles, and the world is noticing.

The Pinehurst area is known for its more than forty-one championship golf courses. Courtesy, N.C. Division of Tourism, Film, and Sports Development

10

CHRONICLES OF LEADERSHIP

In 1584, English explorers returning from the New World described "The Goodliest Land Under the Cope of Heaven." Eager for new colonization and expanded commerce, England responded by establishing its first colony in the New World on Roanoke Island, North Carolina.

By the time North Carolina celebrated its bicentennial, it was still the focus of new business and international commerce. According to the state department of commerce, in 1983 more companies—both foreign and domestic—announced plans for new facilities in North Carolina than in any other state in the union.

As with most new and underdeveloped countries, colonial North Carolina's principal economic pursuit was agriculture and related industries. The colony's first major enterprises naval stores and lumber—were based on forest products. Naval stores, which included tar, pitch, rosin, and turpentine were the colony's most valuable exports, hence North Carolina's nickname, the "Tar Heel State."

Production of these stores dovetailed into the whole agricultural economy because farmers could carry on naval stores operations when the weather prevented ordinary farm work. The use of trees aided the farmer in clearing his land, and since these stores were shipped in barrels or hogsheads, a very important cooperage, or barrel-making, industry developed.

It wasn't until the first quarter of the twentieth century, however, that the economic value of

The North Carolina Biotechnology Center was established in Research Triangle Park in the mid-1980s to foster and attract the biotech industry to the state of North Carolina. Courtesy, Research Triangle Foundation of N.C.

manufacturing industries really began to exceed that of the traditionally agriculture-based economy in North Carolina. During that time the state saw a remarkable development in industry, becoming the leading industrial state in the Southeast and the nation's largest producer of cotton textiles, tobacco products, and wooden furniture. Although manufacturing had superseded farming as the state's chief source of wealth, the leading industries were all closely associated with the local abundance of raw materials produced on the farm.

By the late twentieth century, the state had moved from a primarily agricultural based economy to an industrial one. At the dawn of the new millennium new industries joined traditional tobacco, textile, and furniture manufacturers to rank North Carolina among the top states nationwide for technological industries.

According to the Urban Institute of the University of North Carolina at Charlotte, a combination of factors have contributed to North Carolina's emergence as a leader in industry. The development and improvement of transportation systems have increased the region's accessibility to other markets. Relatively low labor costs, reliable and economical utilities, and low construction costs add to the appeal. Educational improvements have been noted nationwide, and North Carolina is becoming known as an innovator in the field. And finally, the climate and appeal of the beautiful natural environment are bringing more people and industry to North Carolina—a trend that is projected to continue well into the future.

The organizations whose stories are detailed on the following pages have chosen to support this important literary and civic project. They illustrate the variety of ways in which individuals and their businesses have contributed to the state's growth and development. The civic involvement of North Carolina's businesses, institutions of learning, and local government, in cooperation with its citizens, has made the Tar Heel State an excellent place to live and work.

AMMONS INCORPORATED

Ammons Incorporated, located in Raleigh, North Carolina, is not just one company, but an assemblage of several different successful businesses ranging from construction and land development to real estate and health care. The leader of this substantial corporation is Justus (Jud) Murray Ammons, a man as full of character and charm as he is gifted with entrepreneurial skills and business prowess. The Raleigh based developer has numerous successes of which to be proud. However, his pride is reserved for his four children who have not joined the family business, but have continued his legacy of pursuing entrepreneurial endeavors of their own. "Do not judge me by what I do, but by what my children do for others," states Ammons in an easy Southern drawl. His achievements and benevolent community developments are renowned throughout the Raleigh community. But Ammons will refer to one of his children's business successes before mentioning his own awards for excellence in land development. Although his accomplishments are many, Ammons' story begins as humble as his North Carolina hills upbringing.

Born in 1935 in the town of Mars Hill and raised on a farm in the mountains of Western North Carolina, Ammons is no stranger to hard work. From an early age, he and his brothers and sisters were expected to help with everything from raising hogs to hauling eggs. "It wasn't a matter of being told what to do. You looked for something to do. Doing your

Justus Murray (Jud) Ammons.

part was expected. We'd get up in the morning and work for one or two hours before we'd eat breakfast," reflects Ammons upon his childhood. The work ethic instilled by his parents was instigated out of necessity, as it was the difficult years following the Depression. However, those early years set forth the foundation for a work philosophy that holds true for Ammons and his family, today. Simply put: hard work pays off. Even when Ammons wasn't working on the farm, he found ways to make extra money doing odd jobs and creating small business opportunities. These experiences taught Ammons valuable lessons he would use in his future entrepreneurial endeavors.

Ammons learned early that charging by the job would earn more money than working by the hour. He would race to finish one project then move on to the next one, therefore making more money in a shorter period of time. He also learned that taking risks was the only way to increase earning potential. As a boy, he attended an auction and bought a couple of goats, which appeared to be nothing but a nuisance to the other

bidders. Ammons paid $2.75 for the animals. The young entrepreneur brought his goats home and, within a few days time, a man came by asking if Ammons would sell him goat's milk. He agreed to sell the man a quart of milk a day at $.80 each. Young Ammons turned a profit for his purchase by the end of the week.

Some might think that Ammons' ability to quickly see ways of making a return on his investment is luck—not business acumen. His older brother, Roy Ammons, once jokingly commented, "Jud could flip up a nickel and it would come down a quarter." But Ammons friend, Adam Lucas added, "That might be true. But while that nickel was in the air, he'd be doing everything he knew how to do to turn it into a quarter. And if it came down a quarter, he'd immediately begin thinking about how to turn it into a fifty-cent piece." His keen sense of business was evident, even at an early age.

Soon young Ammons was off to college where he developed great skills at multi-tasking. In addition to a full load of classes, Ammons worked his way through North Carolina State University with several part-time jobs. One foretelling position was building model farm buildings for the North Carolina Depart-

The Factory, eat, play, shop, developed by Jeff Ammons.

Jud Ammons is a former president and now serves as an advisor to the FarmHouse Fraternity. Jud was chairman of the building committee and Jeff Ammons was the contractor for the new house.

ment of Agriculture. He also designed and drew plans for structures at state research farms. Another entrepreneurial endeavor was starting a laundry pickup business. In a short period of time, the one-person company grew to a twelve location business.

A natural born leader, Ammons served two terms as president of the NC State FarmHouse Fraternity Chapter. His loyalty to the Chapter remained constant and fifty years later he helped the fraternity build a new forty-man fraternity house. After assisting the young men in charge of the project with challenges such as design, zoning, building permits and fund raising, Ammons celebrated with his young "fraternity brothers" at a groundbreaking on October 12, 2003. With the help of Ammons' son, Jeff, who was hired as contractor, the project was completed in August of 2004.

Before graduating with an ROTC commission to the U.S. Airforce, Ammons met a very special woman, JoEllen Williams, a Meredith College student from Monroe, North Carolina. Not only did JoEllen become Ammons' wife and life partner, she is also credited with "keeping Jud focused" and contributing to the company's projects in significant and practical ways such as the

The Village at Nags Head is a golf course community that includes residential and commercial areas.

interior design and decorating of his numerous developments.

The two married shortly after graduating in 1957 and were off to France for Ammons' Air Force assignment. Their first son, Andy, was born there. After Ammons four year tour of duty ended, the growing family settled in Dunn, North Carolina. There, Ammons accepted a job with Carolina Power and Light (CP&L), North Carolina's largest electrical utility company. His position was as an Agricultural Development Engineer and his leadership qualities did not go unnoticed. Groomed for top management, he was promoted to the company's home office in Raleigh.

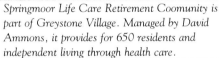

Springmoor Life Care Retirement Coomunity is part of Greystone Village. Managed by David Ammons, it provides for 650 residents and independent living through health care.

Although his advances with CP&L came quickly, Ammons soon learned that the conventional route was not to be his career path. Not only were his risk-taking skills stifled, his independent nature and forthright approach were not qualities that fit into a corporate structure. "You'd spend a third of your day getting permission from your boss to do something, a third of your day doing it, and a third reminding him you did it so you could get a raise," quips Ammons. To release the stresses from the work day, he relaxed in the evenings by designing houses. The opportunity came to turn those designs into homes and Ammons took a chance. Ammons trusted his past entrepreneurial successes and made a career of being a risk taker.

"I wish more people would rather be broke and starting over than scared to take a chance," remarks Ammons. He "started over" by forming Ammons Construction Company. His first projects were small. Ammons began by building a few residential homes in West Raleigh. Then he wisely invested profits into larger projects and soon tackled developments such as Hidden Valley II, Trotters Ridge and Lake Park subdivision.

Over the years Ammons Construction Company has blossomed into several independent sister companies which have worked in tandem to complete projects. The reason for the number of businesses is two-fold; building on old successes and addressing new needs. For instance, when he saw that the elderly members of his church had no suitable place for retirement, Ammons built them one. Because of his past development successes and his ever-present optimistic approach, he knew it could be done. Springmoor Retirement Center, a retirement community with 650 units for the elderly, became a reality. He planned the project, then built and managed the Center for over twenty years.

Not only does he complete projects effectively, he makes them beautiful. "'Let it be pretty' is his motto," states James Seay of Seay and Horne Law Offices. "It is reflected in all of his work." This is certainly true of Springmoor and Greystone Village, a 500-acre mixed-use development, another landmark project for Ammons. Both are marked by the deliberate preservation of parks, greenways, trees, streams, and beautiful stretches of green grass.

Some other past and present projects of Ammons in North Carolina are: NorthChase in Wilmington, a 900-acre housing and industrial development; Nags Head Village in Nags Head, a 400-

Mars Hill Retirement Community, an assisted living facility developed by Jud Ammons. It is managed by David Ammons and provides for approximately sixty residents.

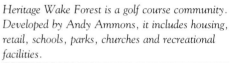

Heritage Wake Forest is a golf course community. Developed by Andy Ammons, it includes housing, retail, schools, parks, churches and recreational facilities.

acre mixed use development including beach houses, commercial buildings and a golf and swim club; EagleChase in Raleigh, a residential community of 225 homes; LakePark in Raleigh, a residential community with 200 homes surrounding a lake; EastPark in Raleigh, a 600-acre industrial site with offices and industrial development; Tadlock Planation in Wake County, a residential community with ninety lots and homes; and Mars Hill Retirement Community in Mars Hill, an assisted living facility with seventy units on the campus of Mars Hill College.

Ammons was a trail blazer. He helped to write original ordinances for Planned Unit Developments (PUDs.) The PUD approach mixes shopping centers,

churches, day care facilities, recreational facilities, offices, retirement living and schools to form a more cohesive community. With this type of community plan, residents can live, work, play and go to school in one general area, thereby reducing travel and congestion and saving time for leisure and family.

His land developments have not only benefited the community, they have gained Ammons significant recognition for his expertise. In 2001 Ernst and Young named him Carolina Entrepreneur of the Year in acknowledgment of his exceptional skills. He was named Builder of the Year and served as president of the Raleigh Wake County Home Builders Association. He also was the national director for the organization for over fifteen years. During his presidency he began the Raleigh Wood for Warmth Program, encouraging other builders to bring wood to a central site for cutting and delivering. In addition, he served on the Raleigh Bicentennial Commission which developed New Year's First Night Celebration and the Acorn, two popular seasonal events.

Impressive land developments and accolades aside, Ammons, at heart, is a family man. His four children and twelve grandchildren are his main source of pride. He has three sons and a daughter;

all are entrepreneurs in their own right. Andy, David and Jeff have followed in the family tradition of acquiring land and developing it, but they don't work for their father's company. "Once they got out of school, they never worked for me," states Ammons, "It's hard to be creative and innovative when someone is telling you what to do." All of his children are vocationally independent and creative in their own endeavors.

Alma, his daughter, specializes in education. She earned her Master of Education degree from Meredith College and creates and coordinates summer workshops for continuing education. She also teaches motivational techniques to teachers who, in turn,

As an educator, Alma Ammons Hoffmann has written books, designed material taught and facilitated numerous educational seminars.

inspire their students in creative writing.

Andy, the oldest son, developed Heritage Wake Forest which is the town's largest and most upscale residential and commercial subdivision. Like his father, he didn't just complete the job; he considered the needs of the community. He provided nearly $8 million in road improvements and he sold land at a reduced price to Wake County Public Schools for three school sites. Also, like his father, he paid special attention to the beauty of the development and set aside 200 acres for parks and greenways. Andy Ammons was named Wake Forest's 2005 Citizen of the Year in recognition of his successful efforts and positive contributions to the community.

David Ammons, the middle son, builds senior citizen homes and plans to build in Wake Forest, as well. He created SpringShire, a continuing care retirement community being built in Greenville, North Carolina. The resort-style community will offer a variety of floor plans for deluxe homes, cottages, villas and apartments. It also will have amenities including a pool, movie theater, computer lab, fitness center and health and educational programs.

Ammons youngest son, Jeff, developed The Factory, a thirty-eight-acre redevelopment project off South Main Street in Wake Forest. The 222,000 square-foot facility which was the former Athey sweeper manufacturing plant was converted into a recreational and shopping complex complete with indoor hockey and ice skating rinks, basketball courts and spaces for soccer games and gymnastic competitions. Although the facility is clearly youth friendly, it is designed to appeal to adults, as well. Parents can enjoy a workout at the gym while their kids play a game of basketball, all within the same structure.

Ammons is clearly an inspiration to his children, grandchildren, and all others who aspire to make a difference in the

Greystone Village developed by Jud Ammons, provides residences shopping, office recreational, schools, churches, lakes and parks.

lives of those around them. He has built, owned and operated major subdivisions, day care facilities, golf course communities, retirement communities, nursing homes, assisted living communities, industrial parks and shopping centers throughout North Carolina. His philosophy is summed up in the simple and direct title of his book, *Don't Wish You Had, Be Glad You Did.* Ammons is a glad man, and so are the beneficiaries of his home developments throughout North Carolina— the many people whose lives he has greatly improved and profoundly influenced.

Justus Murray (Jud) Ammons' book on his life and philosphy.

BUCK STOVE CORPORATION

Celebrating its thirty-first year in business, the Buck Stove Corporation is situated in the small rural town of Spruce Pine, North Carolina in the majestic Blue Ridge Mountains. Known as the "Christmas tree capital of the world," many beautiful evergreens from these mountains have been chosen to be the official White House Christmas tree. About 7,500 residents call Spruce Pine home, a number of whom are employees of Buck Stove. The company is the oldest privately held national gas and wood heating manufacturer in America.

Buck Stove has ninety employees, rests aside the Toe River, and has been located in Spruce Pine since its inception in 1975. Originally, Robert Bailey and Alvin Barrier opened a small country store called Minpro Supply in the town in 1971. They sold gasoline, refurbished appliances and baloney sandwiches made by Robert and his mother.

In 1975 Mr. Carol Buckner of Asheville approached the two men about selling a new wood-burning stove that he had built, which included a three-speed motor. Buckner was searching for a company that could manufacture the stove, which he called the "Regular Buck," as well as set up a dealer network for its sales. He had created the stove in the midst of the

Robert L. Bailey, *president of Buck Stove Corporation.*

national energy crisis, when people were desperately looking for heating alternatives to gas and oil. He made Bailey and Barrier an offer: if they could not sell the stove within thirty days, he would buy it back from them, no strings attached.

Bailey and Barrier used the stove as a floor model, and in just a short time they had so many orders they decided to start a Buck Stove manufacturing operation as well. Within two months they had sold 200 stoves. They transformed their

store into a manufacturing facility, selling the stoves faster then they could get them off the finishing line. Robert's sister, Betty Bailey Carswell, even learned how to weld to help keep production moving. They set a goal of producing thirty stoves a week, but the demand was so high they quickly fell behind.

Rapidly running out of physical space, the company moved about a mile or so down the road, purchasing a property with an existing larger structure. Bailey and Barrier set a new goal of manufacturing 200 stoves a week, but again found they still were not meeting the demand. To solve their dilemma the two men decided to hire more employees and build a new structure on the property that could keep up with their ever-increasing sales. In less than twelve months the company went from manufacturing thirty stoves a week to 3,000 stoves per month. Shortly after, other stoves were added to the production line, including the "Big Buck," and the "Little Buck." All three models were triple-wall stoves with three-speed motors and fans.

By the early 1980s the wood stove business began to level off as the energy crisis waned. Suffering from health prob-

Original Regular Buck.

Built in the early 1900s, the former Harris School was bought and renovated into the area's premier hotel and conference center.

The 400 foot long footbridge, connecting Spruce Pine to the school property, hence the name, "Pinebridge."

lems, Alvin Barrier sold his share of the company to partner Robert Bailey and Buck Stove became a sole proprietorship. Bailey began to look for new product ideas. At the same time, he was approached by a number of community officials asking for assistance raising funds for a football field for Spruce Pine's new Mitchell High School. Bailey was a natural choice for a partner, since he was a native of the town and Buck Stove had become a leading employer of the community. With his customary business acumen, Bailey analyzed the situation and came up with a great solution. He first bought up the land and buildings of the old high school, which had been condemned four years earlier and was standing vacant. A good portion of those funds were used to create the new football stadium and field, helping the community to realize its dreams. Bailey's ingenuity went one step further by providing benefits to the community beyond the school in ways no one else had imagined. He took the main building of the old school, built in the early 1900s, and completely renovated it, creating a forty-four-room hotel and conference center. He ran a contest in the town in which residents could submit names for the new complex, with the winning name being the Pinebridge Center Complex. The name is derived from a small, 400-foot long footbridge that crosses the Toe River onto the old school property.

Today, the only daughter of Robert Bailey and his wife Donna Andrews Bailey, Claudia Bailey Pittman, runs the Pinebridge Center Complex with her husband, Gerald. Over time Bailey added an 80,000 square foot, privately-owned community sports complex to the property, which includes a fitness center, indoor swimming pool, sauna, steam room, Jacuzzi, and the largest ice skating rink in the South. There is also an impressive attention to detail in addressing the needs of certain segments of the local population. An example of this is the indoor pool, which is kept at eighty-seven degrees so that Spruce Pine's elderly citizens, who suffer from ailments such as arthritis, can take advantage of the physical benefits of swimming and exercise. Each year the North Carolina Mineral and Gem Show is held at the complex and it also hosts the annual statewide high school wrestling tournament, as well as several Christmas-related festivities.

Claudia Pittman, whose official title is Director of Operations for Pinebridge Center Complex, has known Buck Stove all her life. She specifically recalls a day when she was in first grade and attended the ribbon-cutting ceremony for the Inn. "I remember the Governor was there and a bunch of news crews and it was all really exciting," said Pittman. "But even more than that I specifically remember standing on the front steps and looking up at the Inn and saying to my parents that I was going to run Pinebridge someday. My childhood dream has actually come true."

The Inn itself has also become an integral part of two Christmas traditions in Spruce Pine, which grew out of a best-selling children's book authored by Dr. Gloria Houston, who grew up in the town. *The Year of the Perfect Christmas Tree* is a story about a little girl in Appalachia whose father is about to go off to war. The child is worried that her father will not be back in time to help cut down the family Christmas tree and so he takes his daughter up into the mountains to choose the perfect tree, which he marks with a ribbon. When her father does not make it home for Christmas, the little girl trudges off into the night with her lantern to find the tree they chose to-gether.

On the book cover is an illustration of the little girl with her lantern. The Chamber of Commerce and Mitchell County Economic Development Commission made arrangements with the author and illustrator of the book to commission the products. Buck Stove manufactured the first licensed product of the project with part of the proceeds going to local, underprivileged high school students to assist in paying their college tuition. The idea was such a success that the Chamber of Commerce and the economic development commission in Mitchell County started an arts and crafts program, which hires out-of-work people with crafts abilities as well as artisans from the nearby Penland School of Craft to create products based on the book, which are then sold in shops in Spruce Pine and are also part of the scholarship program.

Visitors began to come to Spruce Pine from far away during the Christmas

The Year of the Perfect Christmas Tree *book*.

The Lantern made by Buck Stove.

holidays, and the Pinebridge Center Complex responded by creating the perfect Christmas weekend. Upon arrival, guests are given a copy of the book, which they can read to their children and then head out into the nearby tree farms, take a hayride and find their own "perfect Christmas tree."

While Buck Stove has also continued to produce state-of-the art products, including wood stoves, vented heaters, vent-free heaters, gaslights, fireplaces, oil circulators and designer log sets, one of their best-selling products is the Model 91 Catalytic. The model is a wood-burning stove, which can be used as a masonry fireplace insert or as a freestanding unit, heating up to 3200 square feet. As fuel costs rise to all time highs in the twenty-first century, the company has seen a 400 percent increase in the sale of their wood stove models in the past year.

In 2003 Buck Stove bought out Tharrington Oil Stoves in Rocky Mount, which was about to close its doors. In taking over the company, Bailey added fifteen new employees, saving them from unemployment, which has become a serious issue for many people in the

Carolinas as more and more businesses move their plants overseas.

Buck Stove is committed to remaining in the Spruce Pine community and has not had a layoff or a decrease in employment for the last twenty years. More importantly, they have actually added employees twice during that time, acquiring new product lines, new networks, and new distribution points. The company currently has a nationwide distribution network, including ten national distributors that have their own dealer networks, which range from 50 to 500 dealers. Part of the sales and customer service team is Bailey's only son and Claudia's younger brother, Robert Andrew Bailey, better known as Andy. Buck Stove also has an extensive online parts store.

The company's biggest challenge is, and has always been, its location. Buck Stove rests some forty miles from the interstate and transporting parts and product up and down a two-lane mountain road presents a unique set of problems. Unlike similar companies located in larger urban areas like Atlanta, employees are harder to come by and transportation fees are much higher being in a rural location. Still, Buck Stove has managed to keep its products competitively priced and prides itself on its wide selection of models.

To celebrate the company's thirtieth anniversary, Buck Stove fully sponsored "School Days," an annual community event held in Spruce Pine. Attended by more than 700 people, Buck Stove hosted a special catered event and gave out $10,000 in door prizes throughout the

Buck Stove's top selling wood burning stove, Model 91.

weekend, including Buck Stove fireplaces, lanterns, stoves, and Buck Stove jackets. The company also conducted special factory tours and held an awards ceremony to honor longtime company employees.

As business continues to boom for Buck Stove, they are always aware of the importance of giving back to the community, whether locally or much farther away. During hurricane Katrina, two of Buck Stove's dealers in Gulfport, Mississippi were completely wiped out. Bailey immediately arranged for 100 stoves from its Spruce Pine plant to be sent down to the dealers to distribute free of charge to employees and other local families.

One of the more rewarding aspects of running a business, for both Robert Bailey and his daughter, Claudia, is in seeing employees who grow into strong, responsible members of the community through what they have learned at Buck Stove. Claudia Pittman gives an example. "It's like the person you hire at seventeen and you wonder if they will show up after the first day. And they come back and they come back again and before you know it you are promoting them and then you promote them again, this time to manage a whole department of their own. Twenty-seven years later they are sitting right beside you and they have made a life for themselves because

of what they have been able to do at Buck Stove. That's pretty fulfilling."

Over the years, Buck Stove has distinguished itself as a private, family run business (almost unheard of these days), and Robert Bailey and his wife, Donna and their family are living proof that real success only comes if you share that success with your surrounding community and beyond. Claudia Pittman says one of the most important lessons she learned from her father is "If you're going be successful you have got to live it. And that does not mean that you've got to be at work every second of every day. It means you always have to be thinking, you always have to be moving. You don't have

Robert L. Bailey, president of Buck Stove Corporation and Claudia Pittman.

time to sit and stare, you don't have time to sit and wonder what if, you have to move forward all the time."

You can find more information about Buck Stove and the Pinebridge Center Complex online at: www.buckstovecorp.com.

A stove being welded in the production area.

A sample of over fifty products made by Buck Stove today.

CALLOWAY JOHNSON MOORE & WEST

Calloway Johnson Moore & West celebrates its centennial in 2006—100 years of architectural, engineering and interior design excellence. The 100-person firm headquartered in Winston-Salem is among the largest firms of its type in North Carolina. The company has grown through a series of partnerships; each successfully completing exceptional projects over the decades. CJMW serves the diverse needs of its clients utilizing the resources of a large firm, including in-house engineering and interior design. However, because of the firm's philosophy of using focused, project-driven design teams, clients have also benefited from hands-on attention and flexibility usually only possible in smaller architectural boutiques.

Clients are impressed with the firm's ability to provide creativity in design while meeting functional needs and budget. But clients are only part of the story. Buildings have a life of their own, and many generations of building users have benefited from CJMW's work. A performing arts student premiering on a college stage, an Alzheimer's patient meandering down a corridor looking more like a street in a charming village than an assisted living facility, or a WWII veteran reminiscing in the awe-

The clubhouse at The Cedars of Chapel Hill, a continuing care retirement community. 2005. Photo by JWestProductions.com

Lowe's Companies new headquarters in Mooresville, North Carolina, overlooks landscaped terraces. 2004. Photo by JWestProductions.com

inspiring lobby of the Airborne & Special Operations Museum, these are the people who truly benefit from the time, care and grace put into each building designed by Calloway Johnson Moore & West.

In the last half century much of the firm's work has been concentrated in college and university buildings, buildings for the performing arts, retirement communities, healthcare, corporate offices, museums, historic adaptive re-use facilities, and libraries.

Originally founded in 1906 by Willard Northup, the company was then a small architectural firm in Winston-Salem. One of its largest commissions was the design for the original North Carolina Baptist Hospital, which opened in 1923. This commission began a partnership between the two entities that continues to this day. His partner, Leet Alexander O'Brien, joined him a few years later; the firm then was called Northup and O'Brien. The partners designed Winston-Salem's Union Station in 1926. That structure, now the Davis Garage, still maintains its strong architectural features in the classical entry portico and the interior plaster work.

Luther Lashmit, a native of Winston-Salem who studied architecture at

Carnegie Tech, joined the firm in the early thirties. He was educated in the Beaux-Arts tradition in which architects studied the rules of classical architecture, created their own designs based on these studies and then competed for prizes that included trips to Europe for further study. Several of Lashmit's entries still hang on the walls at CJMW. Lashmit's first project at the firm was "Graylyn" built between 1927 and 1932. The mansion, which was the personal home of the

The lobby of CompRehab Plaza, part of the Wake Forest University Baptist Medical Center. 1995. Photo by Rick Alexander

prominent Gray family, is considered one of the finest examples of Norman Revival architecture in the U.S. "Imagine that for your first commission," comments Alan Moore, one of CJMW's current principals who remembers Lashmit. "Luther said that the Gray family was traveling around the world shopping for interior furnishings. From time to time they would buy an entire room—paneling, doors, and furnishings—from a European or Asian architectural landmark. Huge boxes would arrive at the construction site and Luther would have to change the plans to make it all fit."

After Northup and O'Brien the firm became Lashmit Brown and Pollock. Under that name the firm grew in prominence throughout the state. Notable projects completed by the company at this time include many of the buildings at Salem College, Davidson College, and NC Wesleyan College. Many Winston-Salem and surrounding area churches, schools, homes and commercial buildings were also projects of the firm.

Lashmit, Brown and Pollock all retired in 1972; the firm became known as Newman VanEtten Winfree Associates, after the principals who remained with the practice. The Southeastern Center for Contemporary Art (SECCA) is credited to this partnership, as is the NCNB Plaza, the entire block at Third and Liberty Streets. Under this leadership, the firm also designed the adaptation of the old Carolina Theatre in downtown Winston-Salem to become the Roger L. Stevens Center, a multi-purpose performance hall for the North Carolina School of the Arts. At the Stevens Center grand opening, Leonard Bernstein conducted the orchestra, and Gregory Peck was the Master of Ceremonies.

Members of CJMW's present day key management team are Tom Calloway, Alan Moore, P. Michael West, John Drinkard, Peter Epermanis, and Dave Moore. The firm was incorporated as Calloway Johnson Moore in 1986 and became Calloway Johnson Moore & West in 1994. The Lynchburg, Virginia office was established in 1997, Asheville's office in 2002, and the Columbia, South Carolina office in 2005.

The firm has maintained an incredibly diverse practice throughout the years. Along the way, it has received official recognition for its design work, winning awards for a wide range of projects including the Airborne & Spe-

Granite pavers commemorate military units at the Airborne and Special Operations Museum in Fayetteville, North Carolina. 2000. Photo By Rick Alexander

CJMW's design of the interior of the Clay Center's lobby provides a vibrant backdrop for performances and events. 2002. Photo by JWestProductions.com

cial Operations Museum, The Forest at Duke Special Care Unit and Assisted Living Addition, SciWorks Science Center and Environmental Park, The Cedars of Chapel Hill Retirement Community, the Schiele Museum of Natural History, North Carolina School of the Arts Performance Place, and Winston-Salem's Ronald McDonald House.

Designing a successful building requires both creative and technical skills. It also requires consideration, care and appreciation for the end-user. The current leadership of Calloway Johnson Moore & West is acutely aware of the company's tradition of care for those who will experience the buildings the firm designs. Whether it be a college campus educational building, a performing arts center, a memorial museum or a senior living center, CJMW's design team puts the user of the building above all other considerations. One hundred years in existence means thousands have appreciated and enjoyed the benefits of CJMW's building designs.

View of "Main Street" at The Forest at Duke's Assisted Living Addition. 2003. Photo by JWestProductions.com

Michael West, who led the design team for the Airborne & Special Operations Museum in Fayetteville, North Carolina, had a respect for the individuals he would be honoring with the design of the building. "The museum immortalizes and commemorates the U.S. Army's airborne and special operations forces—their accomplishments and the sacrifices they made for our country," states West, whose interest in military history prompted him to write two books on the subject. In addition to civilians, thousands of military, present and past, visit the museum with their loved ones— over 1 million visitors in the last five years.

The Forest at Duke Assisted Living Center in Durham, North Carolina, is also a project in which the special needs of its inhabitants were considered. A large percentage of the elderly who live in the center suffer from dementia. Environments with familiar, non-institutional features have a positive impact on these individuals. This means less dangerous behavior and less need for medication. The design of the project creates separate "neighborhoods" connected by an indoor street. This delightful, sky-lit "main street" has trees,

benches, fountains and lampposts. The typical community spaces found in a building of this type are redefined as the amenities, such as a neighborhood bistro, a spa/salon, and a theater, that one would find in a small town main street. The design was so distinctive it was featured on the cover of *DESIGN for Senior Environments 2005.*

CJMW is particularly proud of its forty-year relationship with the North Carolina School of the Arts. Lashmit Brown & Pollock designed the school's first dormitory—a rush job to prepare for the School's opening. As the school grew, CJMW and its predecessors designed performance and rehearsal facilities for drama, dance, and music, and in doing so acquired special expertise in the functional needs of each performance type. As the firm developed this expertise, it found opportunities to design other such buildings. Significant examples include the RiverPark Center for the Performing Arts in Owensboro, Kentucky, new music buildings at UNC-Greensboro and East Carolina University, and the renovation of Memorial Hall at UNC-Chapel Hill. The firm recently completed a master plan for new music facilities at The Ohio State University.

In addition to the examples already described, CJMW has designed buildings for many of North Carolina's most respected institutions and businesses, among them: eight campuses of the University of North Carolina, North Carolina Baptist Hospital/Wake Forest University Medical Center, The Center for Creative Leadership, The Presbyterian Homes of North Carolina, BB&T, Lowe's Corporation, and many more. CJMW has also provided pro-bono services to local community organizations like The Ronald McDonald House, the Samaritan Soup Kitchen

and The Children's Center for the Physically Handicapped.

Throughout its history CJMW and its predecessor firms have made a major impact on Winston-Salem's architectural environment. Projects like Old Salem's Visitor Center and BB&T's building at Five Points have become Winston-Salem landmarks. CJMW continues this tradition as the architects and planners of The Gateway, a new mixed-use development that will completely transform a formerly blighted area.

Many have benefited from the design work of Calloway Johnson Moore & West. General James J. Lindsay (U.S. Army-retired) had this to say about a visit to the Airborne and Special Operations Museum: "During the recent 82nd Airborne reunion a large number of WWII veterans visited the site. More than one broke into tears as they entered the spacious lobby area. That says more than I could ever say about the impact of your design."

Watson Chamber Music Hall, an intimate performance space in NCSA's School of Music. 2004. Photo by JWestProductions.com

Greensboro Skyline. Courtesy, N.C. Division of Tourism, Film, and Sports Development

CLEVELAND COUNTY HEALTHCARE SYSTEM

Cleveland Regional Medical Center (CRMC) located in Shelby, North Carolina has been serving the medical needs of Cleveland County and surrounding communities since its opening in August of 1923. In existence for more than three quarters of a century, the hospital has seen growth in physical structure, sophistication in equipment and services and in the numbers of patients served. But, perhaps its greatest accomplishment has been evidenced in the past decade through the benevolence of its leadership and the collaborative nature of its community. In fact, the joining together of the Medical Center's leadership with willing members of the community brought about the most noteworthy transformation in the hospital's history: the merger of Cleveland Regional Medical Center with Kings Mountain Hospital (KMH.) Both now serve as the Cleveland County HealthCare System.

CRMC, first called Shelby Hospital, began as a two-story red brick building on Grover Street in Shelby. The hospital was long awaited, with patients traveling to Rutherfordton, Charlotte and even Baltimore, Maryland for their healthcare needs. A bond referendum was passed in 1921 with voters approving the construction of Shelby Hospital, which was to serve as a memorial to

New Women's Life Center addition in 2002.

Cleveland County war veterans.

On August 17, 1923 the facility opened with forty-three beds and patient rooms decorated in ivory and mahogany. Three days before the opening, the community was invited to tour the $100,000 building. Close to 4,000 people lined up with great anticipation to see the facilities. They were not disappointed. "It has been the dream of the county for years to have an institution of this kind, and at last our hopes are realized. Our money is there and our heart also," wrote the *Cleveland Daily Star* at the time of the opening.

In its first year of service, 472 patients were treated at the hospital. A private room was priced at $3; a bed in a hospital ward was $2.50. The early years brought about quite a few improvements and changes. A laundry room was added. A steam plant and sprinkler system modernized the facility, and a new maternity unit was dedicated after a generous $10,000 was donated for that purpose. By 1945 the hospital property, now in the ownership of Cleveland County, was valued at an estimated $375,000.

The 1950s witnessed great changes as the hospital added a new wing with a price tag of $600,000, a new surgical suite, new kitchen and dining rooms, two floors for medical and surgical patients and six rooms equipped with up-to-date X-ray facilities. In 1957 the name of the hospital was changed to Cleveland Memorial Hospital, as the institution secured a place as one of North Carolina's forerunners in modern healthcare.

Ribbon cuttings and dedications became a common occurrence—as the

Shelby Hospital 1923.

CRMC today.

hospital made expansions every decade for the next forty years. In 1967 a $3.8 million, 100-bed wing was added, making it the most ambitious expansion program to date. In May of 1972 a plan for a $1.5 million dollar addition was unveiled with the assurance that more expansions would soon follow. A 290-bed capacity was reached in 1975 and the purchase of a $150,000 linear accelerator, one of the first in the state of North Carolina, made it possible for Cleveland county residents to receive extensive cancer treatment without having to travel outside the county.

The hospital had purchased four surrounding pieces of property and by 1987 the trustees voted to build a new, substantially expanded facility. In September of 1992 a new $35 million, five-story, 230-private room hospital began operations. In 1994 the hospital joined the Carolinas HealthCare System. Two years later, in 1996, Cleveland Memorial Hospital became Cleveland Regional Medical Center.

By the 1990s the strong foundation of this great hospital was an assurance to the community that its healthcare was secure and trust in its leadership solidified. A mutual appreciation between community and hospital leadership led to collaborative efforts through committee-lead programs. Other hospitals and medical practices followed CRMC's lead and soon entities began working together. One such successful joining of forces was with Kings Mountain Hospital.

The merger between the two medical institutions, Cleveland Regional Medical Center and Kings Mountain Hospital, culminated in January 2003. However, preparation for this monumental step began years earlier. The coming together of these two institutions was an awesome challenge. The willingness of the two hospital communities to make this union a positive reality was imperative. The process began a decade before through the collaborative efforts of both institutions' superior leadership.

C. Bridges, former chairman of KMH Advisory Council and CCHS Community Trustee Council Member; John Young, CCHS president and CEO; Larry Corry, CCHS Community Trustee Council chairman continue working to provide the best in healthcare to the residents of Cleveland County.

Esteemed leaders and key members of Cleveland County's medical community and surrounding townships began to realize the need and the advantage of coming together in strategy and purpose for the betterment of the whole. The formation of this partnership encouraged collaborations such as: Alliance for Health, CLECO, the HealthCare Enterprise and others, which were powerfully effective in bridging communities and encouraging interdependence.

The late Dr. T. Reginald Harris was one of the foremost internal medical physicians in the country and a well-respected physician in Cleveland County. Dr. Harris spearheaded a group, which included Austin Letson, CRMC's CEO at the time; Denese Stallings, Cleveland County Health Department director;

and several other key community leaders, to form a preventive healthcare initiative known as the Alliance for Health. The Alliance, although not initially a legal organization, was considered a "virtual" committee formed for preventative health issues. This group, now a separate 501c3 healthcare non-profit entity, has more than forty organizational members and has raised more than $2.5 million for the community.

Prior to 1995 there were three acute care providers in Cleveland County and several other not-for-profit healthcare providers. Medical staffs from each of these institutions were diligent in their care for patients and in their desire to help the community. However, lack of communication between these entities often resulted in replication of tasks. "There was very little collaboration between these 'community based' healthcare providers with various missions and competitive strategies," states John E. Young, president and CEO of CRMC. "Even though resources were scarce, duplication of effort abounded. Today there is the HealthCare Enterprise and an Alliance for Health."

The HealthCare Enterprise includes Cleveland Pines Nursing Center, Crawley Memorial Hospital, Hospice and Palliative Care of Cleveland

Beautiful fountain welcomes patients and visitors to the newly renovated Kings Mountain Hospital.

County, Cleveland Home Health Agency, CLECO Primary Care Network and Cleveland Ambulatory Services, all of which are either owned or managed by the Cleveland County HealthCare System. In turn, the HealthCare Enterprise, along with many community organizations that provide services to citizens of Cleveland County, are partners in the Alliance for Health.

The Alliance serves as a steering committee for Cleveland County's Healthy Carolinian Task Force and helps organize, operate and fund a unified system to improve community health. Denese Stallings remains chair of that committee and CRMC is a partner in helping fund a staff employee for the Alliance, providing a continual focus on prevention and community health education initiatives.

A key initiative of the HealthCare Enterprise is CLECO, a primary care network of clinics with rural health status. The steering committee came together to discuss the need for more physicians in outlying rural communities. Now, four rural health clinics exist in the surrounding areas including: Shelby, Fallston, Grover and Kings Mountain. One also exists in the Gaston County Community of Cherryville. The CLECO networks' vision is to "…actively coordinate, integrate and improve access to quality primary and preventative healthcare services for the citizens of Cleveland County and surrounding communities, regardless of their ability to pay."

Programs such as these have helped pave the way to setting the standard of trust between communities. When the idea of merging the two hospitals surfaced, both communities relied on the

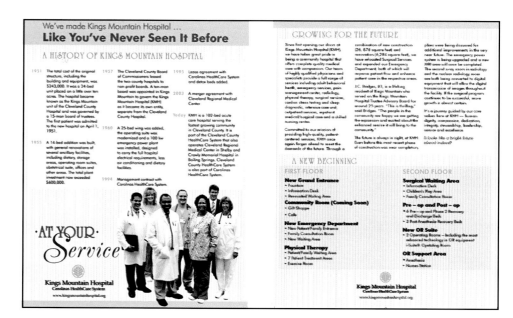

track record of successful interdependence. "I see no reason to delay...I feel confident we have a great thing for Cleveland County and Kings Mountain Hospital and Cleveland Regional Medical Center," stated J.C. Bridges, KMH's Trustee Advisory Board Chair at the time of the merger.

The union is certainly mutually beneficial. "Kings Mountain is situated perfectly in the middle of a region that is growing and well connected with infrastructure," comments Young. Under the umbrella of the Cleveland County HealthCare System, CRMC is therefore extended to that geographic location through KMH. A promise to help grow programs and expand the Kings Mountain facility has been made and kept. "...our commitment to grow acute care services and make significant capital investments at KMH is absolute. This will be an exciting place to be over the next ten years," stated Young at the time of the merger.

Larry Corry, chair of the CRMC Trustee Council during those discussions added, "We're growing in our ability to trust each other; and those opposed will soon see that we are people of integrity and will honor this agreement." The first investment into the KMH facility was an impressive $11 million capital project which included out-patient surgery and

Kings Mountain Hospital.

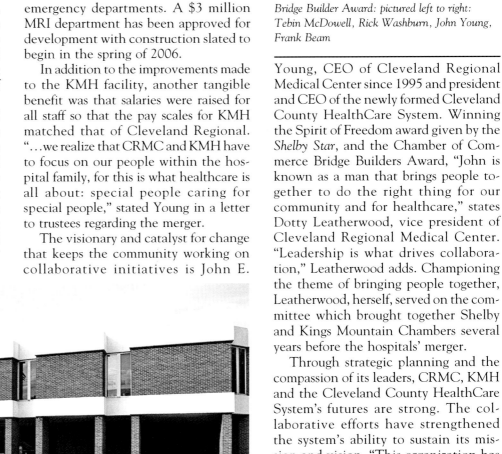

emergency departments. A $3 million MRI department has been approved for development with construction slated to begin in the spring of 2006.

In addition to the improvements made to the KMH facility, another tangible benefit was that salaries were raised for all staff so that the pay scales for KMH matched that of Cleveland Regional. "...we realize that CRMC and KMH have to focus on our people within the hospital family, for this is what healthcare is all about: special people caring for special people," stated Young in a letter to trustees regarding the merger.

The visionary and catalyst for change that keeps the community working on collaborative initiatives is John E.

Bridge Builder Award: pictured left to right: Tebin McDowell, Rick Washburn, John Young, Frank Beam

Young, CEO of Cleveland Regional Medical Center since 1995 and president and CEO of the newly formed Cleveland County HealthCare System. Winning the Spirit of Freedom award given by the *Shelby Star*, and the Chamber of Commerce Bridge Builders Award, "John is known as a man that brings people together to do the right thing for our community and for healthcare," states Dotty Leatherwood, vice president of Cleveland Regional Medical Center. "Leadership is what drives collaboration," Leatherwood adds. Championing the theme of bringing people together, Leatherwood, herself, served on the committee which brought together Shelby and Kings Mountain Chambers several years before the hospitals' merger.

Through strategic planning and the compassion of its leaders, CRMC, KMH and the Cleveland County HealthCare System's futures are strong. The collaborative efforts have strengthened the system's ability to sustain its mission and vision. "This organization has a long history of strong leadership and we want to leave a quality provider of health care services to the next generations. Sometimes the right people come together at the right time to do the right thing" Mr. Young says. For Cleveland County HealthCare System, the right time continues to be now.

HOCK DEVELOPMENT CORP.

Gary Hock's rise from a poor farm boy to the owner of a development corporation that's built a half billion dollars worth of buildings since the late 1960s has all the makings of a classic rags-to-riches story. As a young boy, the Pennsylvania native lived on a small farm with his family. Wheat and corn were grown on the farm where Hock would carry wood for the family's wood-burning stove. In addition, he would gather eggs from dozens of chickens and help feed the animals, including about forty milking cows and about twenty pigs.

Life growing up on the farm was not easy, and the family worked from sunup until sundown. His father, Horace Henry Hock, milked cows at 4:30 a.m., drove a school bus later in the morning, then drove milk trucks, and *then* worked the second and sometimes the third shifts at a local carpet company called the Magee Carpet Company. To young Gary, it seemed like his father was always working and never slept. The work ethic he learned from watching his father toil day and night stuck with him, and Hock continues to be a hard worker to this day.

Independence Park, Durham, North Carolina, home of Hock Development Corp.

Habitat for Humanity project.

The carpet company where his father worked, and the gentleman who owned it, Harry Magee, had a lasting impression on the young Hock. The Magee Carpet Company was located just a few miles from the family farm in Bloomsburg, which had a population of about 10,000 at the time. In those days, Magee Carpet Company was the largest business in the area, at one point in time employing between 3,000 and 4,000 people. One day, when Hock was about

six years old, his mother took him and his older brother into Bloomsburg and while walking down Main Street, he looked up and saw Harry Magee pass by slowly in a beautiful gray Rolls Royce. Everyone on the street stopped and stared. At that moment, Hock was struck by the notion that someone could have such wealth and power. To this day, he's sure that this brief encounter had an impact on his success in years to come.

When Hock was twelve years old, the family moved from his Grandfather's farm to a new home that his father built several miles up the road. He began helping out at neighboring farms and working nights and weekends at a farm equipment store, cleaning old tractors and farm equipment, refurbishing and painting them. Also as a twelve year old, he spent two summers working on a nearby migrant farm that grew tomatoes. This became the setting for Hock's first entrepreneurial endeavor. The teenager had always been mechanically inclined, and he decided to purchase an old car and paint and repair it. When he got it in working condition, he sold it to one of the migrant farm workers.

With the money he earned, he bought more junk cars and repaired and painted them. Again, he sold them to the migrant farm workers. This practice of putting his profits back into the business would stick with him and would eventually become one of the cornerstones of his development company.

The notion of entrepreneurship and business ownership was actually something Hock grew up with. At one point during his childhood, all of his father's five brothers were in business for themselves. The businesses were all unrelated and included forestry, farming, fuel oil delivery, well drilling, and road construction. With so many entrepreneurs in the family, it was only a matter of time before Hock went into business for himself.

After graduating from high school in 1962 at the age of seventeen, Hock was ready to join the business world. In spite of his young age, he managed to convince the Gulf Oil Company to allow him to purchase a Gulf service station business. The enterprising youngster had saved about $1,000 from working and selling cars and had accumulated a fair amount of mechanical equipment that counted as assets. With that, he bought a Gulf service station business and remained in that enterprise for about three years before selling it to his brother-in-law.

Hock took a job as a machinist at a manufacturing corporation after selling

First purchase, a gas station, 1973.

Farm where Gary Hock grew up.

the service station. But his days of working for someone else didn't last long. At the age of twenty-one, Hock purchased an old house and started remodeling it. He worked on the remodeling project during the day then worked the night shift at his job as a machinist. To say that remodeling the house was a learning process is putting it mildly. Hock is the first one to admit that he had no idea what he was doing. In fact, he would drive to other construction sites to watch what other contractors were doing and then emulate their actions. In spite of his inexperience, Hock managed to complete the project with satisfactory results. Although he had lived in the house during the remodel, he decided to sell it once he had completed the project. The young man he sold it to eventually become Hock's first employee and remained with the company for twenty-two years.

The house was located on a fairly large piece of property and Hock realized that there was enough land to build a three-unit apartment building. He decided to take the profit he made from selling the house and put it into the apartment building. This marked the turning point in Hock's career. He quit his job to dedicate all his time to building the three-unit apartment building. Hock needed more workers, and the second man he hired also remained with the company for twenty-two years. While building those first apartment projects, Hock had about four or five men working for him, plus subcontractors.

Although Hock had little experience in construction, he was a fast learner. Combine that with his work ethic, and it didn't take long for him to gain expertise. Once the apartment projects reached completion, he sold them and pocketed a substantial profit. Based on that success, he looked for more construction opportunities.

Hock's next purchase was in Espy, Pennsylvania, where he acquired about thirty-forty acres of land. His plans were to create a development of townhouse units to rent as well as twenty-five single-family homes. To complete this far more demanding undertaking, Hock brought on approximately seventy employees, most of whom earned about $3.50 an hour. Once he completed this project and sold off the homes and townhouse units, he set his sights on a piece of adjoining land. There, he built more townhouses and apartment projects. Things were looking good at Hock Development Corporation, which incorporated in 1972, about three years after being launched. But that same year, Hurricane Agnes hit and Hock's office, warehouse, and base of operations were flooded with six feet of water. Fifty percent of his stored materials and equipment were either completely destroyed or floated down the Susquehanna River never to return. Unfortunately, Hock didn't have any flood insurance at the time. In fact, he admits he didn't even know what flood insurance was at the time. In spite of the setback, it didn't slow the growth of the operation by much.

Hock's first foray into office construction came in 1976. That's when the

Pennsylvania Department of Public Welfare hired him to build and lease office buildings. Over time, Hock built about twenty office buildings for them, ranging from about 10,000 to 30,000 square feet. But Hock didn't just build the facilities; he maintained ownership of them and leased them back to the Department. This practice of maintaining ownership of the office buildings became the foundation of Hock Development Corp., and continues to be one of the main things that differentiate the business from its competitors.

Throughout most of the 1970s, Hock's development projects were concentrated in Pennsylvania. Projects during that time included buildings for Hewlett Packard and the Internal Revenue Service in Harrisburg. At one point, Hock was one of the largest landlords for the State of Pennsylvania Department of Public Welfare.

In 1979 Reliance Insurance Company in Harrisburg, Pennsylvania hired Hock to develop a service center. A year later, the company wanted a 28,000 square-foot facility in Durham, North Carolina. At the time, Hock didn't know where Durham was. Over the coming years, Hock built several buildings for Reliance Insurance, including a 67,000-square-foot building and a 54,000-square-foot building in Durham. Eventually, the Reliance projects inspired him to pull up his Pennsylvania roots and relocate to

The removal of the Bonnie Brae house in Durham, North Carolina, to make room for a retirement community.

the North Carolina town where his firm has been based ever since.

During the 1980s Xerox Financial Services sought out the newly relocated Hock Development Corp. to build multiple projects. These major endeavors included multi-story office properties in Durham and Charlotte, North Carolina, and St. Louis, Missouri, ranging in size from 56,000 to 140,000 square feet. The relationship proved to be a profitable one for Hock, who continued developing for Xerox Financial Services for about a decade.

By 1985 Hock was leasing 146,000 feet of building space in Pennsylvania, 600,000 feet in North Carolina and had multi-million-dollar projects in St Louis, Missouri. The following year, the builder embarked on some of his most important projects to date.

The year 1986 saw the development of a 40,000-square-foot medical facility in Durham. That same year, Hock embarked on one of his biggest projects ever, a 250-acre mixed-use development called Independence Park in northern Durham. The park represents a $120 million mixed-use development investment and boasts a large medical complex and undeveloped land with complete infrastructure for future development of healthcare-related facilities.

The Independence Park project sparked controversy in the community. A historic 10,000-square-foot Colonial Revival-style home known as the Bonnie Brae house was located on the land. Hock, at that point in time, had no intention of incorporating the home into the proposed medical office facilities and considered razing it. When that possibility drew loud protests from

Women's Dormitory project 1973.

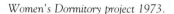

Hock Development Corp.'s private jet.

preservationists and concern from city officials, Hock came to the realization that he couldn't demolish and remove it.

Hock had to get creative to develop a solution for the problem, which had become a so-called political hot potato in the local community. After two years of public debate, Hock made a decision. In order to preserve the home while also preserving his vision for Independence Park, he decided to enlarge and renovate the house and make it one of the centerpieces of the Park where it still proudly remains today. With that obstacle out of the way, Hock was able to move forward with his plans for a sprawling complex of mixed-use development consisting mainly of medical office, medical labs and retail.

Building these medical facilities represented a new focus for the firm that had previously concentrated on government and insurance office buildings. Since 1989 the developer has specialized mainly in the construction of biotechnology laboratory and healthcare facilities. However, the company also continues to build facilities for clients who aren't involved in healthcare. Since 1991, Hock has completed more than thirty-five projects, including medical buildings for national health systems, nationally ranked teaching hospitals, and cell and gene therapy labs for biotechnology pharmaceutical companies. Clients for these facilities include Duke University Medical Center, HCA, Inc., Cogent Neurosciences, Clinical Trial Services, Merix Bioscience, Rhone-Poulenc Rorer, Centeon Bio-Services, Duke Central Core Laboratory, and Health Trust Inc. Some of the non-healthcare-related clients have included First Citizens Bank and Golden Corral Corporation.

To date, Hock Development has built and developed nearly two million square feet of property in the Southeast, Midwest and Northeast. Clients range from Fortune 500 companies to venture capital-funded firms and from hospitals to individual medical practices. Today, the firm is a full-service real estate development company specializing in office building and medical office building development.

With construction projects in North Carolina, Pennsylvania, Florida, Missouri, Virginia and Kentucky, Hock was forced to branch out with additional offices. The man who launched his business with a home currently main-

Hock Plaza Building.

205

tains offices in St. Louis, Charlotte and Raleigh-Durham. This way, he can serve clients across the country. In addition to the satellite offices, Hock makes use of his private jet to allow him to be quickly accessible to clients no matter where they are.

Just as he did with those junk cars repaired and sold as a youngster, and just as he did with that very first house he remodeled back in the late 1960s, Hock has continued to invest profits from all his projects back into the business. Ultimately, this has allowed the builder to finance projects on his own and avoid bank debt. The ability to self-finance projects really separates Hock Development from its competitors.

In the development industry today, most companies require the client to take on the financial risk associated with developing properties. But clients often don't want to undertake the financial burden that comes with building new offices. By self-financing projects, Hock Development becomes much more attractive to clients.

The builder has also found a unique niche with his turnkey approach to development. Hock offers architectural,

Building leased to National General Insurance, Saint Louis.

engineering and full-service construction along with its leasing and self-financing capabilities. Because the developer combines a full-service construction company with development capabilities, Hock maintains absolute control over project costs and project completion. By taking responsibility for the entire venture, Hock makes it easier on clients. Instead of having to juggle working with several different construction and development-related companies, they have a single source that's in charge of every aspect of the project.

Hock Development's turnkey approach goes beyond the building phase of a project. Since Hock Development maintains ownership of each building, the firm also manages the facilities once they're completed. What this means is that clients can focus on what they do best rather than undertake the tasks necessary to manage a facility.

Maintaining ownership of the facilities he builds means that Hock approaches each project with a long-term mindset. Because he holds the equity in a facility, he wants it to be the absolute best that it can be. This ensures a superior level of quality in both the design and the construction of each project, something clients really appreciate. To provide all of these services, Hock employs a host of seasoned professionals. Depending on the number and scope of projects underway, he'll employ anywhere from 50 to 200 construction workers and professional staff. On some

Home built in Covington, Virginia, in 2002.

projects, he brings in subcontractors, but he still maintains control and takes responsibility for all the work completed. During the more than thirty-six years he's been in business, Hock has also employed each of his four children. His oldest son worked side-by-side with the founder for twenty-three years and eventually decided to start his own firm, proving that entrepreneurship truly does run in the family. Hock's daughter ran the St. Louis operation for about eight years before relocating to Charleston, South Carolina. His middle son, a computer whiz, worked with the developer while going to college and helped set up Hock Development's AutoCAD, a computer program for architecture and design. Hock's youngest son worked in his father's business during college before leaving to become a teacher.

Although each of Hock's children has spent time at the firm their father created, none of them are currently involved on a day-to-day basis. However, they do own large real estate holdings of the company so they maintain a connection to the business. Hock doesn't have plans to retire anytime soon so he doesn't have a succession plan set in stone.

While Hock has reached a level of success he never could have imagined as a poor young farm boy, he has never forgotten his roots or what it's like to grow up poor. Because of this, he's consistently sought ways to give back to the community and especially to young

Hock Scholarship contribution in Pennsylvania, 1979.

children in need. The developer served as a board member of the Patrick Henry Boys and Girls Plantation, a home for displaced children in Virginia. In addition to his role as a board member, he helped the home computerize its operations, and he donated Christmas gifts each year to the children.

That orphanage isn't the only one to benefit from his charitable donations. Each year Hock has contributed between $25,000 and $50,000 for Christmas gifts for the children at the Durham County Public Housing Authority. He also donated funds for several years to allow these children to participate in the Send a Kid to Camp program.

Besides helping children, Hock has focused his philanthropic efforts on education. The fact that Hock never had the opportunity to go to college may be

Reliance Insurance, Durham, North Carolina, 1986.

part of the reason why he's so determined to help other young people reach their educational goals. Over the years, Hock has donated to North Carolina Central University—where he was a North Carolina Governor-appointed member of the board of trustees—Elon College, Durham Academy and Duke University. In fact, he donated $1.5 million to Duke University to create a professorship in global healthcare.

In addition to making cash donations, Hock has found other ways to contribute to those in need. As a builder, he sometimes has excess building materials that he offers to various charities. The developer also donated fifty-four acres of land now valued at $2 million to the Durham YMCA. And he donated two houses to the Durham Habitat for Humanity.

With these actions, it shows that the developer is interested in building goodwill in addition to building facilities and building long-lasting relationships with clients. This combination makes Gary Hock and his Hock Development Corp. one of the standout firms in North Carolina. And with the same amount of enthusiasm for the business that he had from day one, Hock should continue building on his current success for years to come.

HOUSE-AUTRY MILLS, INC.

When William House settled in North Carolina nearly 200 years ago, establishing what was to become House-Autry Mills, Inc., he laid the cornerstone for his family's legacy as well as a time-honored Southern cooking tradition.

House, a native of England, had left North Carolina for Tennessee with his father in 1790. He returned to Sampson County some time later and took over the construction of the mill first begun by Blake Warren in 1795, completing it in 1812. The land he chose was indicative of the region, picturesque with abundant agricultural resources. Just sixty miles southeast of Raleigh, the site provided House a viable vocation while the country was embattled in the War of 1812.

House's Mill was built from the area's long leaf pine, which was hand-hewn and held together by wooden pegs. The original mill also featured grinding stones that were shipped from England to Wilmington and transported by Cape Fear River to Fayetteville, and finally carried by mules and oxen to the mill.

As the United States was still a young country, most settlements were built around communal service providers, including flour and corn mills. So House's Mill, located on a 116-acre pond in Newton Grove, quickly became a gathering

Aerial photo of the new mill.

Ground level of the old mill as it currently stands.

place. The mill established itself as the center of the community, a place to come together not only for staple food needs, but social interaction as well.

On grinding day many residents would bring their own corn for milling, leaving a small portion of the finished product for payment. The grinding process was time consuming, but allowed for a bit of freedom and fun for the area's people, who worked hard from dawn to dusk. It took an hour for the water-driven stones

to grind three bushels of corn, so the residents, waiting for their turn, would dance, sing, fish and swim in the pond.

The mill successfully serviced Sampson County for more than fifty years after opening, and continued production even through the Civil War and the local Battle of Bentonville in March 1865. During the battle, the largest fought on North Carolina soil and waged just seven miles from the mill site, the Union Army spared House's Mill, operating it for their troops' use.

After the war the mill was returned to the ownership of the House family. Although it was badly damaged, the original structure was quickly repaired and the mill continued to be a valuable food source and meeting place for the community.

During the mid-to-late 1800s, a second generation of the family took the company's helm. Frank House, William's son, ran the mill until 1920, following in his father's footsteps with the tradition of superior quality and service.

In 1920 House's grandson, Edgar, became the third generation to operate the still growing mill. Edgar House ran the company for thirty-two years.

House-Autry Mill's product lined up in their packages.

One of the very few changes that occurred in the mill's first 150 years of service was replacing the operating method for the grinding stones. The millstones were turned with power generated by water from the pond until they were replaced with an electric version in 1947. One of the last original mill stones now serves as a monument at the burial site of William House.

In 1952 the fourth generation of Houses took ownership of the mill. The founder's great granddaughter, Eleanora House, and her husband, Sherrill Williams, received ownership of the company. Under their direction, the mill began to develop into a competitive food manufacturing facility.

In November of 1967 the company merged with Autry Bros. Milling Com-

pany, and the name became House-Autry Mills, Inc. The family bought out the Autry interest just five years later, but retained the combined name.

Although the daughters of Eleanora and Sherrill Williams had ventured into making hushpuppy mixes in the '50s and '60s, House-Autry Mills' experienced its first significant expansion of its product line in the '70s. The American lifestyle was significantly changing with women joining the workforce and more single family households being established. House-Autry met the evolving needs of its consumers by introducing high-quality value-added mixes. These mixes, including breaders for seafood, chicken and pork as well as hushpuppy mixes, quickly became popular with their ease of use and made-from-scratch taste.

Eleanora and Sherrill Williams successfully ran the mill for thirty-eight years until 1990. On July 17 of that year

the House family, having no more heirs interested in the milling business, sold the 178-year-old family firm to a group of corporate investors.

The mill went through changes in the structure of its parent company ownership over the next four years and is now held by a group of individual investment partners.

Perhaps the most pivotal change in business operations occurred for the company in 1994 under the leadership of Richard M. Justice as president, Roger F. Mortenson as vice president of finance and Kenneth C. Gilbert as vice president of sales. At that time House-Autry eliminated its direct-store delivery method of distribution, electing to transport its products via common carriers to distribution centers for grocery chains as well as selling to retail and food service distributors.

By employing the new delivery approach, House-Autry radically reduced fixed operating costs, including the expenses of owning and maintaining more than thirty vehicles. The economically beneficial move also allowed for the company to broaden its exposure to markets outside of its core three states, North Carolina, South Carolina and Virginia, to about thirty states.

The decision to outsource the delivery of the company's product coincided with the effort to streamline their offerings, which had multiplied through acquisitions over time. The company restructured its forty-two brands to one, simply named House-Autry, to further standardize the company's efforts.

Aerial photo of the old mill.

As the company streamlined its operations, it expanded its sales. The growth brought more positive change for the company.

Roger Mortenson, who had been with the company for five years, was promoted to president in 1996. Mortenson lead the organization through its first location change in its 184-year history.

Relocation from the founding site was a decision of necessity. In September of 1996 Hurricane Fran devastated the North Carolina coast, pushing water inland. The old mill was completely surrounded by water from the on-site pond and neighboring Seven Mile Swamp. Because the possibility of water damage was obvious, a move was considered, but a location to suit the company's needs was yet to be identified.

In 1999 Hurricane Floyd hit the area and the water took out a dam that provided essential protection to the mill. This time water damaged the original mill and other support structures.

With the high-risk of further damage from more hurricane-related weather and the company redefining its operations and developing a strategy for growth, a move was needed. Mortenson found a new site in neighboring Johnston County, outside of Four Oaks and northwest of the original mill.

The new eighteen-acre site proved to be ideal. It was high and removed from natural water sources. The parcel was located less than ten miles from the intersection of highways I-40 and I-95,

New mill elevation.

which was convenient for truck distribution. Rail transportation was also readily available due to the CSX rail line that ran directly behind the mill.

But most important to House-Autry's executives was the location for the company's forty-plus employees. Due to careful planning, the new site, with its $8-million, 49,000-square-foot plant, was within the immediate area, allowing all staff members the opportunity to stay with the company.

In early 2001, when House-Autry opened its doors for the first time in its new state-of-the art facility, every staff member joined Mortenson, ready for work. Not one staff member left the mill due to the location change. That fact is far from surprising, as House-Autry values every employee on their sixty-five-member team. Through the evolving business strategies, Mortenson's goal has always included treating his employees like individuals, treating them with respect and recognizing a job well done.

The mill's guiding philosophy of valuing its employees is extended to investing in the community House-Autry calls home. The company is the lead sponsor for the annual Four Oaks Acorn Festival and is a presence at the North Carolina state Fair every year; a sponsor of local university athletic programs; a business partner and host to area community-based organizations, such as the Johnston County Tourism Council and the Four Oaks Chamber of Commerce; and, a supporter of the Goodness Grows in North Carolina program, a program sponsored by the North Carolina Agriculture Department.

House-Autry is committed to providing a good place to work and being a great corporate neighbor, all while maintaining a focus on producing quality products that raise its brand's profile on grocery store shelves. The mill has retained the number one market position in the breaders category in the company's three core states, with a strong grasp on the number five position nationally.

The future holds unlimited growth for House-Autry Mills. With research and development as a constant strategy and unique and innovative marketing and advertising tactics, the company has an eye on national distribution and position expansion within the marketplace.

But central to the company's promising future success is its past. William House's earnest effort to create a quality product and solid customer service was a family legacy for four generations of Houses. His goal continues to be honored as the present owners and employees of House-Autry Mills, Inc. have created a new family, carrying on a true tradition for Southern cooks.

Flood in front of the mill.

Fish Market, Morehead City. Courtesy, N.C.
Division of Tourism, Film, and Sports
Development

JOHNSON C. SMITH UNIVERSITY

With approximately 1,500 students, Johnson C. Smith University (JCSU) may not be as well known as some of the region's larger universities, but it is making a name for itself as one of the best small colleges in the South. Beginning in 2001 and each year since, *U.S. News & World Report's* "America's Best Colleges" issue has identified JCSU as a "top tier institution" among comprehensive colleges in the South that offer bachelor's degrees.

The university, which sprawls across 100 acres in Charlotte, has earned other accolades as well. JCSU is one of only two Historically Black Colleges and Universities (HBCUs) in the Carolinas listed in *Black Enterprise Magazine's* list of the "Top 50 Best Colleges for African Americans." *Black Issues in Higher Education* recently named JCSU as the top university in North Carolina that produces African American students with computer science degrees. On the national level, the university ranks twenty-second in producing African American students with computer science degrees.

With all of these honors, it seems that JCSU is wired for success. And it is, literally. In 2001 *Yahoo Magazine* named it one of the nation's "50 Most Wired Small Colleges. That is a source of pride for university President Dr. Dorothy Cowser Yancy, who has placed an emphasis on technology in the classroom since taking over the leadership role at the school in 1994. Thanks to her efforts, JCSU became the first HBCU to

Historic Biddle Hall, recently renovated and reopened in 2005

earn the honor of being an IBM ThinkPad university in 2001.

Each of the university's students is provided with a laptop computer, and wireless Internet access is available in the library, dorm rooms, and multimedia classrooms. By incorporating technology into the coursework, Dr. Yancy has made it possible for the students at JCSU to compete globally with others when they graduate.

Dr. Yancy, who is an alumna of JCSU herself, has ushered in an era of growth and progress since becoming the first female to be elected as president of the university. During her tenure, applications to the university have tripled. In part, prospective students are attracted to the innovative educational programs she has spearheaded.

One of Dr. Yancy's educational initiatives is a program called the Freshman Academy, designed to help students succeed in college. The program was created to ease the transition from high school to college by offering support to new students on both an academic and a social level. As part of the program, JCSU staff members serve as case managers, helping new students register for classes and find their way around campus. In addition, case managers make sure that freshmen are attending classes and excelling in their coursework. With this additional support and attention, Dr. Yancy expects new students to benefit both academically and socially.

However, at JCSU, succeeding as a student requires more than just good grades. Participating in community service is a requirement for graduation for all students. Since 1994, nearly 15,000 JCSU students have completed 660,000 hours of community service. The college's service learning program has benefited numerous organizations, including the Charlotte Mecklenburg

JCSU President, Dr. Dorothy Cowser Yancy.

School System, Habitat for Humanity, the American Red Cross, and the Urban League of Central Carolinas Incorporated.

With its innovative programs and commitment to technology, JCSU is a thoroughly modern institution. As such, it bears little resemblance to the tiny college that first opened its doors back in 1867. The school was founded shortly after slavery was abolished in the southern states. At the time, many white missionaries and ministers established schools and churches to educate and evangelize former slaves. Such was the case with JCSU.

The college was founded by three ministers: Reverend Samuel C. Alexander, Reverend Sidney S. Murkland, and Reverend Willis L. Miller. Alexander and Miller assumed posts as professors with Murkland taking on the role of financial agent for the school. Initially created as a school for men only, the first session of classes began on May 1, 1867 with approximately eight men in attendance.

At the time, the school's campus consisted of no more than a few lots on "C" Street in Charlotte and a single building that had been transferred to that land by the Freedmen's Bureau. Efforts to acquire more land resulted in the donation of eight acres on Beatties Ford Road. In 1868 the college relocated to this site, expanding to its current size of 100 acres.

An additional $10,000 was donated by Mrs. Mary D. Biddle in honor of her late husband, Major Henry J. Biddle, who

All JCSU students have access to technology on campus.

Graduating class of 1895.

died from injuries received in a Civil War battle. With these funds, construction began on two professor's houses and the main building. To honor Mrs. Biddle and her late husband, the school was named the Henry J. Biddle Memorial Institute. The couple's name was also bestowed on the institution's oldest surviving structure: Biddle Hall, completed in 1883. With more than 40,000 square feet, the building recently underwent renovations to modernize it for the twenty-first century. It currently serves as the institution's general administration building.

During the late nineteenth and early twentieth centuries the Biddle Memorial Institute made some landmark moves that have earned it a place in history. In 1886 the university appointed the first black professor at a four-year college for blacks in the South. Five years later the institution elected the first black president of such a college. Other firsts followed, including the first black football game in 1892, the first gymnasium on a

black campus in North Carolina in 1928, and the first black college in North Carolina to receive national accreditation in 1932. That same year marked the first time women were allowed to enroll in courses, making the university fully coeducational.

The college changed its name to the Johnson C. Smith University in 1923. The name change came in recognition of the generosity of Mrs. Jane Berry Smith. The widow of Mr. Johnson C. Smith, Mrs. Smith donated more than $700,000 for the construction of nine campus buildings and the establishment of a permanent endowment during the 1920s.

Considered a tremendous amount of money in those days, that sum pales in comparison with today's fundraising efforts. Since 1994, the institution has raised more than $125 million, and the school's endowment has more than doubled from $14 million to $47 million. Thanks to these funds and the efforts of JCSU's visionary president, Dr. Yancy, the college has been able to build on its long history of innovation and progress to earn a place as one of the best small colleges in the South.

LOUISBURG COLLEGE

Located in the small, quiet town of Louisburg, North Carolina and only thirty minutes from the major metropolitan area and state capital, Raleigh, Louisburg College is the only private, residential two-year college in the state. Founded in 1787, the roots of Louisburg College began in the days when the United States was just beginning to form and the Methodist religion was first emerging in America.

When Louisburg was established, a public common was set aside on the town's highest point. The common became famous for its beautiful oak grove and by the late 1700s was chosen as the site for the Franklin Male Academy, now Louisburg College. Early students were taught by Yale graduate Matthew Dickinson, with a curriculum of twenty subjects and five languages. The student body soon reached ninety members.

On December 27, 1814 the state legislature ratified an act to charter the Louisburg Female Academy, another milestone in the evolution of Louisburg College. This was followed in 1855 by

Students enjoy Louisburg College's picturesque campus.

The Franklin Male Academy building was constructed in 1804, and opened classes on January 1, 1805. The oldest surviving building on campus, it was restored by the Louisburg College Golden Anniversary Club and is used for meetings and conferences.

another state charter authorizing the transfer of property owned by the Louisburg Female Academy to the Louisburg Female College Company.

In August 1857 Louisburg College officially opened under the guidance of Professor James P. Nelson. The college had both primary and college departments and offered courses in drawing, painting, needlework, piano, guitar, French and Spanish. The Greek Revival building completed in 1857 and known as "Main," is still in use today as the college Administrative Building. The college remained open during the years of the Civil War and for a brief period afterwards the groves of the campus served as a camp to 500 Union soldiers during May and June of 1865.

The school underwent major changes at the onset of the 20th century. The college became officially linked with the Methodist Church. The relationship resulted when the college property then owned by the estate of Durham philanthropist, Washington Duke, was deeded to the North Carolina Conference of the Methodist Church.

The Southern Association of Colleges and Schools accredited Louisburg College in 1952, and in 1956 during the presidency of Dr. Cecil W. Robbins, the North Carolina Conference of the Methodist Church established two co-educational senior colleges, recommending that Louisburg merge into one of them. This merger was strongly opposed by the local citizens and alumni of the college and a "Keep Louisburg at Home" campaign was launched with such success that the Conference agreed to retain Louisburg College as an accredited junior institution.

In 1980, during the presidency of Dr. J. Allen Norris, a major fundraising campaign was initiated resulting in the building of the E. Hoover Taft, Jr. Classroom Building. This was followed in 1986 with the construction of the Clifton L. Benson Chapel and Religious Life Center, a generous gift from the

The Reverend Dr. Reginald W. Ponder.

The Old Main building used for administration, is a four-story brick building completed in 1857. With its greek revival facade, the building has symbolized the historic Louisburg College to generations of alumni.

United Methodist Men of the Raleigh district, which was matched by Clifton L. Benson. The campus also saw the addition of a new auditorium and theater complex. During this period, the school published its first history of the educational institution, *Louisburg College Echoes*.

In 2002 the Board of Trustees elected Dr. Reginald W. Ponder as president of the Junior College. Under Dr. Ponder, an ordained United Methodist minister and a local church pastor for twenty-three years, the school has experienced tremendous success in the growth of its student enrollment (approximately 100 percent in three years), an increase in faculty and staff, and improvement to the physical plant, including the renovation of residence halls and the school's dining center.

The majority of Louisburg College students come from within a 100-mile radius, but an ever-increasing number of students are coming from the Northeast and beyond. Additionally, a large number of students attend Louisburg on the strength of its athletic programs. Louisburg College has produced scores of All-Americans and many of the school's teams have been involved in regional and national tournament play on a regular basis. Many Louisburg students have been awarded athletic

scholarships at senior institutions, including NCAA Division I schools, and at least seventy-five Louisburg alumni have gone on to play professionally. Twelve of the school's baseball players have had major league careers.

Thus far, Louisburg College has participated in twenty-one NJCAA National Tournaments. The women's basketball team ranks second nationally in number of national tournament appearances, winning the Region Championship fifteen times in the last seventeen years, including each of the last ten years. Other school teams including men's basketball, women's fast-pitch softball, women and men's soccer, and men's golf have experienced similar successes.

Since Plato's *Republic*, it has been argued that training the body and training the mind are mutually supportive. Cecil Rhodes recognized this relationship in establishing the Rhodes

Louisburg College students study in front of the main building.

Scholarship Program at Oxford University, making athletic involvement a condition of consideration, though now more broadly interpreted. An unusually high percentage of Louisburg's scholars participate in athletics. In the fall of 2005 44 percent of the students with 4.0 averages were intercollegiate athletes; 54 percent of the students on the Dean's list were athletes, and 40 percent of the students on the Honor's list were athletes. Collectively, Louisburg athletes constitute 46 percent of all students with grade point averages greater than 3.0.

At the heart of this diverse and athletics-oriented school are the lessons it offers in living a spiritually healthy and morally strong lifestyle. For many students, attending Louisburg is a major step in their lives and has proven to be a solid confidence builder and a place where the discovery of self-esteem and self-respect are equally as important as the academic lessons learned in the classroom. Some 90 percent of students receive some form of financial aid while attending Louisburg, making it possible for those financially less fortunate to get a quality college education. The college has also proven to be a firm stepping stone in helping students become better prepared when moving on to a four-year educational institution.

MARS HILL COLLEGE

Located in the Blue Ridge Mountains of western North Carolina, Mars Hill College combines its Baptist roots and Appalachian heritage to create a unique educational experience that integrates faith with learning and community service. In many ways, the history and growth of this small liberal arts institution mirrors the development of the region itself. From a fledgling rural school to its emergence as a thriving center of academic excellence, Mars Hill College celebrates its 150th anniversary in 2006 and looks forward to exploring new frontiers in the future.

In the mid-1850s a small group of pioneer citizens from Madison County, North Carolina sought to make education and religious instruction available to students in their remote mountain community. Edward Carter, a devout Baptist, donated a tract of land, and a modest brick building was erected on the site. The school opened in the fall of 1856 as French Broad Baptist Academy.

From the start, the school's Christian roots have shaped its mission to intersect matters of faith with matters inside the classroom. In 1859 the school was chartered by the North Carolina General Assembly as Mars Hill College. The name is derived from the Biblical reference in the Book of Acts, in which the

Mars Hill College President, Dan Lunsford.

apostle Paul engages in a dialogue about faith and reason with Greek philosophers on a hill in Athens in the first century.

The college continued to operate as an academy or boarding high school until 1921 when it was organized as a junior college. In 1960 the Baptist State Convention of North Carolina approved plans to convert Mars Hill into a senior college and in May 1964 the first baccalaureate degrees were awarded to 146 graduates.

Today, the private four-year college has an enrollment of 1,000 traditional students and 400 part-time students. The majority of the student body is from North Carolina, with significant numbers from Florida, South Carolina, and other states throughout the Southeast, but also includes students from as far away as California and South Dakota. Two percent of the current freshman class are international students.

Because of its small size the average student-to-teacher ratio is sixteen. Over thirty majors are offered with more than sixty concentrations. Students can receive bachelor degrees in art, science, social work, fine arts, and music.

The history of western North Carolina and the southern Appalachians plays an integral role in the modern identity of Mars Hill College. To preserve and promote this heritage, its acclaimed Regional Studies program crosses academic disciplines so students will gain a broad appreciation for the area's rich culture.

In 2002 the Southern Appalachian Center was renamed the Liston B. Ramsey Center for Regional Studies in honor of a Madison County native and Mars Hill College alumnus who served in the North Carolina State Legislature for forty years. The Center supports the regional studies focus of the college's curriculum, houses archival resource materials, and sponsors special programs and events.

The Rural Life Museum, located in the Montague Building on campus and easily recognized by its stone structure, is an important component of the college's educational services. From Native American artifacts to pioneer farming implements to handmade crafts, the exhibits showcase the culture and history of Madison County and of the Southern Appalachians. The museum offers tours, workshops, and internships that enable patrons and students alike to gain a deeper appreciation for the area's rural heritage.

For the past thirty years the Bailey Mountain Cloggers have served as ambassadors of goodwill for the school. One of only a few college-based performing clog teams in the United States, the folk dancers have performed on Broadway and in the Kennedy Center, as well as internationally in Canada, Austria, the

Montague Building, home of the Rural Life Museum.

Marshbanks Hall.

United Kingdom, and Ireland. Their reputation for excellence has garnered them national champion honors twelve times.

In addition to the school's regional studies programs, Mars Hill is perhaps best known for its commitment to service learning. Students are encouraged through the LifeWorks Learning Partnership to connect what they study inside the classroom to real life experience with the local community. Opportunities for involvement include tutoring and mentoring a child, building a Habitat for Humanity house, designing hiking trails, and doing an internship at one of over seventy-five sites.

The Bonner Scholars program awards scholarships to students who are the first in their families to attend college. In exchange, the students participate in community service projects, thereby equipping them with the skills and values to improve lives as well as to earn a living. In 2005, two scholarship recipients helped build a Habitat for Humanity house in South Africa.

With more than forty campus clubs and organizations, outstanding musical and theatrical productions, and a vast array of outdoor recreational opportunities, the college offers something for everyone. Mars Hill competes in eighteen intercollegiate sports at the NCAA Division II level and is a member of the South Atlantic Conference.

Distinguished Mars Hill College alumni include Dean Propst, a retired chancellor of the University of Georgia system, LaVonda Wagner, a 1986 graduate who was recently named the women's basketball coach at Oregon State University, and Archie Campbell, a writer and entertainer who is best known for his work on the long-running television variety show *Hee Haw.*

During the course of its sometimes tumultuous history, strong leadership has sustained the college and enabled it to flourish. Some of Mars Hill's most influential presidents include W.A.G. Brown (1856–1858), Dr. R. L. Moore (1897–1938), Dr. Hoyt Blackwell (1938–1966), Dr. Fred Bentley (1966–1996), Dr. A. Max Lennon (1996–2002), and Dr. Dan G. Lunsford (2002–present).

A year-long celebration is planned for the school's sesquicentennial anniversary during the 2006–2007 academic year. An original drama about the college has been commissioned and an updated history of the school is being written. A new entrance arch and a memorial to the mountain families who started the college will be dedicated during the year.

A campus master plan is also being developed to preserve and accentuate the beauty of the college's historic buildings, such as Founder's Hall, the oldest structure on campus which was built in 1892, and the Marshbanks Building, with its signature bell tower. Construction is underway for a new residence hall and a major addition to the math and science center is expected to begin in 2006.

Students gathered in front of McConnell Hall.

MONROE METAL MANUFACTURING, INC.

Monroe is the seat of Union County, with a population of more than 30,000. In that community filled with tree-lined streets and historic properties, Mr. Bobby Pope decided to open Total Comfort Inc. in 1968. For twelve years the company provided air conditioning, insulation service, and installation. In 1974 Pope expanded the operation to include the manufacturing of rectangular ductwork, opening Monroe Metal Mfg. in the same location, off Highway 74.

A native of Boomer in Wilkes County, Bobby Pope got his start in the service area of the heating, ventilation, and air conditioning (HVAC) business working for a company called Temperature Control, Inc., also located in Monroe. He eventually became one of the owners of the company, and built an impressive reputation as a heating and air conditioning service person. Qualified, professional HVAC service personnel were in short supply in the state, making Pope a busy man. In fact, the area of residential and commercial cooling was so new in the Carolinas at the time, it was next to impossible to find people to install and service the sought-after units.

Pope sold his share of Temperature Control and started his own service

Bobby Pope, founder of Monroe Metal Mfg.

business, a sole proprietorship called Total Comfort Inc. One day he received a call from an area hospital in need of a new HVAC unit for one of its wings, but at that time, Pope was only running a service business. The hospital administrator convinced Pope that he was the right man to handle the installation and handed him a purchase order for a new unit. Pope went to Charlotte and found a new air-to-air unit (without any water involved), perfect for the hospital's needs. This twist of fate pushed Pope in a direction he never imagined working in, and within months, he had the

beginnings of a thriving installation and service business.

Pope's installation business continued to grow, and in 1974, he began manufacturing rectangular ducts to meet the specific needs of his customers, and Monroe Metal Mfg. Co. was born. Pope bought new, hand-operated metal manufacturing equipment to make ducts for gas and oil furnaces, as well as heat pumps. In the beginning, Monroe Metal operated out of a 1,200 square-foot space with only four employees, including Pope and his first wife, Betty, who handled the company's accounting and bookkeeping. The company quickly found itself working on new residential and commercial construction projects, both large and small.

Within less than a year, business was exploding so rapidly that Pope leased a 7,500 square-foot building that was once a car dealership and service station. The space allowed for a much larger manufacturing plant. In 1969 the company began getting a regular stream of work from a local contractor, which expanded the reach of Monroe Metal Mfg.'s clientele to now include projects in both North and South Carolina as well as Virginia.

In 1974 Pope bought five acres of land in Monroe and built a 20,000 square-foot facility, and hired an additional seventy-five employees to run the business, including installers, field personnel, machine operators and administrative staff.

Pope again saw the need to expand in 1979, and added 18,000 new feet to his existing plant, spending more than $500,000 on new equipment, including automated manufacturing machines, welding machines and machines for rolling round pipe.

In 1980 Monroe's duct manufacturing division became so successful that Pope eliminated the installation division all together in order to focus on manufacturing, and also to avoid competing with its own customers. This turned out to be a very wise business move and sales at Monroe Metal Mfg. increased by volumes. Between 1980 and 1984, Pope expanded the plant's physical space twice more, adding 10,000

In 1975 Monroe Metal Mfg.'s facilities moved to a location that had formerly served as a car dealership and service station.

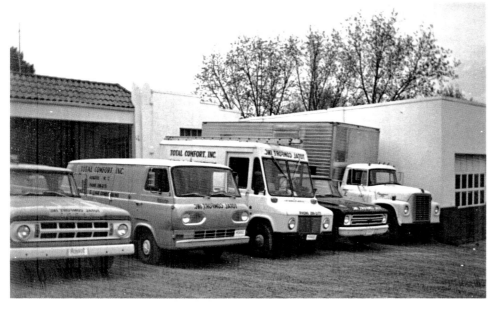

square feet to increase work and staging areas and then building an additional 27,000 square feet. He also purchased an additional five acres of land next to his current property.

Now covering 75,000 square feet in four separate buildings, Monroe Metal Mfg. was still not the ideal space for the business that Pope envisioned. He was determined to create a working plant that was both efficient and that streamlined the manufacturing process. In the spring of 1985, Pope purchased another seventeen acres and built a 100,000 square foot fabrication structure that contained no partitions and had twenty-six-foot high ceilings. Ideally suited for the use and transport of any size or type of equipment, the added space made the company one of the largest duct manufacturing facilities in the country.

Pope bought the best manufacturing equipment available for the new plant and hired computer programmers to create custom software, based on his specifications for use in cutting systems. Using CAD drawings, client jobs can be entered into software programs that directly download to the cutting machines, greatly reducing lead-times.

Pope says his biggest challenge has always been in finding enough good employees while maintaining a business in

Monroe Metal Mfg.'s manufacturing facilities.

Monroe Metal Mfg. is the leader in spiral pipe manufacturing.

a small community. But the length of time employees have stayed with Monroe Metal Mfg. is surely a testament to the good work environment the company offers. Many of the company's sixty full-time employees have been with Monroe for as long as twenty-eight years. Though it is not a family business as such, Pope's second wife, Janice, oversees all of the office personnel and works very closely with the accounting department, the company's CPA and all banking business. "Part of the challenge," Pope confides, "is that young people are no longer interested in learning a trade, but a good benefits package, like we offer at Monroe, is a strong attraction for an employee looking for some security."

Total Comfort Inc. and Monroe Metal Mfg. separated into two individual entities in 2005. Monroe Metal Mfg. manufactures rectangular, spiral and oval ducts to meet any specification and has the ability to produce spiral duct up to eighty-four inches in diameter, and oval duct to forty-eight by ninety-six inches, which many fabricators cannot produce. Monroe Metal Mfg. operates two fully automated duct lines, three spiral machines, three ovalizers, and four plasma machines with coil lines that allow for quick, accurate and efficient production. In addition to the fabrication shop, Monroe Metal Mfg. has two warehouses, yard storage and business offices.

MOSES CONE HEALTH SYSTEM

For more than fifty years, Moses Cone Health System has fulfilled a legacy of honor and integrity credited to its namesake, while providing unparalleled healthcare to the community of Greensboro.

Moses Cone, one of thirteen children of Bavarian immigrant Herman Cone and his wife Helen Guggenheimer Cone, founded the Greensboro-based Cone Mills Corp. with his brother, Caesar. The mill eventually became one of the nation's largest textile manufacturers, as well as a catalyst for growth and prosperity in the region. The Cone family achieved the American dream, but their gratitude and generosity would become the traits for which they are best remembered. One of the greatest gifts bestowed by the Cone family to the community was created by Moses' wife, Bertha L. Cone following her husband's death in 1908.

Bertha established a trust fund in 1911 to build The Moses H. Cone Memorial Hospital to honor her late husband. When the articles of incorporation were drafted, Bertha included the statement, "No patient shall be refused admittance because of inability to pay," thus creating the foundation for the hospital's culture of quality care and unwavering service.

Bertha died in 1947, and her entire inheritance was bequeathed to the trust.

*Moses Cone Health System
Behavioral Health Center.*

The Moses H. Cone Memorial Hospital.

Two years later construction began and on February 20, 1953 the doors of the hospital were officially opened by the board of trustees president—Moses' nephew, Herman Cone. Forty-two years after the trust was founded, Bertha's wish to memorialize her husband was realized.

At the 1953 board of trustees meeting, Herman Cone stepped down as president. The helm of the hospital remained in the family however, as Benjamin Cone, another of Moses' nephews, assumed the presidency. Benjamin served on the board until 1971.

The need for the new hospital, which had 231 employees and daily rates ranging from $8 to $20, quickly became apparent. By the end of the hospital's first year of operation 592 babies had been delivered.

Moses Cone Hospital soon found another way to provide an important community service. Through the dedication and leadership of Dr. Joseph Lichty, the hospital established itself as a teaching facility. Just one year after opening, the hospital founded its first clinical study program, The School of Medical Technology. More successful educational efforts followed, including an independent one-year internship program and a two-year associate degree in association with Woman's College. (now The University of North Carolina at Greensboro.)

The late '50s and early '60s were not only a time of change for the nation, they were decades of growth for Moses Cone Hospital. In 1960, under the direction of Harold Bettis, who served as director from 1956 to 1979, the hospital embarked on the first of many expansions. Two floors were added to the original building increasing the number of beds to 484. One year later, the hospital opened North Carolina's first intensive care unit, which was also one of the first ICUs in the country.

As the '60s progressed, Moses Cone Hospital maintained its dual focus on providing the best possible healthcare to its community while creating a viable teaching facility. In 1965 the cardiopulmonary laboratory was opened, furthering education and research for cardiovascular disease and treatments. In 1967 the hospital opened a cardiac acute care unit. These efforts were the foundation for the hospital's evolution as a world leader in the treatment of acute heart attacks and primary angioplasty. Also in 1967, Moses Cone Hospital and the University of North Carolina at Chapel Hill formed a post-graduate training program for medical and pharmacy students. This affiliation between the college and the hospital continues today.

In 1974 expansion continued with a $16.5 million construction project. A 236,000-square-foot wing was added, providing a location for primary care clinics, radiology and emergency departments and an additional floor to serve more patients. More innovative technical, program, and facility changes occurred over the following years and by 1981, another expansion was needed. More than $32 million was dedicated to renovating the existing facility as well as adding a five-story wing.

Dennis Barry became hospital director in 1979 and led the hospital's efforts to provide high quality healthcare at an affordable price. Barry would lead the Health System until he retired and Tim Rice took the helm in 2004.

During the 1980s, Moses Cone Hospital introduced many new healthcare

Wesley Long Community Hospital.

options for the residents of the Greensboro area. Surgical laser procedures were initiated, oncology care was added, the first cochlear implant surgery in the Triad was performed and the state's first inpatient hospice unit was opened. And during the '80s, for the first time, the reach of the hospital's services were broadened beyond its original facility. The freestanding Greensboro Diagnostic Center and the 12,000-square-foot Family Practice Center opened.

In 1988 the hospital's first acquisition occurred with the purchase of Greensboro's Humana Hospital. The facility would become The Women's Hospital of Greensboro, the state's first free-standing facility dedicated exclusively to healthcare for women and newborns. During its first year of operation in 1990, more than 3,500 babies were delivered and more than 10,000 women received specialized care.

The Women's Hospital of Greensboro.

The late 1990s brought more expansion and more groundbreaking events for Greensboro's major healthcare provider. In 1991, the Neuroscience Center became the first of its kind in the Triad, treating acute head and spinal injuries, brain and spinal tumors, seizures and other neurological disorders. The founding of the Moses Cone Heart Center occurred the following year.

Today's Moses Cone Health System encompasses five hospitals, including Moses Cone Hospital, Wesley Long Community Hospital, The Women's Hospital, Annie Penn Hospital in Reidsville, and the Behavioral Health Center. The system and its 7,500 employees are focused on providing quality care for residents in Alamance, Guilford, Randolph, and Rockingham counties as well as the city of Kernersville while continuing to serve as a state-of-the-art teaching facility.

In the more than half a century since opening its doors, Moses Cone Health System has been a steadfast community partner in the Triad, much like its namesake, Moses Cone. And the future for this hospital system will follow its respected past, with Moses Cone Health System owning the leadership role in introducing the finest and most up-to-date services by some of the country's top healthcare providers in the Triad area.

NC MONROE CONSTRUCTION COMPANY

Established in 1951 by N. Carl Monroe, the NC Monroe Construction Company is a well-known licensed general contractor in Greensboro, North Carolina, recognized for performing work throughout the southeastern United States. The company is especially noted for its expertise in commercial and industrial, large and small-scale projects in both the private and public sectors, consisting of general contracting, design/build, "fast-track," and program management. The company is a licensed general contractor in the states of North Carolina, South Carolina, Georgia, Kentucky, Virginia, Tennessee and Maryland.

The roots of this highly successful and enduring company come from one man, N. Carl Monroe. A twelfth generation descendant of Richard Warren, who was both a passenger and investor in the *Mayflower* in 1620, as well as a merchant who became the twelfth signer of the "Mayflower Compact;" N. Carl Monroe comes from a long line of millwrights, builders and carpenters. Raised in Garland, Maine, and the eldest of five brothers with two older sisters, Monroe is proud of the fact that the descendants of the Warren line include Sir Winston Churchill, the Roosevelts and the Bush

N. C. Monroe Construction Company headquarters in Greensboro, North Carolina.

N. Carl Monroe.

family. Born in 1921, Monroe worked part time most of his teenage years honing his skills as a tradesman and carpenter and working for nearby businesses, including a large fur farm, building structures such as breeder houses.

In 1941 the government put out a call for skilled workers to help build military bases overseas. Monroe answered the call and was sent to Bermuda on a two-year contract where he was qualified as a carpenter, ironworker, and a certified welder. Recognizing his great skills,

Monroe's employers soon placed him in a supervisory role, managing crews and overseeing the construction of the facility's underground fuel storage tanks.

Having spent fourteen months in Bermuda, Monroe was released from his contract and enlisted for military service in 1943. He trained as an Army Air Corp pilot on the B25 and the B17. While stationed in Alabama, Monroe was among many B29 pilots with assigned crews on stand-by for the invasion of Japan, when the atomic bomb ended the war. Monroe was stationed in Greensboro, North Carolina in 1943, the place where he met his future wife, Marjorie Thomas. They were married in 1944 and by 1945 Monroe was discharged from the service and headed back to Maine with his new wife and a strong and impressive resume in building and construction skills. But there were few job opportunities in Maine and the possibility of opening a construction business and keeping even a small group of workers employed full time was not a realistic goal.

In February 1948 Monroe and his wife, Marjorie, headed back south to Greensboro to try their chances there and from the moment they arrived it was clear they had made the right decision. After spending two years working for a contractor, Monroe formed his own company, NC Monroe Construction Company, in 1951.

The company's first project was the construction of the Congregational United Church of Christ in Greensboro, which also happened to be Monroe's own parish. Being chosen to build the church was a surprise to Monroe because he had never been approached about whether he was qualified to do the job, but the 700-member congregation thought otherwise, selecting him for the project before he had even been consulted. Since he didn't have his contractor's license yet, it meant that he had to approach the licensing board about getting permission to proceed, which the board did grant. Monroe was honored that the church chose him and his new business and that his first construction project was his own place of worship.

NC Monroe Construction Company also participated in the design of the church. In addition to the sanctuary, the project included the construction of an educational facility, kitchen, church offices, and a fellowship hall. One of the more unique features of the church's Early American design was its high steeple and cross, which are completely made of stainless steel. By the time the project was finished, N. Carl Monroe had his contractor's license and was on his way to building what would become one of the most recognized construction businesses in North Carolina and the southeast.

For the first two years Monroe ran his business out of the lower level of his home. In 1954 he acquired a tract of land in Greensboro that contained a small office building, a shop, and a warehouse. He started with himself and a few contract employees. By 1960 his workforce grew to nearly 300.

The slogan "Tradition of Change" at NC Monroe Construction Company is a reflection of over fifty years of growth and development, coupled with a progressive attitude to meet the needs of their clients. Always thinking "outside the box," Monroe and his company have developed a solid reputation for excellence and dependability to the great satisfaction of their myriad of clients.

Currently operating throughout the southeast, Monroe and his company have served a diverse list of owners by

Congregational United Church of Christ, Greensboro, North Carolina.

building a variety of projects, including hotels and other lodging projects; retail and shopping centers; office buildings; schools and universities; warehouse and distribution facilities; laboratories; computer centers; churches; foundries; manufacturing facilities; correctional facilities; food processing and cold storage facilities.

Many of the company's projects are done using a design/build approach, enabling them to "fast-track" the projects. Managing projects this way has resulted in substantial savings in both time and money for their clientele, while also eliminating much of the client's administrative burden.

Often a business owner will contract with Monroe and his company to do the design, engineering and contracting for a project, rather than awarding separate contracts for their construction project. This approach provides single source responsibility, and allows the owner to benefit from NC Monroe Construction Company's vast experience early in the planning and design process. Through careful analysis of the scope of work, NC Monroe Construction Company is able to team up with highly qualified designers and engineers to provide clients with the optimum quality at the lowest possible cost.

In heading design/build projects, Monroe's company brings in qualified subcontractors in specialized fields to add even more benefit to the owner, from the earliest stages of each project. Significant savings are realized this way in both time and money. This makes it possible to "fast-track" projects, building in phases if necessary. The company also "value engineers" each component of the project to evaluate initial cost as well as long-term operating costs and quality of materials.

NC Monroe Construction Company also prides itself on its commitment to understanding the needs of each client from the onset of the project all the way through to its completion. Their general contracting services are offered to a wide spectrum of industries, including lodging, retail, churches, industrial and specialty construction.

Understanding the special needs of clients in the hotel and lodging industry has given NC Monroe Construction Company uncommon success in the hospitality field. The company is known for the quality of the work they have done in the industry, as well as for delivering projects on time and under budget. Hotel clients include companies such as Sheraton, Ramada, and LaQuinta. Their resort and high end condominium clients include the Atlantic Towers in Carolina Beach, North Carolina and Ocean View Towers and Holiday Towers

Owens-Illinois, Winston-Salem, North Carolina.

structure of superior quality, completed in a manner that offers substantial savings in both time and labor.

The SECTRA system is especially suited for mid to high-rise hotels, condominiums, apartments, senior housing and other types of multi-leveled structures. The SECTRA system provides an incredibly stable, highly engineered structure, which is one of the most durable systems available. The company has also completed numerous pre-engineered structures, giving clients an economical approach to warehouse, manufacturing, and other structures.

In 2000 the company took on a primary role as the construction program manager for Guilford County Schools' 2000–2003 $200 Million Bond Program. NC Monroe oversaw the construction of twenty-nine separate school projects, while working concurrently with fourteen different architectural firms. "Listen to the Silence" became a company theme with the school construction program as the North Carolina company successfully eliminated the traditional complaints and negative feedback usually associated with construction activity in and around existing school facilities.

Before launching a school project, NC Monroe Construction Company assists in streamlining the design, engineering, management, and construction process. The company offers expertise in site analysis, selection and building placement, coordinating ongoing school operations and addresses other community concerns. Other services include the development of a preliminary budget and comprehensive master schedule, as well as the establishment of a management information and reporting system that meets a client's exact requirements. Development of detailed and complete bid documents to assure timely, responsive and comparable bids is also part of what NC Monroe Construction Company offers clients, including assistance in reviewing bids for architects and contractors.

in Myrtle Beach, South Carolina.

Monroe and his construction company have also built dozens of condominiums, college dormitories, senior apartments, assisted living facilities and retirement homes. In addition, the company has made its mark in the retail industry throughout the southeast, working on commercial projects covering a wide range of facilities, from shopping centers to office buildings and restaurants. In North Carolina, the company is responsible for building the Golden Gate Shopping Center and the Farmers Market, both located in Greensboro, Sears & Roebuck in Durham, as well as Colonial Department Store, Hecht's Department Store and the New Hanover Shopping Center.

N. Carl Monroe, who had made his start in contracting by erecting a church for his local congregation, learned early on that churches and other nonprofit entities require special care. These projects often involve committees with limited construction experience and limited funding. NC Monroe Construction Company takes pride in the fact that like N. Carl Monroe, their management team has not only built churches, many Monroe Construction Company employees

have served on boards or committees themselves. This gives the company a special affinity for those on "the other side of the table." Among the other churches that the company was responsible for building is the Sedgefield Presbyterian Church in Greensboro, N. Carl Monroe's current place of worship.

In the area of industry, Monroe's company has built laboratories, manufacturing and distribution facilities, processing plants, and post offices. Clients include such major firms as: Levi Strauss & Co, the world's largest brand-name clothing maker; IBM, which has its largest company site in Triangle Park, North Carolina; and Ingersoll Rand, an internationally renowned maker of construction and mining machinery.

Throughout the years, NC Monroe Construction Company has developed a special expertise in concrete construction. In 1972 the company began using a "tunnel form" system first created in England by John Laing & Company called SECTRA, which has been used on many concrete structures and has also set a standard for concrete construction throughout the United States.

Utilizing specially designed forms, the system creates cast-in-place concrete buildings of exceptionally high dimensional accuracy. The result is a

The company represents and works with clients in many of the more critical aspects of the construction process including the release and management of funds throughout the duration of the project, project scheduling, the contracting and procurement of outside goods and services, and organizing onsite inspections to make sure that the project is being built to the client's exact specifications. NC Monroe's professional team has also successfully built a solid track record in keeping construction delays, disputes and cost overruns to a minimum.

Another area in which NC Monroe Construction Company has distinguished itself is as construction program manager for the building of new prisons in the State of North Carolina from 1987 to 1996. In 1987 the North Carolina legislature passed the Emergency Prison Facilities Development Program to construct new dormitories and support facilities. The program involved $300 million of prison building, including site acquisition, facilities analysis, design, construction and the renovation of a number of older facilities.

The construction of correctional facilities is a very demanding and highly specialized branch of the building indus-

LaQuinta Inn & Suites, Cary, North Carolina.

Lee Hall Dormitory, North Carolina State University, Raleigh, North Carolina.

try that requires familiarity with prison planning, programming, design, and operations, as well as an intimate understanding of the complexities of constructing secure facilities. Monroe's company did extensive research in security systems used in both state and federal settings throughout the country. One result of this research was the installation of a state-of-the-art Perimeter Intrusion Detection System, the first such system ever used in a North Carolina prison facility.

Over the years, NC Monroe has built up tremendous knowledge and experience in every detail involved in correctional facility construction, which results in the highest safety standards for prison staff and for the inmate's daily existence in the facility.

Building such sophisticated structures requires an intimate working relationship between the facility operator, the planner, and the builder to successfully build a quality penal facility. NC Monroe Construction Company has worked collaboratively with operators and designers and has built a solid reputation for constructing state-of-the-art facilities that are as secure as any prison built today.

In building the facilities for the North Carolina Department of Corrections, NC Monroe Construction Company acted as construction program manager, led in site evaluation, building evaluation, program establishment, designer and contractor solicitation, oversight of construction, closeout and turnover.

The success of the NC Monroe Construction Company comes from Mr. Monroe's belief in a strong work ethic, integrity, honesty in business, and in the freedom to do business in a professional manner. Many of Monroe's 100 employ-

ees have been with the firm for forty or more years. Monroe himself stresses the importance of looking after his employees and in giving them the authority to do their work with the understanding that whenever they come up against a problem that they share that problem with their superiors so that they receive the proper support in finding the appropriate solutions. The company awards employees who have excelled on a project with a bonus immediately after the project is completed instead of waiting until year's end.

N. Carl Monroe has also been a major proponent of the "open shop" philosophy, which he initialized in North Carolina back in 1965. He was elected by his fellow contractors to organize and promote the concept of open shop construction in the Carolinas and later the country. When this was undertaken, approximately 75 percent of the construction was done union. Some fifteen years later, this was revised to 75 percent open shop.

Foothills Correctional Facility, Burke County, North Carolina.

Bell Laboratories office building, Greensboro, North Carolina.

N. Carl Monroe served as president of the Carolinas Associated General Contractors (AGC) chapter and as life director and on committees of the national organization. Monroe also served on the board of directors of the National Right To Work Committee (NRTWC) for thirty years. Established in 1955, the NRTWC is a nonprofit, nonpartisan, single purpose citizen's organization. One of its main principles is that no worker should ever be forced to affiliate with a union in order to get or keep a job. Monroe also served on the National Chamber of Commerce labor committee.

It is clear that N. Carl Monroe and the NC Monroe Construction Company have left their mark on the landscape of the southeastern United States by building state-of-the-art schools, secure prisons, luxury hotels, and other commercial and industrial facilities. And through the efforts and perseverance of N. Carl Monroe, the face of how business is done has changed, and the "open shop" movement is now a solid part of the American construction industry.

*Airborne and Special Operations Museum,
Fayetteville. Courtesy, N.C. Division of
Tourism, Film, and Sports Development*

NORTH CAROLINA ACADEMY OF TRIAL LAWYERS

The North Carolina Academy of Trial Lawyers was established to advance the skills and education of its members, to build a community of like-minded professionals and to support trial lawyers in their efforts to help injured individuals across the state of North Carolina. Four decades later, these aspirations are being realized. As a result, the Academy has helped level the playing field for North Carolinians in disputes with powerful interests. Although the Academy's present members carry the torch of advocacy, it is the founding members of the Academy who are responsible for this community's existence.

In December of 1961 a group of trial attorneys gathered in Winston-Salem for an educational seminar hosted by the National Association of the Claimants Compensation Attorneys (NACCA). After the well-received program, a few attendees discussed the possibility of starting a North Carolina chapter. Eugene H. Phillips spearheaded the group whose initial goal was to form an organized educational program. The NACCA, now known as the Association of Trial Lawyers of America (ATLA), gave Phillips $200 as seed money to start the affiliated organization. Just a few months later, in early 1962, Phillips called a meeting—and the North Carolina organization began.

In addition to Phillips, other founding members of the Academy included James Clontz, who served as its first president from 1962–1969; Charles Blanchard;

Former U.S. Senator John Edwards (third from right) at one of the Academy's mock trial events.

The Academy's flagship publication. Each issue focuses on diverse topics throughout the year.

William Thorp; and Allen Bailey, who each served a term as president in the 1970s. These distinguished members honed the Academy's mission statement and determined the three areas of focus that have remained to this day: education, community, and advocacy.

Phillips served as president of the Academy from 1972–1974. Because of his continued guiding presence and leadership throughout the following decades, he was later named the Academy's first president emeritus. "Gene Phillips was the brains behind the Academy's initial formation," says Dick Taylor, chief executive officer of the Academy. "He envisioned what it could do for North Carolina…and kept it functioning

through his office in the early days." Taylor adds this about another founding member, "Bill Thorp was like the Academy's heart…inspiring lawyers around the state to believe that they could succeed and make things better for the average North Carolinian."

If Phillips was the mind, and Thorp its heart, the second president emeritus, Allen Bailey, would likely be considered the Academy's soul. He was there at the initial meeting in 1961, and he played a significant role until his death in February 2006. "This organization has been Allen's and his wife Ebbie's life's mission," says Clifford Britt, 2005–2006 Academy president. "We are their family. Their generosity is unequaled." Named for Mrs. Bailey, "Ebbie" awards are presented by Academy presidents to members who have gone beyond the call of duty in their service to the Academy.

Bailey said of the early days of the organization: "The Academy was formed basically with one goal in mind—to provide educational opportunities for trial lawyers." Education remains at the center of the Academy's mission. Continuing Legal Education (CLE) workshops are held at the Raleigh headquarters' building almost on a weekly basis. Seminars include issues such as medical malpractice, auto torts, the death penalty, workers' compensation and pre-trial procedures. These programs are not only a chance to further the members' education, they also are an opportunity to gather and network, share ideas and enjoy camaraderie with like-minded professionals. There is an inclusive, collegiate spirit among Academy members who are interested in helping each other as well as their clients.

The Academy also takes a role in public education with the goal of informing the community about the legal process, an individual's rights within the justice system and the role plaintiffs lawyers can play. One of the Academy's most successful community efforts has been the annual Wade Edwards High School Mock Trial Competition, named in honor of an exceptional young man tragically killed in an auto accident. This high school student was the son of

then Academy member and former U.S. Senator and presidential candidate, John Edwards. Gordon Widenhouse, an Academy member who has helped coordinate the mock trial program from its beginning, explains its purpose: "It is not geared to producing lawyers, but to developing better citizenship."

The North Carolina Academy of Trial Lawyers' history would not be complete without sharing some of the stories of those helped by the Academy's members. For example, there is the story of James Milon, a fifty-three-year-old independent truck driver from Louisburg, who was admitted to Duke University Medical Center for what he was told would be routine prostate surgery. Instead, he suffered a "spinal cord stroke" and left the hospital paralyzed.

Another heart-wrenching story is that of Macy Messer, a bright, beautiful six-year-old girl who, because of a preventable medical error, must spend her life in an electronic wheelchair, able to communicate only through a special computer screen. She will never be able to hold her head up, walk, talk, or eat solid food.

Finally, there is the case of the wrongful conviction of Alan Gell, who with the help of Academy criminal attorneys, was released from death row after spending nearly a decade behind bars. In 2004 a judge ruled that prosecutors withheld key evidence in his case and Gell was

Governor Hunt signs the Automobile Liability Insurance Limits Bill (SB756) into law at the Capitol. The law was a top legislative priority for the Academy.

granted a new trial. A second jury found him not guilty within forty-five minutes of deliberation. These stories illustrate the importance of the work carried out by trial lawyers every day.

Academy members persevere, advocating for North Carolinians every day—both in the courts and in the General Assembly. For example, a half dozen measures were introduced in 2005 that would have stripped injured patients of their rights and enriched insurance companies. The Academy helped make certain none of these unjust bills moved forward.

Another victory in 2005 was the safeguarding of injured workers' rights in a highly-contested legislative battle over workers' compensation. In addition, the Academy helped criminal defendants in North Carolina receive fairer trials and better counsel by advancing procedural reforms and pushing forward the institution of an independent indigent defense system. Through its advocacy efforts, the Academy stays true to its mission of ensuring there is justice for all, not just for a privileged few.

The Academy exists through the collaborative efforts of its members who

Past presidents Howard F. Twiggs and Eugene H. Phillips discuss the work of the Academy.

are among the most skilled and compassionate trial attorneys in the state of North Carolina. "As trial lawyers, we are not just defending our clients; we are defending all of us by making the justice system possible," proudly states Rebecca Britton, 2006–2007 Academy president.

This belief—that trial lawyers protect people's rights—has been true since the Academy's inception, and it remains a driving force behind the association today.

At a luncheon given in his honor, Bailey reflected on his years as a member. "I've found that what matters most when you are looking back—it's not what you have, but what you've given away—what you've done for others."

President emeritus Allen Bailey, the "soul" of the Academy.

NORTH CAROLINA BIOTECHNOLOGY CENTER

The North Carolina Biotechnology Center, located in Research Triangle Park, is the world's first government-sponsored organization dedicated to developing the biotechnology industry. The state of North Carolina created the Biotechnology Center in 1984 and the organization is supported mostly through General Assembly funding.

The Biotechnology Center's mission is to provide long-term economic and societal benefits to the state through the support and growth of biotechnology research, business and education throughout North Carolina.

These goals are met by the Biotechnology Center's staff of fifty-seven professionals fostering industrial development in the state, strengthening the state's existing biotechnology academic and research capabilities and by establishing North Carolina as the preeminent international site for the rapidly growing field of biotechnology.

The Biotechnology Center accomplishes much of this through three core programs: Science and Technology Development, Business and Technology Development and Education and Training.

Working to strengthen the state's biotechnology research infrastructure, one critical way in which the Science and Technology Development Program provides invaluable support is through offering grants, which include: faculty recruitment grants, institutional development grants, collaborative funding grants, multi-disciplinary research grants, event sponsorship and regional development grants

Since the creation of the Biotechnology Center more than $50 million in grants have been awarded to enhance the research and intellectual capabilities of North Carolina colleges and universities and nonprofit institutions. This financial support ultimately results in scientific breakthroughs creating further advances in commercial products and applications.

The Biotechnology Center also sponsors several intellectual exchange groups that provide a forum for those involved in bioscience to discuss issues pertaining to their respective fields.

The Biotechnology Center works

closely with the North Carolina Department of Commerce for biotechnology-related economic development. The Biotechnology Center's staff helps the state's more than 200 bioscience companies with a myriad of issues including: financing; technology assessment, development and transfer; business planning; networking opportunities; and venture capital, marketing and regulatory strategies.

The Biotechnology Center fosters economic development through low-interest loans to emerging life-science companies. These awards support research projects by companies that may not qualify for more conventional forms of financial assistance.

The Biotechnology Center also partners with many organizations throughout the state in helping existing businesses and entrepreneurs open new facilities and establish new businesses. Although the Biotechnology Center does not contain a business incubator, it maintains relationships with a number of incubators and companies and organizations offering laboratory space to start-up ventures.

The two goals of the Education and Training program are to develop a workforce within the state to support North Carolina's biotechnology industry and to educate the state's citizenry about the science of biotechnology, in-

Established by the state in 1984, the North Carolina Biotechnology Center is the world's first government-sponsored biotechnology center.

cluding the issues surrounding it and its uses and applications.

There are a number of ways in which the program continues to successfully achieve these goals. The K-12 Enrichment Program is an initiative currently geared toward high school science and technology educators. Weeklong summer biology workshops are held throughout the state to instruct teachers on how to incorporate hands-on, enjoyable science activities into the classroom.

These workshops reinforce biology concepts by providing an excellent introduction to some of the essential elements needed for a career in biotechnology. Participating teachers receive daily stipends, free room and board, continuing education credits and comprehensive materials that can assist them in teaching in their classrooms what they've learned at the workshop. The program has prepared more than 1,200 teachers to instruct hundreds of thousands of students in biotechnology-related subject matter.

The support of teachers is not limited to the summer workshop offerings. Through an equipment loan program, teachers who graduate from the Biotechnology Center-sponsored summer teacher workshops receive an order form allowing them to receive lab supplies and ready-to-use kits from Carolina Biological Supply Company. Teachers may also borrow biotechnology videos from the Biotechnology Center for up to two weeks, a coordinated inter-library loan program made available through school media centers.

In addition to its ongoing core programs and services, the Biotechnology Center staff is working on several special initiatives including strengthening biotechnology statewide and implementing workforce training program for biomanufacturing—all priorities mapped out by *New Jobs Across North Carolina: A Strategic Plan for Growing the Economy Statewide Through Biotechnology*.

The plan, developed at the request of Governor Mike Easley, was crafted by 120 leaders across the state and released in January 2004. The document includes fifty-four strategic recommendations for improving such areas as research, workforce development and creating jobs. The plan's goal is to have 48,000 biotechnology-related jobs by 2013 and 125,000 jobs in 2023.

As the industry expands statewide, the Biotechnology Center has begun the Project to Strengthen Biotechnology

Job-seekers attend a BioWork job fair at the Biotechnology Center.

Across North Carolina. As part of the project, the Biotechnology Center has opened regional offices in Wilmington, Greenville, Winston-Salem and Asheville. The Biotechnology Center will open a Charlotte office in 2006.

The project is guided by regional advisory committees and the Biotechnology Center offers Regional Development Grant program to assist economic development efforts in such areas as strategic planning and infrastructure building.

Leading the effort to strengthen biotechnology in North Carolina is Dr. Leslie Alexandre, the Biotechnology Center's president and chief executive officer.

Before joining the Biotechnology Center in 2002, Dr. Alexandre was the assistant director for industrial relations at the National Cancer Institute in Bethesda, Maryland. Her skills and talent for building relationships and facilitating scientific collaborations with industry while at the National Cancer Institute made Dr. Alexandre a perfect candidate for leading the Biotechnology Center. Prior to her time at the National Cancer Institute, she was the vice president for corporate affairs and marketing for Oncormed Inc., also in Maryland, a provider of cancer-related genetic testing and pharmacogenomic services.

Dr. Alexandre has been the recipient of numerous awards, including the 2005 Council for Entrepreneurial Development Chairman's Service Award, the Triangle Business Journal's 2004 Women in Business Award and the 2003 Business Leader's Women Extraordinaire

With more than twenty years of sustained investment in biotechnology research, business and education statewide, the Biotechnology Center has helped North Carolina become the nation's number three state for biotechnology, based on number of companies, according to Ernst & Young.

Award. In 2005 Dr. Alexandre was also inducted into the Triangle YWCA Academy of Women.

To date, the Biotechnology Center has provided $16 million in financial assistance to more than ninety early-stage biotechnology companies, which has led to follow-on funding from other sources of more than $1 billion.

The Biotechnology Center has invested another $50 million to recruit forty-six leading faculty, purchase multi-user research equipment and sponsor more than 450 research projects in North Carolina universities. Additionally, through $8 million in special appropriation grants, the Biotechnology Center has tripled the enrollment in the biosciences at six of North Carolina's top minority-attended universities.

Currently 387 biotechnology, pharmaceutical, device, and contract research companies operate in North Carolina, employing 46,153 people, with one-third of these companies considered major, multinational biotechnology companies. North Carolina ranks third nationally in biotechnology, according to the 2005 Ernst & Young report on the industry.

For more information, visit the Biotechnology Center online at www.ncbiotech.org.

NORTH CAROLINA SYMPHONY

The North Carolina Symphony exists to enrich, enlighten and entertain the Triangle area of Raleigh, Durham, Chapel Hill and the many communities beyond. Since its humble beginnings almost seventy-five years ago, the symphony has grown from a group of volunteer players into a sophisticated ensemble of highly esteemed professional musicians. Perhaps that is why the world-renowned, newly appointed music director, Grant Llewellyn, accepted at once the opportunity to lead the artistically superb group. But what Mr. Llewellyn joined was not just a sixty-five member orchestra; he became a part of the North Carolina Symphony's legacy of perseverance and its mission of servitude to the state's greater community. The Symphony's heritage began in the midst of the Great Depression with the aspirations of Lamar Stringfield followed by the determination of Benjamin Franklin Swalin.

A native of North Carolina and a winner of the Pulitzer Traveling Fellowship Award, Lamar Stringfield had a passion for music and a dream of a state symphony. He recruited forty-eight musicians to perform a demonstration concert at Hill Hall Auditorium in Chapel Hill on May 14, 1932. The volunteer musicians came from sixteen communities across the state to prove their worth in hopes of permanent employment. Although

Lamar Stringfield, North Carolina Symphony founder and music director, 1932–1935.

North Carolina Symphony in its early days.

the concert was a success, funding the endeavor remained an obstacle. Over the next two years, the financially struggling yet committed musicians, continued to perform more than 140 concerts in fifty towns. Finally, in 1934 the Symphony applied to the Federal Emergency Relief Administration (FERA) and received a grant for $45,000. This gave the Symphony enough money to pay the now sixty-five member orchestra salaries for eight months! One of these original musicians, John Schnyder states in his memoir, "We were overjoyed at the time because more money was coming into the house and the Symphony paid me for something I loved to do." Unfortunately, the grant money ran dry and Stringfield found it necessary to take a position out of state. The fledgling Symphony began to deteriorate.

In the late 1930s, the Symphony served as a Works Progress Administration (WPA) project and hope for its future was revived. Benjamin Franklin Swalin, an associate professor of music at the University of North Carolina, and his wife, Maxine, took it upon themselves to revive the dream of a state orchestra. A persuasive suggestion from Swalin to Governor J. Melville Broughton led to the approval of Senate Bill No. 248, affectionately referred to as the "Horn Tootin' Bill." The endorsement of this bill on March 8, 1943 marked the first time in America that an orchestra was recognized as a state agency

under patronage of the state as an educational institution. To this day, the North Carolina Symphony has the distinction of being the first continuously state-funded Symphony. Presently, it receives approximately one quarter of its annual budget from the state. Swalin retained the position of music director of the Symphony from 1939–1972. For the first six years of his appointment he drew no salary from the orchestra, but lived instead on his income as a professor.

There was a small succession of music directors upon Swalin's retirement, but it was the appointment of Gerhardt Zimmermann in 1982 which launched a new era for the North Carolina Symphony. Zimmermann's local debut occurred at the first of a series of fiftieth anniversary

Audience members file into a tobacco barn to hear the North Carolina Symphony in concert.

concerts, during which the program from the very first concert on May 14, 1932, was repeated. Zimmermann graced the Symphony with his leadership for twenty-one years until he stepped down from the podium in 2003.

Today, the North Carolina Symphony is the thirty-second largest orchestra in the country. It is singularly unique in its commitment to statewide performances and its dedication to the music education of North Carolina's school children. The orchestra travels approximately 14,000 miles a season throughout the state of North Carolina and reaches nearly 250,000 people per year. Nearly one-third of those are school children. The Children's Concert Division of the North Carolina Symphony, which began in 1945 with the help of the beloved Maxine Swalin, has grown into the Symphony's most cherished accomplishment. "I was stunned at the number of groups prepared to sing "Ode to Joy" in German, the gasps of anticipation from the children when the name Shostakovich was mentioned," exclaims Suzanne Rousso, director of education for the Symphony. The students are excited because they have been prepared for the concerts by their enthusiastic teachers. The Symphony's education director meets with participating school

Benjamin Swalin, North Carolina Symphony music director, 1939-1972.

teachers in advance, discusses the upcoming concert programs and distributes teaching aids which help make the concert experience more understandable and potent for the children.

In addition to its extensive traveling schedule, the Symphony also performs at home in the acoustically outstanding Meymandi Concert Hall at the Progress Energy Center for the Performing Arts in Raleigh. The new concert hall dedicated in 2001 is considered to be one of the finest performance venues in the country, rivaling Boston's Symphony Hall and New York's Carnegie Hall. The Koka Booth Amphitheatre at Regency Park serves as the Symphony's new outdoor facility in Cary. The grand facility boasts acoustics by Lawrence Kirkegaard's world-renowned firm and was designed by William Rawn, the architect of Ozawa Hall at Tanglewood in Lenox, Massachusetts.

One of the Symphony's finest additions in the past decade is its newest music director, Grant Llewellyn. The magnetic forty-four-year old Welshman is praised for his charisma and musicianship. "Llewellyn combines artistic discipline and creative risk, exciting the musicians and compelling them to play their best," states Bruce Ridge, a double bass player who led the music director search committee. There was an international search which lasted almost three years, but when Llewellyn returned

Grant Llewellyn, current music director.

for a guest-conducting visit, the search ended. "North Carolina has an outstanding orchestra," exclaims Llewellyn, "I think the North Carolina Symphony is well-positioned to take its place beyond North Carolina and enjoy a nationwide profile." Llewellyn's coveted appointment clearly is a mutually beneficial one.

North Carolina Symphony's sixty-five member, full-time professional orchestra performs more than 170 concerts each season. One-third of those concerts are generously performed free for children through the Symphony's extensive educational programs. The objective of the Raleigh based Symphony is to present the beauty of music and superb artistry of its orchestra to the people of North Carolina and beyond, regardless of background, age, economic status, or geographic location. The future for the North Carolina Symphony is clear: exposure to a wider audience base. "We want to share this great organization beyond the borders of North Carolina and have it gain the attention of national and international press," states David Chambless Worters, President and CEO of the Symphony, "We want to take this already very accomplished orchestra and create America's Next Great Orchestra." The North Carolina Symphony is well on its way.

OLD DOMINION FREIGHT LINE, INC.

Old Dominion Freight Line was founded in 1934 by Earl and Lillian Congdon. That fateful year the Congdons had no way to know they were starting what would ultimately become a billion dollar nationwide, less-than-truckload company. Instead, for the Congdons, the company simply began out of necessity.

Lillian and Earl Congdon, Sr. were married in 1929, the year the Great Depression began. Not surprisingly, due to the poor economic state of the country, Mr. Congdon was having a difficult time finding work. With no prospects of a job, the Congdons took matters into their own hands.

In what would prove to be a significant decision, the Congdons traded their car for a truck believing that Mr. Congdon would work for himself as a truck driver until the Depression ended. His plan was to resume his employment search and find work elsewhere. They

Lillian and Earl Congdon, Sr.

Lillian and Earl Congdon, Sr.in 1948.

began with a route that ran between Richmond and Norfolk, Virginia and called the company Old Dominion after the nickname for the state of Virginia, "The Old Dominion State."

In those early days, Mrs. Congdon completed the necessary paperwork on their dining room table. She dispatched the single truck, driven by Mr. Congdon, who would often drive day and night. Some of the first products they transported were coffee beans, bales of burlap, canned goods, paper products and chemicals.

Unfortunately, their route was limited due to the restraints imposed by the Interstate Commerce Commission's regulation of the trucking industry. The law, enacted in 1935, required ICC certificates for each trucking route. Certificates were automatically granted as long as detailed documentation of prior service in that lane was provided. Old Dominion's ICC certificate allowed it to handle export/import traffic from Norfolk or interline (partnership) traffic because the operating certificate granted the company an interstate route only, which meant that the shipments must move from or to Virginia. They could not move within the state.

Despite this operational challenge, Old Dominion (OD) began to grow and by 1940 had forty-five em-

ployees who worked in three Virginia service centers: Newport News, Norfolk and Richmond. Old Dominion operated at this time as a union company. In 1946 a union strike occurred along the East Coast, which negatively impacted OD. The business was on strike for ten weeks. This was a dire time for Old Dominion as unpaid bills increased and there was no income. At last, an over-the-road driver telephoned Mr. Congdon and stated that the drivers wanted to return to work. He asked if Mr. Congdon would reopen the company as a non-union carrier. Mr. Congdon agreed. The Richmond drivers left the teamsters. However, the Newport News and Norfolk drivers remained in the union. As a result, Old Dominion operated as both entities. Thankfully, the two groups worked together well and there was no conflict.

The year 1950 was marked by tragedy for the family when Mr. Congdon died suddenly. Left behind were his wife, Lillian, age forty-one and two sons, Earl, age nineteen, and Jack, age seventeen. Offers to purchase the company poured in but Lillian steadfastly refused each and every one. She was adamant that the company she and her husband had founded together would not be sold. Lillian immediately took over the daily operations of the business and, with that, assumed a new and greater level of responsibility. Earl was attending Business College and Jack was still in high school, but both quickly became immersed in the day-to-day operations of the company. Earl and Jack continued their education and at the same time managed to maintain a daily presence in the operations of the company. They both drove trucks and worked on the docks in the afternoon, at night, and on the weekends.

The company persisted by virtue of the Congdons' hard work and dedication. The family realized that in order for Old Dominion to survive it needed to expand. Regulation caused the process of acquiring additional operating certificates to be lengthy and expensive. The most feasible option for OD was to acquire these much-needed certificates through the acquisition of another trucking company's assets.

David and Earl Congdon. David is the third generation president and COO of Old Dominion. Mr. Congdon is still very active as chairman and CEO.

The Bottoms-Fiske acquistion started the real growth rate for Old Dominion in 1957. Bottoms-Fiske was larger than Old Dominion at the time.

In 1957 the opportunity for expansion arrived through the purchase of Bottoms-Fiske Truck Line. OD had maintained its three service centers in Virginia but the acquisition of Bottoms-Fiske would provide an additional fourteen service centers throughout North Carolina and southern Virginia. Some might say it was a risky move for OD to purchase a company priced at twice its own net worth but the acquisition proved to be a smart business decision.

The agreement called for the two companies to operate separately until the end of an eight-year payoff period. Be-

fore the end of the payoff period the drivers of Bottoms-Fiske allied themselves with the union, which resulted in a strike that lasted one and a half years. This was a turbulent period in the history of Old Dominion as the strike resulted in numerous episodes of violence. Over the course of time, however, the strike gradually phased out and eventually ended with OD maintaining its non-union status.

The buyout of Bottoms-Fiske was completed in five years and Old Dominion moved its headquarters from Richmond, Virginia, to High Point, North Carolina. This move allowed OD to take advantage of a general office that was adjacent to its newly acquired service center in High Point. Along with the new headquarters, Old Dominion also installed a new president. In 1962 Earl Congdon, Jr. became president while Lillian Congdon moved into the role of chairman of the board. Earl's brother, Jack, served as vice president but remained in Richmond. He began operating Old Dominion Truck Leasing, which today remains a very successful Richmond based company.

Old Dominion enjoyed a period of unparalled growth between 1969 and 1979. In 1969 OD acquired Barnes Truck Line, Nilson Motor Express and White Transport. Two years later, in 1971, the company acquired Star Transport followed by the acquisition of Deaton Trucking in 1979. These five major acquisitions allowed Old Dominion to open service centers in New England, Alabama, Georgia, Louisiana, Mississippi, and South Carolina. With this growth came the need for larger corporate headquarters, which precipitated the move to a newly constructed office building located on Westchester Drive in High Point.

By 1979 Congress had begun to consider deregulation of the trucking industry. As a leader in the transportation field, Earl Congdon was invited to attend a weeklong meeting held at Harvard University along with twenty-four of his peers. The purpose of the gathering was to discuss the potential effects, both positive and negative, of deregulation.

Old Dominion truck used for pick up and delivery in the city operations and in linehaul operations, pictured in 1940.

Congress, based on its success in deregulating other industries such as the airline industry, moved forward with the deregulation of the trucking industry in 1980. This was an important milestone for Old Dominion as deregulation allowed OD to expand as never before, since it no longer needed the previously required operating certificates. As a result, in the early 1980s, Old Dominion expanded its services to Florida, Tennessee, California, Texas, Illinois, Ohio, and Indiana. This exciting time of growth was soon marred by the realization that OD had expanded too quickly. As a result, by the mid 1980s, OD found it was struggling financially. A halt to all further expansion and a renewed focus on existing service areas allowed the company to rebound and by 1988 Old Dominion again posted a profit.

Once its fiscal stability had been maintained for several years, the company began to focus on the need for financial flexibility, which would allow for regional expansion. A public stock offering was deemed the best solution and, as such, Old Dominion went public in 1991. Prior to this time, the primary operational empha-

sis of the company had been on long haul business or on shipments that moved more than 500 miles. This additional influx of capital allowed the operational focus to include short haul business, or shipments that move within a 500-mile radius, an important and growing sector in the trucking industry.

In 1997 Earl Congdon became chairman and chief executive officer when his

son, David S. Congdon was named to the position of president and chief operating officer. Like his father, David grew up in the company and after graduating from college worked in many different areas throughout the Old Dominion system. The vast experience David gained prior to succeeding his father provided him with the vision necessary to navigate OD through a period of carefully planned, yet aggressive growth. From 2001 to 2006, under his skilled guidance, Old Dominion acquired the assets of Fredrickson Motor Express, Goggin Truck Line, Skyline, Carter and Sons Trucking, Wichita Southeast Kansas Transit, and UW Freight Line, effectively solidifying OD's national footprint.

The growth continues as Old Dominion expands globally with direct service to Canada as well as service to Mexico, the Caribbean, Europe, the Far East, Central America, South America, Oceania, and to points in between. This period of dramatic growth again fostered the need to relocate Old Dominion's

Lillian Congdon at the ribbon cutting ceremony for the new corporate office, May 1980.

corporate headquarters into a much larger facility. The company moved to a completely renovated sleek and modern 162,000 square foot building located at the intersection of Business 85 and National Highway in Thomasville, North Carolina. This new complex provided OD with much needed space as well as secure housing for its advanced technological systems. OD has emerged as a leader in transportation technology and is constantly developing new and innovative ways to assist customers while continually making operational improvements.

The future is indeed bright for Old Dominion. From its humble beginnings in 1934, OD today has grown into a company with more than 12,000 employees working in over 170 service centers across the nation. Throughout the years, Old Dominion has maintained a unique position in the transportation industry; a position that differentiates OD from all of its competitors. The company is not made up of separate operating groups or business entities. Old Dominion is one company with one highly qualified and committed management team. It is one company dedicated to the goal of becoming the premier transportation solutions company in domestic and global markets served. This goal is the driving force

David and Earl Congdon.

Old Dominion employees.

1956 Old Dominion truck used for pick up and delivery in the city operations and in linehaul operations.

behind the company and guides each one of Old Dominion's valued employees every day.

Companies often boast of a family-like atmosphere but, at Old Dominion the family atmosphere is a reality. The close bond between all who work at OD harkens back to the earliest days of the business when Earl, Jr. was only nineteen, working on the docks side by side with the employees. This spirit remains a cornerstone of the Old Dominion way. It is nurtured through the handwritten birthday cards that Earl sends to each employee every year, as well as letters of congratulation that David sends to employees on their anniversaries with OD. Many are often amazed that in this fast paced, results-oriented world, senior management at Old Dominion takes time to personally connect with their employees. Actions such as these have created a completely unique company climate that is Old Dominion.

Interior of Old Dominion service center dock.

Old Dominion's history is truly inspirational. From one truck and a husband and wife's dream of making a decent living, to the financially solid company today boasting more than 20,000 trucks and over 12,000 employees, OD is the epitome of the American success story.

Old Dominion corporate office from May 1980 until November 2001.

Opposite page, top
New corporate office, whick Old Dominion moved into in November 2001.

Opposite page, bottom
New 2006 Old Dominion equipment.

PIKE ELECTRIC, INC.

With more than 7,000 employees and a customer base that extends into nineteen states, Pike Electric, Inc. is one of the largest power line contractors in the nation. The sixty-year-old company owes much of its success to the gritty determination of three generations of one Mount Airy family—and to a waterlogged truck that helped the dream become a reality.

After years of working as a lineman, Floyd Pike was eager to start his own power line construction business. He knew he had the skills and experience to get established. What he lacked was equipment. It was 1945 and World War II had recently ended. The production of light and heavy duty vehicles had been dedicated to the war effort. Trucks were almost impossible to obtain.

Floyd thought he had exhausted all possibilities—until he heard a story that grabbed his attention. A line truck had fallen from a barge into the Intracoastal Waterway near the town of Beaufort, North Carolina. The truck had been submerged for several months. Floyd checked into the options and cost of salvaging the abandoned vehicle. In a matter of days, he and a friend were on their way to the coast. Together, they raised the truck from the bottom of the waterway, somehow managed to get it

In earlier years, line work was labor intensive and energized conductors could only be handled with insulated hot sticks.

Pike family members and senior management officials of the company share the podium of the New York Stock Exchange as Eric Pike rings the bell to open public trading for Pike Electric.

running, and drove it across the state to Mount Airy in freezing November temperatures—without a windshield.

That 1939 Ford became the first truck used by the business. For years after it was retired from service, the vehicle was covered with tarp and stored in a corner of the company garage. It was painstakingly restored in 1995 in time for Pike Electric's fiftieth anniversary. Today the bright yellow truck is prominently displayed in the lobby of corporate headquarters—a testament to the drive and unique vision of the company's founder.

The original business was named "Floyd S. Pike, Electrical Contractor," and an office was set up in the Pike family kitchen. Once Floyd had a truck and workspace, all he needed was a customer. He contacted Mr. H. E. Carter of Duke Power Company. Carter was familiar with Floyd's work ethic during his years of service with Duke Power and a contract was soon awarded to the budding entrepreneur.

Experienced linemen were paid $1.25 an hour, a handsome wage in 1945. Floyd hired associates he had worked with during his career at Duke Power and with other contractors at Cherry Point Marine Corps Air Station near Camp Lejeune. His initial crew stayed busy as service contracts multiplied. Power companies had postponed maintenance and

expansion during the war, so there was a pent-up demand for contractor assistance to rebuild and extend power grids.

But it was Floyd's solid reputation as a hard worker and a man of integrity that helped catapult the company over its initial financial hurdles. Individuals who believed in Floyd and his entrepreneurial vision underwrote some of the start-up costs. Eventually more conventional financing was secured. Crews were added to the Duke Power system, then to Carolina Power and Light (now Progress Energy). The company expanded into Virginia and West Virginia on the American Electric Power system and later into Georgia.

Eventually, the makeshift office in the kitchen of the Pike home was no longer adequate for the burgeoning company so the business moved into a separate facility. Over the years the building was repeatedly expanded, and a garage was added so equipment could be maintained and repaired. In less than a decade, Pike Electric had grown to several hundred employees. The young company was reaping the benefits of an excellent reputation, both for its outstanding

The corporate office for Pike Electric rests on the company campus of approximately 125 acres south of Mount Airy, North Carolina.

personnel, and its quality equipment and services.

The company evolved with the industry as technology ushered in safer and more productive types of equipment. In the early years power lines were built by manual labor. Holes were dug by hand, and poles were set by groups of men using hand-held sticks with spikes in one end to grab the wooden pole. It was strenuous work. In the late 1950s and early 1960s, major technological advances in equipment revolutionized the industry. Manufacturers and suppliers developed hydraulic-powered line trucks with augers and booms to both dig and set the poles. Shortly after the introduction of hydraulic line trucks, insulated bucket trucks were designed to allow safer access to energized power lines that were undergoing a transformation to higher and higher operating voltages. Pike Electric was among the first contractors to accept the new technology.

The company continued to expand in the 1960s as its service territory widened to encompass more southeastern states. In addition, Pike Electric developed several initiatives during this decade that were unique to the industry. Crews and equipment were spread over a large geographical area, and returning to Mount Airy for maintenance or repair

became impractical. The solution was to establish satellite garages with a staff of field mechanics throughout the company's service area. This approach to fleet maintenance remains today and has set Pike Electric apart from its competitors. Floyd also oversaw the creation of a Safety Department and strict adherence to specific procedures to ensure a healthy work environment for his employees—a full decade before OSHA came into being.

The unexpected death of Floyd Pike in 1975 was an emotional blow to the company. Floyd's son, Joe, had grown up

with the business and was thoroughly familiar with its day-to-day operation. Unfortunately, the timing could not have been worse for him to assume leadership of his father's business. The nation was in the midst of one of its worst recessions since the Great Depression of the 1930s. Several utilities were on the verge of bankruptcy. Work had slowed to a trickle. Some utilities released all of their contract companies in a desperate cost-saving measure.

Power restoration following hurricanes and ice storms is a visible part of Pike's business

Pike Electric managed to weather its most difficult season with the same resolve that its founder possessed when he started the company. Personnel were laid off and management accepted pay cuts to survive the down period. As bleak as the situation appeared, Joe Pike believed the industry would rebound. Sure enough, the demand returned in the late 1970s and the company responded with a renewed desire to grow.

The work Pike Electric performs has a tendency to go unnoticed by the typical consumer. Its base of utility, cooperative, and municipal clients often have more visibility with their customers than does a contractor working on their system. In the event of a major disaster such as a hurricane or ice storm, however, Pike Electric becomes highly recognizable.

The company has responded to such events with personnel and equipment since the early 1950s. But their massive response to the hurricane-devastated areas of the Gulf Coast in 2005 has brought unprecedented exposure to the firm. Some 3,000 employees and over 2,000 pieces of equipment were mobilized to these ravaged areas to restore power. Crews typically worked sixteen hours a day, seven days a week, until power was restored. The distinctive yellow service trucks were seen throughout the affected areas. Pike Electric has received hundreds of thank you letters, cards, and

The introduction of specialized equipment and insulated rubber gloves allow line personnel to safely handle energized conductors.

The company's first truck was restored for the fiftieth anniversary in 1995 and is on display in the lobby of the Corporate office.

emails from utility customers expressing their appreciation for the dedication of these hard-working men and women.

"Our response to disasters has been our biggest sales tool," says Barny Ratliff, the chief administrative officer for Pike Electric. "We send out line personnel, supervisors, safety representatives, and our fleet staff. That really makes an impression on customers, and has done more to expand our business over the past two decades than anything else."

In 1998 J. Eric Pike assumed the presidency of the company and became the third generation leader of Pike Electric. Like his father, Eric grew up with the company, and he began his career at age sixteen working in the commercial department during summer vacation. He later gained practical experience working on line crews out in the field and earned the top classification for linemen.

Pike Electric continues to be a leader in the utility industry, and has expanded its service region to include western states such as Texas and Oklahoma. The company has over 10,500 pieces of equipment, and with its six garages strategically placed in North Carolina, Georgia, and Texas, Pike Electric is able to ensure low downtime no matter how remote the location.

Some of the company's competitors have attempted to diversify by expanding into the cable television and telephone industries. Pike Electric, on the other hand, has stayed true to the original mission of the company—electrical distribution and transmission work.

"We have stayed focused in that market and we have become very good at what we do," says Ratliff. "We want to be the best contractor that a company can choose. We may not necessarily be the one who offers the lowest price, but you won't find anyone who will bring better value to the table."

"Our mantra is to continue to grow and expand, but not beyond the capability of maintaining our reputation for quality," Ratliff added.

A milestone was celebrated in July 2005 when the company that had been privately run for fifty-nine years became listed on the New York Stock Exchange. J. Eric Pike, along with family members and a delegation of company management, visited the New York Stock Exchange and were honored to ring the opening bell.

Resource: *Climbing to the Top* by Anne Pike

THE YORK COMPANIES

When C.V. York co-founded his small North Carolina construction company in 1904, he built more than structures of brick and mortar; he built a solid foundation for The York Companies.

Today, The York Companies, led by Smedes York, C.V. York's grandson, is a group of industry-leading real estate development and related businesses dedicated to serving the Triangle area of Raleigh, Durham and Chapel Hill. Without a doubt, the privately held group of businesses has grown and prospered to be a billion-dollar organization, while continuing to honor C.V. York's commitment to quality and customer satisfaction made more than a century ago.

The legacy was established when C.V. York's company, York and Cobb, built the first five buildings in 1908 at what is now East Carolina University in Greenville. Two years later C.V. purchased the remaining interest from his partners, the Cobb brothers, and reestablished the business as York Construction Company in Raleigh. C.V.'s son, J.W. "Willie" York, joined the company, and the two men focused the business on the evolving Triangle area, building some of the most notable landmarks, including the Sir Walter Hotel, Memorial Auditorium, the Velvet Cloak Inn, the Bell Tower at North Carolina University and the York Industrial Center. Most notably, in 1949, the company developed Cameron

Phyllis York Brookshire (COO of York Simpson Underwood).

Village—the Southeast's first shopping center and planned community.

The successful business of construction naturally led to a venture in the real estate industry. York Properties Inc., formed under the leadership of Smedes York as president, is a comprehensive real estate company, providing commercial sales and leasing, retail leasing and property management.

York Construction Company became McDonald-York after a merger in 1994, and today operates as a leading regional general contracting firm, continuing the focus on quality and customer satisfaction. Co-owned by Smedes York and Jack McDonald, the company, which is one of the oldest firms in the area, has a

G. Smedes York, George York, Jr. and Smedes York, III. Smedes is president of York Properties. George is vice president of retail for York Properties.

proven history of building on time and within budget.

In 2000, York Properties established York Simpson Underwood Realty, and refined its focus on residential services. With multiple offices and almost 300 dedicated and experienced agents, York Simpson Underwood, a Christie's Great Estates affiliate, extends professional but personal assistance to homebuyers in the Triangle area.

Through the award-winning York Simpson Underwood, the independent real estate company further assists in buying and selling services, with YSU Lending offering the most up-to-date mortgage alternatives and efficient financial tools to fit a variety of individual needs.

Portrait of J. Willie York.

At the core of all these business ventures is the York commitment to its community. The York family has always recognized the value of giving time and talents to the Triangle region that their growing companies have called home for so many years. J.W. York served the area as a member of the Raleigh School Board, the North Carolina Board of Conservation and Development and the Raleigh-Durham Airport Authority. Smedes York followed in his footsteps by becoming a political and community leader, serving as a Raleigh city councilman and a two-term mayor of the town, as well as volunteering with a variety of local charitable and nonprofit organizations. And George York, who joined the company in 1993 and currently serves as vice president of the York Properties retail division, is a board member of Southlight Inc., a substance abuse nonprofit organization and is involved with the Urban Land Institute, an organization which promotes responsible land development.

The future for The York Companies is unlimited as the company excels at its time-tested services and products while looking for new and useful ways to grow the Triangle area. And the century-old focus of quality, in honor of C.V. York, will be the driving force to take The York Companies into another generation of unparalleled success.

R. L. STOWE MILLS INC.

From the time he was a young boy helping work on his father's farm in the 1860s and 1870s, Robert Lee Stowe was determined to start a business of his own one day. That dream of entrepreneurship would eventually become R.L. Stowe Mills Inc., a textile firm headquartered in Belmont that has expanded to six manufacturing facilities which turn out dyed and natural yarns for the apparel, home furnishings, and automotive textile industries. A success story by any standard, the company Stowe founded has spanned more than 100 years and survived three generations of the Stowe family.

But it took time for the young Stowe to achieve his goal of business ownership. After finishing his schooling, he toiled as a schoolteacher and also clerked in a general mercantile store. Frustrated with the low salary he earned from teaching, Stowe became even more determined to get into business for himself. His experience with the mercantile store convinced him that he wanted to open his own store in what was to become Belmont.

With little more than a few hundred dollars saved up, he couldn't afford the start-up costs associated with launching a retail operation. The young man's enthusiasm helped him convince local investors to partner with him in the venture, and in his mid twenties, he opened the doors to his first business. Stowe's brother-in-law joined him in the operation, in due course, marking the debut of a family business. Stowe began to realize that operating such a store had limits in terms of success and he decided to start a business that could potentially prove more lucrative.

At the time, Gaston County was the site of a growing textile industry. Stowe zeroed in on this field and on the town of Belmont in particular for his next endeavor, one that would prove even more successful than he had ever imagined. A cotton mill was Stowe's goal, and to make it come to life, he once again turned to investors to help finance the business. Thanks to his ambition and his track record with the store, Stowe was able to convince people to become shareholders in the venture. This financing strategy worked so well that Stowe would repeat it many times in the future.

In 1901 he incorporated the first of his textile mills and called it The Chronicle Mills. His brother joined him in the venture, making this a family business that would remain in the family for generations to come. On February 28, 1902 workers opened the first bale of cotton, and manufacturing of 100 percent combed cotton at the mill began in earnest.

R. L. Stowe Mills Inc. plant children's Christmas party in the early 1950s.

Stowe Spinning Company, Belmont, North Carolina in 1965.

Business had barely gotten underway when disaster struck. A tornado hit the approximately 100,000-square-foot mill with such force that it ripped off a major portion of the roof. In spite of the damage the mill was able to continue operating. Just a few months later, in April, the first shipment of yarn was made.

The Chronicle Mills plant also earned a place in history for something other than its yarn-making. It became the first textile mill in the nation to be equipped with a system of ducts and outlets that provided the proper humidity for spinning. This unique system supplied by a young engineer, Willis Carrier, would eventually become known as air conditioning. Air conditioning got its name from the use of high humidity to dampen or "condition" textile fibers.

Today, all textile mills have central air conditioning.

With the mill churning out yarn, Stowe needed to find customers. To do so, he relied on the relationships he forged when he owned the mercantile store. As a retailer, he had been a customer of several apparel makers and fabric makers, buying their wares to sell in his store. With his new venture, he managed to turn the tables and turned these former vendors into his own customers.

The textile industry was then growing and so was Stowe's business. Successful from the start, the plant paid dividends to its investors in its earliest years. It wasn't long before Stowe began adding new products and was forced to expand the plant to accommodate new equipment and additional workers. In fact, business was so good that Stowe was faced with a dilemma: greatly expand the existing mill or build a second plant? Stowe finally decided to build a second

plant and offered stock in the new plant as a way to finance its construction.

Just as Stowe's Chronicle Mills plant made history as the first textile mill to have air conditioning, the new mill would also make history. When the new cotton mill called Imperial Yarn Mills began production in 1907, it became the first cotton mill in all of North Carolina to be powered by electricity. At the time, cotton mills were steam-powered. The electricity proved to be such a success that Stowe converted the Chronicle Mills to electricity as well. And he opted for electricity in every subsequent mill he opened.

Stowe never lost the fervor he possessed for launching a new business. In fact, once his cotton mills were operational, he would turn his attention to opening yet another mill. Within less than two decades after opening his first mill in 1901, he and his brother were the operating executives of seven mills in the Belmont area and had financial

The old Stowe Park, Belmont, North Carolina, located on Main street in the heart of Belmont.

interests in other textile corporations in the area.

In 1928 the second generation of the Stowe family took a leadership role in the family business. That year Robert Lee Stowe Jr. took his place as president of Belmont Hosiery Mills. Stowe Jr. began working in the family business when he was a young man just out of college and his father was determined to teach him every aspect of the business.

One of Stowe Jr.'s first tasks was selling yarn. Stowe had explained to his son that the only way he would really learn the business was by going out and meeting the customers and selling yarns himself. Over time, Stowe handed over the sales and manufacturing duties to his son. While Stowe focused on starting new mills, Stowe Jr. was the one who maintained the facilities once they had become operational. Stowe Jr.'s brother,

Daniel J. Stowe, eventually became involved in the family textile business as well.

It wasn't long after Stowe Jr. joined the firm that the Depression hit. During these trying times, Stowe and his son managed to keep each of the mills operational. Some of them were forced to go to reduced work weeks of only three days a week, but they were still open. By remaining operational, the Stowe mills provided gainful employment to the local community. Mill employees were still able to earn enough money to feed and clothe their families unlike millions of other Americans who suffered from layoffs and a lack of work.

The mills survived the Depression, and Stowe continued looking for opportunities to start new ventures. In 1939 the elder Stowe launched yet another mill, his last. Stowe would live to the age of 96 and even in his 90s, he insisted on staying informed about the daily activities at the mills.

Throughout his lifetime, Stowe felt a

tremendous commitment not only to his employees but also to his community. In fact, he served as chairman of the Gaston County board of commissioners for more than thirty years. As part of his commitment to bettering his community, Stowe was instrumental in transforming miles and miles of rugged dirt roads into smoothly paved roads. In an effort to provide more financial resources to the community, the businessman took a position as president of the newly created Bank of Belmont in 1906. He would hold this position until his death nearly sixty years later. Throughout his lifetime, the entrepreneur would also have a strong association with the local Presbyterian church.

Today, the family business Stowe created is in the hands of the third generation, including Robert Lee Stowe III, chairman and D. Harding Stowe, president and CEO. Although the industry has changed dramatically since the founder's time, the current leaders have

President Bush visited the Helms Plant in July 2005. Shown in the photo with him (right) is Harding Stowe, president & CEO of R. L. Stowe Mills.

revealed a shared passion for opening new mills and acquiring others.

In 1988 the Stowes built a $23 million, 100,000 square-foot spinning plant filled with automated machinery. The Helms plant, named after a longtime employee, was the first new spinning plant in the U.S. to be opened in years. Unlike the early days when the plants operated only during the daytime and never on Sundays, the Helms plant was designed to be operational twenty-four hours a day, seven days a week. This thoroughly modern plant's automated machinery sparked interest within the industry, so much so that the company began fielding numerous requests to tour the facility. The most important person ever to visit the facility is President George W. Bush, who toured the plant on July 15, 2005.

The current leadership has also acquired a competitor's three plants, bringing the current total to six plants, four in Belmont and two in Tennessee. With about 800 employees, the company spins, twists, dyes, and mercerizes cotton and cotton synthetic blended yarns. The yarn is used primarily in the apparel,

home furnishing and automotive textile industries.

In the recent past, the textile industry has gone through difficult times. The industry as a whole has shrunk by about 50 percent. This has forced the current leaders at R.L. Stowe Mills to find new customers both domestically and internationally. Thanks to the entrepreneurial spirit, the Stowe family has managed to keep the business going despite the tough times just as the founder had done during the Depression.

Their strategy for the future? Continue to focus on the customer. Recognition of customers as the most important part of the business is emphasized to all employees. In fact, the company's leaders challenge each and every one of their employees to achieve and exceed the needs of their customers 100 percent of the time. Delivering products on time is a continuous, everyday priority.

Just as the founder's penchant for business has survived the generations, so has his devotion to community involvement. Today's family leaders are equally dedicated to making their community a better place for everyone. Donations have been made to the YMCA, American Red Cross, Salvation Army, Presbyterian

church, and a local Catholic college.

The Stowe family also maintains the Daniel Stowe Botanical Garden, named one of the top ten autumn destinations by *USA Today*. The Garden was created by Daniel J. Stowe, a lifelong nature lover and gardening enthusiast who retired from the family business. In 1989 he reserved 450 acres of prime rolling meadows, woodlands and lakefront property and established a foundation to develop a world-class botanical garden. The garden has since been called one of the nation's "Twenty Great Gardens" in the *HGTV Flower Gardening Book*.

There's no doubt that the Stowe family and the textile dynasty it has created has had a tremendous impact on the city of Belmont and on Gaston County as a whole. For more than a century, the firm has been providing jobs for the local residents and has been giving back to the community in a number of ways. A fourth generation of the Stowe family is currently in college and poised to start their careers, not yet certain if they'll follow in the family business.

The Chronicle Mills smoke stack in June 1968.

TRI-COUNTY COMMUNITY HEALTH COUNCIL, INC.

For more than thirty years, Tri-County Community Health Council, Inc. has been an integral part of the eastern North Carolina region. The success of the nonprofit award-winning organization has depended on its ability to change to meet the needs of those it serves, while remaining steadfast to its day-one commitment: providing quality healthcare to the medically underserved.

Tri-County Community Health Council was founded by humble means for a noble goal—to help the 10,000-plus migrant workers who come to the region annually for the agricultural harvesting of sweet potatoes, tobacco and cucumbers. These farm workers, many of them from Mexico, continue to serve an important role in the agriculturally driven economy of the area. But for decades, the migrant workforce and their families faced language and financial barriers prohibiting many from receiving any type of professional healthcare.

In 1976 through the federally funded Migrant Health Program, the health departments of Sampson and Johnston counties joined together to form a health center for this special-needs population. The Sampson-Johnston Migrant Health Clinic was established in a former country store, located three miles west of the town of Newton Grove, on U.S. Highway 13.

Tri-County Community Health Council. Aerial photo in the 1990s.

Tri-County Community Health Council's second satellite clinic—Bladen Lakes CHC, Dublin, North Carolina.

Family nurse practitioner Juanita Morrison Henderson served as the first medical provider for the clinic, with Dr. Romeo Lewis as the backup physician. In the first year of operation, more than 5,000 people were provided with basic healthcare services. The demand was great, and the clinic was steadfast in offering help to the migrant population.

In 1977 Harnett County joined the alliance, shifting the clinic's impact to a more regional one. During that same year, on November 30, another milestone for the clinic was achieved—it formed its own board and became incorporated as the Tri-County Community Health Council (TCCHC). The formation of the independent clinic provided the opportunity to serve the medical needs of thousands of disadvantaged seasonal and migrant farmworkers in the area.

With an increasing population seeking health care from the center and a broadening slate of services being offered, a bigger building was needed. In 1981 building construction was made possible through a $291,000 loan from the Farmers Home Administration. TCCHC relocated near Timothy Cross Roads at 3331 Easy Street, which continues to serve as home to the council's twelve-acre headquarters campus today.

Growing needs also meant the council's staff had to expand. The year after moving to its new location on Easy Street, the first permanent staff physician, Barbara G. Cler, M.D., joined the center. In 1984 dental services were added, as the council evolved from a focused community program to a broader medical care center.

J. Michael Baker joined the staff as executive director in 1986. Baker, a former corporate finance consultant, educated at Lehman College (CUNY) and New York University in Business Administration, brought a new perspective to operating the council. He quickly set his sites on increasing services and expanding outreach initiatives into eastern North Carolina, while maintaining quality healthcare. Baker envisioned a facility that would provide all the medical needs, including dental and behavioral resources, to the medically underserved and disadvantaged.

Under Baker's direction, TCCHC introduced several much-needed programs, including maternity care. The numbers in the Hispanic community were rapidly rising for both substance abuse treatment and HIV/AIDS care, so the center also sought grants and created programs to meet those specific and urgent needs.

While maintaining medical services—and in many cases a true lifeline to the migrant workers—TCCHC opened its doors to the general population of the community, again, shifting its services, but remained focused on quality care. With the aging of farm workers and the toll of a shifting economy on small family farms, permanent residents were welcomed at the center.

Another significant change for the council was its introduction of Harvest House. First opened in 1994, this ten-bed halfway house, located on the main campus, offered the state's first bilingual

J. Michael Baker at the twenty-year anniversary.

intensive drug-addiction recovery program. Before Harvest House opened its doors, the community expressed resistance and concerns, mostly based on fear of the unknown.

Soon, residents came to understand the important role the facility played in the community. Harvest House has been part of not only saving hundreds of lives from drug addiction, but it has changed perceptions along the way as well.

The new millennium brought substantial growth to the organization. In

2001 the center opened its first satellite site, Carolina Pines Community Health Center, in nearby Salemburg. On track for exponential growth, TCCHC would be able to provide medical care on a more regional scope.

Just two years after opening the first satellite center, a second was introduced in Bladen Lakes Community Health Center in Dublin, N.C. In 2004 the Homestead Health Center in Pender County was opened and in 2005, the company marked its fourth satellite site with the addition of the Four County Medical Center in Harrells, N.C.

The center has been recognized time and time again for its efforts in offering comprehensive care to the tens of thousands of people it serves annually—many of whom would forgo necessary medical attention if the center did not provide it.

Among its distinctions, TCCHC and its staff have been awarded the Cecilia B. Abhold Award for Outreach Services, the Robert Wood Johnson Leadership Award, the Harold E. Hughes Award for Excellence in Rural Treatment Programs, the HRSA Excellence in Cultural Competency Award and the Joint Commission Accreditation for Healthcare Organizations. Mr. Baker was recognized as the 1995 Alumni of the Year for Leadership at the UNC School of Public Health.

Today's TCCHC provides a comprehensive approach to healthcare for the region, providing clients with a vast spectrum of medical, social and behavioral-health services. The center also impacts its community as a real economic driver. With more than 150 employees, a payroll exceeding $5 million and a total operating budget over $10 million, the center has established itself as a viable business partner to the area it serves.

Tri-County Community Health Council has survived the test of time by changing, growing, and adapting to its community and the needs within. In its three decades of operations, the council has stayed true to its commitment and positioned itself as a viable community partner to eastern North Carolina for many years to come.

Tri-County Community Health Council board of directors.

A TIMELINE OF NORTH CAROLINA HISTORY

1500s
Native Americans of the Algonquian, Iroquoian, and Siouan language groups had first contact with Europeans.

1584
Walter Raleigh sent an exploratory expedition to what would become North Carolina. Queen Elizabeth named the region "Virginia" after herself.

1585
Raleigh organized the Lane Colony. Reports, maps, and paintings by John White and Thomas Harriot sparked European interest.

1587
Raleigh sponsored the John White Colony. Virginia Dare was the first English child born in America. Returning after three years, White found only a "Lost Colony."

1629
King Charles named the region "Carolana" after himself.

1650s
Virginians began to settle areas just north of Albemarle Sound.

1663
After the English Civil War, King Charles II rewarded the loyal "Lords Proprietors" with the Carolina Charter.

1665
The Lords Proprietors issued the Concessions and Agreement to lure prospective settlers by improving government and recognizing slavery.

1669
The Assembly rejected John Locke's Fundamental Constitutions of Carolina which proposed a feudal-like system.

1677
Culpeper's Rebellion broke out.

1678
Quakers entered the state.

1695
Baptists arrived.

1710
Nine hundred blacks lived in Carolina.

1711
The Tuscarora Indian War broke out.

1712
Hoping to improve government and quell unrest, the Lords Proprietors formally separated North and South Carolina.

1715
A state law forbade blacks to marry whites.

The Lost Colony *has been performed in Manteo every summer since 1937. It is America's longest running outdoor drama. Courtesy, N.C. Division of Tourism, Film, and Sports Development*

1718
Pirates Stede Bonnet and Edward Teach (Blackbeard) were captured and killed.

1720s
Increased immigration led to the creation of four new counties in southern and western North Carolina.

1729
North Carolina became a royal colony.

1730s
Scots spread Presbyterianism.

1733
Wilmington was established.

1742
The Crown created the Granville District.

1751
The *North Carolina Gazette* began publication.

1753
Moravians settled in "Wachovia."

1765
Crowds in Wilmington formed the Sons of Liberty to thwart enforcement of the Stamp Act.

1766–1769
North Carolina joined Massachusetts and Virginia to oppose Parliament's taxation and political policies. Defying Governor William Tryon, legislators convened as a "convention"—the first such body in the colonies.

1767
Construction began on the controversial "Tryon Palace."

1768
Charlotte was incorporated. Sixty percent of the American colonies' exports of naval stores originated in North Carolina.

1770s
Methodists became established.

1771
The Battle of Alamance ended the Regulator Rebellion.

1774
In New Bern, the First Provincial Congress assembled and elected delegates to the Continental Congress. At the "Edenton Tea Party," fifty-one prominent women signed an agreement to support the American cause.

1775
As royal government effectively ended, citizens near Charlotte wrote the Mecklenburg Resolves in an effort to restore order. Soon after Governor Josiah Martin fled from Fort Johnson, Cape Fear Minutemen burned down the fort.

1776
A Whig victory, the Battle of Moore's Creek Bridge became known as the "Lexington and Concord of the South." The Fourth Provincial Congress submitted the Halifax Resolves, the first formal call for independence in the colonies. The Fifth Provisional Congress

created a constitution and the Declaration of Rights, an important forerunner to the U.S. Bill of Rights.

1780
Lord Charles Cornwallis arrived in the "Hornets Nest" of Charlotte. The "Over the Mountain Men" won the Battle of Kings Mountain.

1781
Although Cornwallis "won" the Battle of Guilford County Court House, his weakened army would surrender later in Yorktown, Virginia.

1784
Four western counties created the new state of Franklin, which collapsed four years later.

1788
Despite Federalist James Iredell's pamphlets, Willie Jones led the Anti-Federalists at the Hillsborough convention against ratification of the U.S. Constitution.

1789
Urged by William R. Davie, the Assembly chartered the University of North

The Battle of Guilford Courthouse is reenacted annually. This Revolutionary War battle set the stage for American victory at Yorktown. Courtesy, Greensboro Area Convention and Visitors Bureau

---

The fate of the Confederacy was sealed when Union troops captured Fort Fisher in 1865, as represented in this 1887 illustration by J.O. Davidson. Courtesy, Library of Congress, Prints & Photographs Division, [LC-USZC4-2384]

Carolina, the first state university in America. North Carolina ratified the U.S. Constitution.

1790
North Carolina was the third most populous state, and the fourth largest slave state.

1792
The Assembly bought 1,000 acres in Wake County to build a capitol named "Raleigh."

1799
Discoveries by the John Reed family set

off a gold rush in the Piedmont.

1804
The state's first banks, the Bank of Cape Fear and the Bank of New Bern, were chartered.

1813
Lincolnton's Michael Schenck opened North Carolina's first cotton mill.

1815
Archibald D. Murphey began a series of reports on internal improvements, public education, and constitutional reform that others helped to realize. Nevertheless, one-third of the population migrated during 1815–1850.

1816
The North Carolina Manumission Society formed, and within a decade had eight branches and 1,000 members.

1818
Joel Battle opened a cotton mill near Rocky Mount.

1819
Rumors circulated nationally that a Mecklenburg Declaration of Independence had been secretly written in 1775.

1830s
Pro-slavery advocates gained control of the debate in North Carolina, and the

Assembly strengthened "black codes."
1834
Wake Forest College was founded.
1835
Whigs helped create a new constitution that gave westerners more power but disfranchised free blacks. The state's first three railroads were formed.
1836
Francis Fries opened the Salem Manufacturing Company.
1837
Davidson College opened. A branch of the U.S. Mint was established in Charlotte. Edwin M. Holt opened the Alamance Cotton Mill. Slave George Moses Horton published the first of three volumes of poetry.
1838–1839
U.S. Troops herded Native Americans, including Cherokees from North Carolina, to Oklahoma. Almost 25 percent died along the "Trail of Tears." The Assembly passed the state's first public school law. Slave Stephen Slade and his master, Abisha Slade, of Caswell

Zebulon B. Vance was a Civil War governor of North Carolina. His birthplace can be visited in Weaverville. Courtesy, Library of Congress, Prints & Photographs Division, [LC-DIG-cwpbh-03823]

One of North Carolina's many private higher education institutions, Davidson College, was established in 1837. The Maxwell Chambers Building, named after an early benefactor, was constructed in 1859. This campus jewel was destroyed in a 1921 fire. Courtesy, Library of Congress, Prints & Photographs Division, [HABS, NC,60-DACSO,1C]

County created "bright leaf" tobacco.
1840
To combat 33 percent illiteracy, North Carolina's first public school opened in Rockingham.
1841
Union Institute (eventually Duke University) was chartered.
1843
William Woods Holden became the editor of the *North Carolina Standard* (Raleigh).
1846–1848
North Carolina native James K. Polk led the U.S. into the Mexican War. North Carolina contributed a regiment.
1848
Dorothea Dix lobbied for a state insane asylum, which opened eight years later.
1853
After Calvin H. Wiley became North Carolina's first superintendent of common schools, the state became a regional leader in education.
1857
Democrats passed a universal (white males) suffrage amendment. North Carolina native Hinton Rowan Helper published the controversial antislavery book, *The Impending Crisis.*
1859
Wesleyan Methodist Reverend Daniel Worth was charged with distributing inflammatory literature to the slaves.
1860
The state's largest city was Wilmington. Methodists and Baptists were the dominant religious sects. A state of farmers, North Carolina's stake in slavery was ambiguous. While slaves constituted about 33 percent of the population, fewer than a third of all farmers owned slaves. Only four of the South's 300 large planters lived in North Carolina.
1861
With Governor John W. Ellis' blessing, North Carolina seceded from the Union on May 20.
1861–1865
Led by Governor Zebulon B. Vance during the Civil War, North Carolina supplied more than its share of troops, provisions, and casualties. Bentonville was the bloodiest battle ever fought in North Carolina. Confederate General Joseph E. Johnston surrendered in April

Land of Cotton *by E.W. Day. At the turn of the twentieth century, low cotton prices led many whites to abandon the fields for factories, while blacks had no such option. Courtesy, Library of Congress, Prints & Photographs Division, [LC-USZ62-56499]*

1865 at Bennett Farmhouse near Durham. President Andrew Johnson appointed William W. Holden as provincial governor.

1867
Holden formed the North Carolina Republican Party. Congress placed North Carolina in the Second Military District.

1868–1870
Republicans dominated the constitutional convention and state government. Democrats turned to the Ku Klux Klan (KKK) to regain control. The Kirk-Holden War broke out.

Invented in 1898 by a New Bern pharmacist, Pepsi-Cola quickly became a popular drink throughout the state. Courtesy, Library of Congress, Prints & Photographs Division, FSA/OWI Collection [LC-USF33-T01-001111-M3]

1871–1872
Holden became the first impeached American governor to be convicted. Federal troops were sent to KKK areas.

1876
Zebulon B. Vance's gubernatorial victory "redeemed" the state and marked the end of significant Republican influence in North Carolina for many years.

1880s
The state began to industrialize with furniture, tobacco, and textiles. Banking, finance, trade, and transportation grew

as well. Agriculture languished as prices declined.

1887
Leonidas L. Polk was a state and national leader of the National Farmers' Alliance. The Assembly chartered what would become North Carolina State University.

1889
George Vanderbilt broke ground on Biltmore in Asheville.

1890
Washington Duke and his sons Benjamin and James formed the American Tobacco Company, and by the early twentieth century controlled 75 percent of the national industry.

1894
Populists and Republicans created a "Fusion" ticket, and gained control of the Assembly. Helen Morris Lewis and others organized the North Carolina Equal Suffrage Association.

1898
New Bern pharmacist Caleb Bradham renames his carbonated fountain drink "Pepsi-Cola." Former slave John Merrick and Dr. Aaron M. Moore formed the North Carolina Mutual Insurance Company in Durham, which became America's largest black owned business. State Democratic chairman Furnifold M. Simmons launched a white supremacy campaign to bring white farmers back

North Carolina has always had a strong sports identity. The rivalry between Duke and UNC-Chapel Hill has a long history, as this photo from a 1939 football game attests. Courtesy, Library of Congress, Prints & Photographs Division, FSA/OWI Collection [LC-USF33-030687-M2]

to the party. The Wilmington Riot claimed at least thirty-nine casualties.

1899

The nation's first African American writer to achieve critical success in literature, Charles Waddell Chesnutt published five books over the next six years.

1900

Charles B. Aycock was elected governor. Democrats passed an amendment to disfranchise blacks.

1903

On December 17 in Kitty Hawk, Orville and Wilbur Wright completed the first controlled, powered flight in a heavier-than-air machine. Trinity College trustees and faculty refused to fire professor John Spencer Bassett for publishing a controversial article on race relations.

1905

Thomas Dixon published *The Clansman*, a racist view of Reconstruction that later became the film, *The Birth of a Nation*.

1908

North Carolina became the first state to ban liquor.

1910

Charlotte overtook Wilmington as the state's most populous city.

1917–1918

During the Great War, over 86,000 North Carolinians served in the military. Three military camps were established. Fort Bragg later became the world's largest artillery base. Billy Graham was born in 1918.

1921

Assisted by Governor Cameron Morrison, Harriet Morehead Berry successfully lobbied for creation of the State Highway Commission in 1921.

1924

James B. Duke endowed Trinity College, which changed its name to Duke University. Angus W. McLean became one of America's most progressive governors.

1924–1926

North Carolina became a battleground in the national debate over evolution, but by 1926 voters rejected several anti-evolution candidates, and the crusade died out.

1929

During the National Textile Workers Union strike at Gastonia's Loray Mill, organizer Ella Mae Wiggins was killed.

A 1902 view of the Kill Devil Hills Lifesaving Station, before it was made world famous by two brothers with dreams of the sky. Courtesy, *Library of Congress, Prints & Photographs Division,* [LC-DIG-ppprs-00600]

1930

During the Great Depression, Governor O. Max Gardner initiated many reforms, including consolidation of the UNC system.

1932

Tobacco prices plummeted to nine cents. Unrest among textile workers caused 150 factories to close temporarily.

1933

Furniture production fell by 50 percent from 1929 to 1933.

1941–1945

About 360,000 North Carolinians served in World War II. North Carolina trained more servicemen than any other state. During the wartime "defense boom," 20 percent of the $10 billion in federal defense contracts went to North Carolina industries.

1950

Resurrecting race as a campaign issue, conservative Willis Smith (with help from aide Jesse Helms) defeated Frank P. Graham in the U.S. Senate Democratic primary.

1953

Hurricane Hazel struck.

1954

UNC graduate Junius I. Scales was arrested for Communist conspiracy under the Smith Act.

1955

Under court order, UNC admitted black undergraduates.

1956

Responding to the *Brown v. Board of Education* case, legislators created the Pearsall Plan to placate segregationists.

1957

Charlotte, Greensboro, and Winston-Salem earned national praise by initiating token integration in public schools. UNC won its first NCAA basketball championship.

1958

The Research Triangle Foundation began acquiring land in Durham and Wake Counties to create Research Triangle Park. A year later, Monsanto became RTP's first large tenant.

1960

Four students from North Carolina Agricultural and Technical College staged a "sit-in" at a Woolworth's in Greensboro. Students at Shaw University formed the Student Non-Violent Coordinating Committee (SNCC) to protest for Civil Rights.

1961

Terry Sanford was elected governor. Duke and Davidson admitted black undergraduates.

1962

North Carolina lost its first soldier in the Vietnam War. By war's end, 1,282 more would die in battle.

1963

Reacting to Cold War hysteria, the Assembly passed the "Speaker Ban Law," prohibiting all state-supported colleges and universities from allowing suspect groups or individuals to speak on campuses.

1968

Henry Frye from Guilford County became the state's first black legislator of the twentieth century, and in 1984, he became the state's first black supreme court justice.

1969

Swann v. Charlotte-Mecklenburg Board of Education received national attention when Judge James B. McMillan ruled that busing should be used to integrate schools in a highly segregated urban district. Two years later, the U.S. Supreme Court upheld McMillan's ruling.

1971

The state constitution was overhauled for the first time since 1868. The "Wilmington Ten"—nine black men and one white woman—were convicted of burning a white-owned grocery store.

1972

The end of one-party politics in the state, Republican Jesse Helms was elected to the U.S. Senate. A year later, James E. Holshouser became the first Republican governor of the century. Jim and Tammy Faye Bakker founded Praise the Lord Ministries.

1974

Susie Sharp became the female Chief Justice of the state supreme court. North Carolina State won its first NCAA basketball championship.

1979

In Greensboro, members of the Communist Workers Party planned a "Death to the Klan" rally. Neo-Nazis and the KKK opened fire, killing five.

The Greensboro Sit-ins

Senator Jesse Helms served in the U.S. Senate from 1972-2002. One of the nation's most prominent conservatives, Helms exerted much influence in the political arena during his thirty year career. Courtesy, The Jesse Helms Center Foundation

1988

The Charlotte Hornets played their first NBA game.

1989

Hurricane Hugo struck.

1991

Duke won its first NCAA basketball championship.

1995

The Carolina Panthers played their first NFL game.

1997

The Carolina Hurricanes played their first NHL game.

1999

Rain from Hurricane Floyd and two other hurricanes flooded eastern rivers.

2002

Elizabeth Dole became North Carolina's first female U.S. senator.

2004

The Charlotte Bobcats played their first NBA game.

2005

Businessman David H. Murdoch announced a collaboration with the University of North Carolina system to create the North Carolina Research Campus, a biotechnology research facility, on the former site of Cannon Mills in Kannapolis.

2006

Charlotte was named the site of the first NASCAR Hall of Fame.

The lunch counter sit-ins of the 1960s brought the Civil Rights movement to Greensboro. These historical events, and more, are depicted at The Greensboro Historical Museum. Courtesy, Greensboro Area Convention and Visitors Bureau

BIBLIOGRAPHY

Abrams, Douglas Carl. *North Carolina and the New Deal, 1932-1940*. University of Maryland. College Park, Maryland. 1981.

Achenbaum, Emily S. "Schools Not Keeping Up With Hispanic Population." *Charlotte Observer*, April 27, 2005.

America's Textile Reporter. Vol. LXX, no. 43, Oct. 25, 1956; vol. LXX, no. 51, December 20, 1956; vol. LXXI, no. 51, December 19, 1957.

American Academy of Political and Social Science, The. *The Coming of Industry to the South*. The American Academy of Political and Social Science. Philadelphia. 1931.

American Cancer Society, The. *Cigarette Smoking and Cancer*. New York. 1963.

Antone, George P. *Labor and Unionism in North Carolina: An Historical Perspective*, a paper for the conference on "Human Values and Public Policy." Raleigh. December 10, 1976.

Associated Press. "Union's Growth Remains Blistering." *Charlotte Observer*, April 15, 2005.

Associated Press. "Textile Layoffs Expected to Continue." *Charlotte Observer*, February 2, 2005.

Atherton, Lewis E. *The Southern Country Store, 1800-1860*. Louisiana State University Press. Baton Rouge. 1949.

Badger, Anthony J. *North Carolina and the New Deal*. N.C. Department of Cultural Resources. Raleigh. 1981.

——. *Prosperity Road—The New Deal, Tobacco, and North Carolina*. University of North Carolina Press. Chapel Hill. 1980.

Baker, Blanche Egerton. Mrs. *G.I. Joe*. The Graphic Press Inc. Raleigh. 1951.

Bank of America Corporation. http://www.bankofamerica.com.

Biltmore Estate. http://www.biltmore.com.

Blaine, J.C.D. and Gentry, James A. Jr. *The Industrial Development Program of North Carolina, 1954 to 1962, With Projections to 1970*. Graduate School of Business Administration, University of North Carolina. Chapel Hill. 1964.

Blythe, LeGette. *William Henry Belk—Merchant of the South*. University of North Carolina Press. Chapel Hill. 1950.

Boyd, W.K. *The Story of Durham, City of the New South*. Duke University Press. Durham. 1925.

Brazeale, William and Scott, John G. "Microelectronics—The New Wave. Planning for the Boom at the Local Level." *N.C. Insight*. Vol. IV, no. 3. North Carolina Center for Public Policy Research. Raleigh.

Buckley, James C., Inc. *A Development Study of North Carolina State Ports for the North Carolina State Ports Authority*. James C. Buckley, Inc. New York. January 8, 1957.

Buncombe County Tourism Development Authority. http://www.exploreasheville.com.

Burlington Industries. "Burlington Industries Reports Substantial Progress in Year of Restructuring." November 21, 2002. http://www.burlington.com/news.

Burlington Industries. "Burlington Names Kunberger, Futterman and Ambler to Key Positions." January 20, 2004. http://burlington.com/news.

Burlington Industries. "Court Approves WL Ross & Co. Bid for Burlington." August 1, 2003. http://www.burlington.com/news.

Burlington Industries. http://www.burlington.com.

Cape Fear Coast Convention & Visitors Bureau. http://www.capefear.nc.us.

Cape Hatteras National Seashore. http://www.nps.gov/caha/lrp.htm.

Cecelski, David. *The Waterman's Song*. Chapel Hill: University of North Carolina Press, 2001.

Charlotte Chamber. http://www.charlottechamber.com.

Charlotte Mecklenburg Schools. http://www.cms.k12.nc.us.

Charlotte Observer, The. "Brown Lung: A Case of Deadly Neglect." Charlotte. February 1-10, 1980.

——. "Carolina Industrial Edi-tion." Charlotte. March 2, 1928.

——. "Carolina Progress Edition." Charlotte. November 22, 1930.

——. "Special Report—Our Tobacco Dilemma." Charlotte. March 25, 1979.

——. "25 Years of Cotton Mill Progress." Charlotte. January 3, 1919.

Charlotte Research Institute of The University of North Carolina at Charlotte. http://www.charlotteresearchinstitute.com.

Chase, Nan. "Tour de Vin." *Our State: Down Home in North Carolina* 71, no. 9 (Feb 2004): 76-81.

Claiborne, Jack and William Price, Ed. *Discovering North Carolina: A Tar Heel Reader*. Chapel Hill: University of North Carolina Press, 1991.

Clay, Howard B. *Daniel Augustus Tompkins and Industrial Revival in the South*. East Carolina College Publications in History, vol. II. East Carolina College. Greenville. 1965.

Clay, James W. et al. *North Carolina Atlas—Portrait of a Changing Southern State*. University of North Carolina Press. Chapel Hill. 1975.

Clayton, Thomas H. *Close to the Land—The Way We Lived in North Carolina, 1820-1870*. University of North Carolina Press. Chapel Hill. 1983.

Clewell, John Henry. *History of Wachovia in North Carolina*. Doubleday, Page and Company. New York. 1902.

Cobb, Collier. "Early English Survivals on Hatteras Island." *University Magazine*. Vol. 40, no. 3. University of North Carolina Press. Chapel Hill. February 1910.

Cobb, Irvin S. *North Carolina—All She Needs is a Press Agent*. George H. Doran Company. New York. 1924.

Cobb, James C. *The Selling of the South—The Southern Crusade for Industrial Development, 1936-1980*. Lousiana State University Press. Baton Rouge. 1982.

Coles, Robert. *The South Goes North*. Little, Brown and Company. Boston. 1967.

Connor, R.D.W. *North Carolina—Rebuilding an Ancient Common-wealth, 1584-1925*. Vol. II. The American Historial Society, Inc. Chicago and New York. 1929.

Coon, Charles L. *North Carolina's Schools and Academies 1790-1840*. Edwards and Broughton Printing Company. Raleigh. 1915.

Cox, Reavis. *Competition in the American Tobacco Industry, 1911-1932*. Columbia University Press. New York. 1933.

Crater, Sophie Hamilton. *Some Important Effects of Mergers and Acquisitions Upon the Competitive Nature of the Textile Industry in the United States 1941-1955*. University of North Carolina. Chapel Hill. 1959.

Crawford, Jean. *Jugtown Pottery*. John F. Blair. Winston-Salem, North Carolina 1964.

Crittenden, Charles Christopher. *The Commerce of North Carolina, 1763-1789*. Yale University Press. New Haven, Connecticut. 1936.

Crystal Coast Tourism Authority. http://www.sunnync.com.

Dabney, Joseph Earl. *Mountain Spirits*. Charles Scribner's Sons. New York. 1974.

Daniels, Jonathan. *Tar Heels—A Portrait of North Carolina*. Dodd, Mead and Company. New York. 1941.

Dillon, Vera W. *Avalon—A Brief History of a Fateful Town*. Vera W. Dillon. 1974.

Dixon, J.K. *Fisheries of North Carolina*. January 28, 1927.

Douglas, Davison M. *Reading, Writing, & Race*. Chapel Hill: University of North Carolina Press. 1995.

Drake, William Earl. *Higher Education in North Carolina Before 1860*. Carlton Press. New York. 1964.

Duke Power. "Duke Power – At a Glance" http://www.dukepower.com.

Duke University Markets and Management Studies. "North Carolina in the Global Economy." http://www.duke.edu/web/soc142/.

Ebert, Charles H.V. *High Point's Evolution as a Furniture Town*. University of North Carolina, Chapel Hill. 1953.

Eliason, Norman E. *Tarheel Talk*. University of North Carolina Press. Chapel Hill. 1956.

Eller, Ronald D. *Miners, Millhands and Mountaineers: The Modernization of the Appalachian South 1880-1930*. University of North Carolina. Chapel Hill. 1979.

Emory, Samuel Thomas. *Bright Tobacco in the Agriculture, Industry and Foreign Trade of North Carolina*. The University of Chicago. Chicago. 1939.

Employment Security Commission Quarterly. Vol. X, nos. 1-4; vol. XI, nos. 1-4; vol. XII, nos. 1-4. Employment Security Commission of North Carolina. Raleigh. 1952-1954.

Federal Emergency Management Agency. "Hurricane Fran's N.C. Strike Five Years Ago Triggered $667.6 Million in Federal, State Aid" no. R4-01-31 (August 30,

2001): http://www.fema.gov/news/newsrelease.fema?id=5381.

Federal Writers Project of the Work Progress Administration. *North Carolina—A Guide to the Old North State.* University of North Carolina Press. Chapel Hill. 1939.

Federal Writers' Project. *These Are Our Lives.* W.W. Norton and Company. New York. 1939.

Fenn, Elizabeth A. and Wood, Peter H. *Natives and Newcomers—The Way We Lived in North Carolina Before 1770.* University of North Carolina Press. Chapel Hill. 1983.

Finger, Bill and Krivosh, Mike. "Stevens and Justice." *Southern Exposure.* Summer 1976.

"Fortune 500 Companies." *USA Today,* March 22, 2004. http://www.usatoday.com.

Fuchs, Victor R. *Changes in the Location of Manufacturing in the United States Since 1929.* Yale University Press. New Haven. 1962.

Gaillard, Frye. "Righteousness Reconsidered." *Tar Heel.* Vol. X, no. 8.

——. "Spoils of Victory." *Tar Heel.* vol. XI, no. 11.

Gant, Margaret Elizabeth. *The Raven's Story.* Glen Raven Mills, Inc. 1979.

Garfield, Ken and Jim Morrill. "Billy Graham Returns for Office Dedication." *Charlotte Observer.* April 24, 2005.

Gilman, Glenn. *Human Relations in the Industrial Southeast.* University of North Carolina Press. Chapel Hill. 1956.

Gilmore, Glenda E. *Gender and Jim Crow.* Chapel Hill: University of North Carolina Press. 1996.

Glass, Brent D. "Industrialization in North Carolina: Sources for Historians." *Carolina Comments.* Vol. XXVI, no. 3. May 1978.

——. *North Carolina—An Inventory of Historic Engineering and Industrial Sites.* U.S. Department of the Interior. 1975.

Gloster, Jesse Edward. *North Carolina Mutual Life Insurance Company—Its Historical Development and Current Operations.* Arno Press. 1976.

Godwin, Walter F., et al. *History and Status of North Carolina's Marine Fisheries.* N.C. Department of Conservation and Development. Raleigh. 1971.

Goebel, W.B. *A History of Manufacturers in North Carolina Before 1860.* Duke University Press. Durham. 1926.

Goerch, Carl. *Pitchin' Tar—Things You Should Know About North Carolina.* Edwards and Broughton. Raleigh. 1949.

Golden Leaf Foundation. http://www.goldenleaf.org.

Gordon, David. *Employer Opposition to Union Growth: J.P. Stevens vs. the Amalgamated Clothing and Textile Workers Union.* University of North Carolina. Chapel Hill. 1978.

Greater Durham Chamber of Commerce. "Announcements 2004 (January-June) Economic Development Department: 2004 Major Development Activity Report." http://durhamchamber.org.

Greater Mount Airy Chamber of Commerce. http://www.visitmayberry.com.

Greater Raleigh Convention & Visitors Bureau. http://www.visitraleigh.com.

Greater Raleigh Convention and Visitors Bureau. "Raleigh Ranks Right On Top." (January 2005): http://www.visitraleigh.com.

Green, Paul. *Dramatic Heritage.* Samuel French. New York. 1953.

Greenwood, Janette Thomas. *Bittersweet Legacy: The Black and White "Better Classes" in Charlotte, 1850-1910.* Chapel Hill: University of North Carolina Press. 1995.

Griffin, Frances. *Old Salem, An Adventure in Historic Preservation.* Old Salem, Inc. Winston-Salem. 1970.

Griffin, Richard Worden. *North Carolina: The Origin and Rise of the Cotton Textile Industry, 1830-1880.* Columbus, Ohio. Ohio State University. 1954.

Grove Park Inn. http://www.groveparkinn.com.

Hall, Joseph S. *Savings From Old Smoky—An Introduction to a Southern Mountain Dialect.* The Cataloochee Press. Asheville, N.C. 1972.

Hammer and Company Associates. *The Economy of Western North Carolina.* Hammer and Company Associates. Atlanta and Washington. 1961.

Hamilton, C. Horace. "The Negro Leaves the South." *Demography.* Vol. I, no. 1. Population Association of America. 1964.

Hamilton, J.G. deR. *History of North Carolina.* Vol. III. The Lewis Publishing Company. Chicago and New York. 1919.

——. *Reconstruction in North Carolina.* Columbia University. New York. 1914.

Hanchett, Thomas W. *Sorting Out the New South.* Chapel Hill: University of North Carolina Press. 1998.

Harrah's Cherokee Casino. http://www.cherokee-nc.com/casino.html.

Harris Poll. "California Overtakes Florida as the State Where Most People Would Like to Live" (September 18, 2002): http://www.harrispollonline.com.

Harris, David and G. Scott Thomas. "Union County Growth Tops in NC." *Charlotte Business Journal,* (June 6 2003): http://www.bizjournals.com/charlotte/stories/2003/06/09/story4.html.

Hart, John R. *Directory of North Carolina Electronic and Electrical Equipment and Component Manufacturers.* School of Engineering, North Carolina State College. Raleigh. April 1962.

Hawkins, The Rev. William G. *Lunsford Lane, Or, Another Helper From North Carolina.* Negro Universities Press. New York. 1863.

Hekman, John S. et al. *Impact of Environmental Regulations on Industrial Development in North Carolina.* Center for Urban and Regional Studies, University of North Carolina. Chapel Hill. 1982.

Helms, Ann Doss. "School 'Choice' Renamed." *Charlotte Observer,* November 24, 2004.

Herring, Harriet. *Passing of the Mill Village.* University of North Carolina Press. Chapel Hill. 1949.

Hipp, Bertha Carl. *A Gaston County Cotton Mill and Its Community.* Chapel Hill. 1930.

Hobbs, S.H. Jr. *Gaston County: Economic and Social.* Edwards and Broughton Printing Company. Ra-leigh. 1920.

——. *North Carolina—An Economic and Social Profile.* University of North Carolina Press. Chapel Hill. 1958.

Hooper, Rose. "Harrah's Cherokee Casino Celebrates its Fifth Year." *Sylva Herald,* November 28, 2002. http://www.thesylvaherald.com.

Hoovers Inc. "Fact sheet on Burlington Industries." http://www.hoovers.com/burlington-industries/—ID__15565—/free-co-factsheet.xhtml.

Hosmer, Charles B. Jr. *Preservation Comes of Age.* University Press of Virginia. Charlottesville, Virginia. 1981.

Hughes, Joseph T. Jr. "Microelectronics—The New Wave. A Healthy Future for North Carolina." *N.C. Insight.* Vol. IV, no. 3. North Carolina Center for Public Policy Research. Raleigh.

Hurt, Chris and Kelly Zering. "Hog Production Booms in North Carolina. Why there? Why now?" http://www.aces.uiuc.edu/archives/experts/swine/0868.html.

Institute for Transportation Research & Education @ North Carolina State Universities. http://www.itre.ncsu.edu.

Jackson, Damien "Resegregating Schools" *In These Times,* January 21, 2003. http://www.tolerance.org.

Johnson, Guy Benton and Johnson, Guion Griffis. *Research in Service to Society.* University of North Carolina Press. Chapel Hill. 1980.

Johnson, Guion Griffis. *Ante-Bellum North Carolina—A Social History.* University of North Carolina Press. Chapel Hill. 1937.

Jones, Mary Virginia Currie. A "Golden Triangle" of Research: Romeo Holland Guest—His Conception of and Involvement in the Development of the Research Triangle Park. University of North Carolina. Chapel Hill. 1978.

Jud, G. Donald and Lamb, Marian P. "The Structure of Industrial Expansion in North Carolina 1950-1973." *The North Carolina Review of Business and Economics.* October 1975.

Kahlenberg, Richard. "Economic School Integration: An Update." *The Century Foundation Issue Brief Series.* http://www.tcf.org/publications/education/economicschoolintegration.pdf.

Kahlenberg, Richard. "Post-Brown Schooldays." *Slate,* May 11, 2004. http://slate.msn.com/id/210028.

Kars, Marjoleine. *Breaking Loose Together.* Chapel Hill: University of North Carolina Press, 2002.

Kelley, Stephen R. "Microelectronics—The New Wave. Easy Angling in Legislative Waters." *N.C. Insight*. Vol. IV, no. 3. North Carolina Center for Public Policy Research. Raleigh.

Kennedy, William J. *The North Carolina Mutual Story*. North Carolina Mutual Life Insurance Company. Durham. 1970.

Kephart, Horace. *Our Southern Highlanders*. The University of Tennessee Press. Knoxville. 1913.

Knapp, John L. *North Carolina—An Economic Profile*. Federal Reserve Bank of Richmond. Richmond, Virginia.

Lacy, Dan Mabry. *The Beginnings of Industrialism in North Carolina 1865-1900*. University of North Carolina. Chapel Hill. 1935.

Landon, Charles E. *The North Carolina State Ports Authority*. Duke University Press. Durham. 1963.

Lefler, Hugh T. *Guide to the Study and Reading of North Carolina History*. University of North Carolina Press. Chapel Hill. 1969.

Lefler, Hugh T. and Newsome, Albert Ray. *North Carolina: The History of a Southern State*. University of North Carolina Press. Chapel Hill. 1973.

Lefler, Hugh T. and Powell, William S. *Colonial North Carolina, A History*. Charles Scribner's Sons. New York. 1973.

Lefler, Hugh T., ed. *North Carolina History Told By Contemporaries*. University of North Carolina Press. Chapel Hill. 1965.

Lemert, Ben F. *The Cotton Textile Industry of the Southern Appalachian Piedmont*. University of North Carolina Press. Chapel Hill. 1933.

——. *The Tobacco Manufacturing Industry in North Carolina*. National Youth Administration of North Carolina. Raleigh. 1939.

Lewis, Mark. "From Lowell To Islamabad, Via Greensboro." *Forbes*, November 16, 2001. http://www.forbes.com/2001/11/16/1116textiles.html.

Lost Colony. http://www.thelostcolony.org.

Love, J. Spencer. Memorandum to Department Heads, Managers and Supervisors, Jan. 22, 1942. *F. Spencer Love Papers*. The Southern Historical Collection, University of North Carolina. Chapel Hill. Ibid., Aug. 17, 1945.

Lowe's Motor Speedway. http://www.lowesmotorspeedway.com.

Luger, Michael I. "Microelectronics—The New Wave. The Economic Hope—Promises and Policies." *N.C. Insight*. Vol. IV, no. 3. North Carolina Center for Public Policy Research.

McLaughlin, Glenn E. and Robock, Stefan. *Why Industry Moves South*. National Planning Association. 1949.

MCNC. http://www.mcnc.org.

McVay, Francis E. *Factory Meets Farm in North Carolina*. Technical Bulletin No. 83. Agricultural Experiment Station of the North Carolina State College of Agriculture and Engineering. Raleigh. October 1947.

Milliken, Matthew E. "Poppies Bloom as Alternative to Tobacco." *Henderson Daily Dispatch*. http://www.tobaccotrustfund.org.

Mitchell, Broadus. *The Rise of Cotton Mills in the South*. Peter Smith. Gloucester, Massachusetts. 1921.

Mitchell, George Sinclair. *Textile Unionism and the South*. University of North Carolina Press. Chapel Hill. 1931.

Mitchell, Herbert Hall. *The Development of Commercial Banking in North Carolina 1865-1935*. University of North Carolina. Chapel Hill. 1954.

Moes, John E. *Local Subsidies for Industry*. University of North Carolina Press. Chapel Hill. 1962.

Morrill, Jim and Danica Coto. "Immigrant Growth Sparks Proposals." *Charlotte Observer*, April 16, 2005.

NASCAR. http://www.nascar.com.

Nathans, Sydney. *The Quest for Progress—The Way We Lived in North Carolina, 1870-1920*. University of North Carolina Press. Chapel Hill. 1983.

National Basketball Association. "Hornets History." http://www.nba.com/hornets/history/history_hornets.html.

National Institute of Environmental Health Sciences. http://www.niehs.nih.gov.

NewsHour with Jim Lehrer, PBS, September 13, 1999. http://www.pbs.org/newshour/bb/education/july-dec99/busing_9-13.html.

Newsome, A.R., ed. "Twelve North Carolina Counties, 1810-11." *The North Carolina Historical Review*. October 1928; January, April, July, and October 1929. North Carolina Historical Commission.

NFL Team History. http://www.nflhistoryguide.com/cp/history.htm.

Noble. M.C.S. *A History of the Public Schools of North Carolina*. University Press. Chapel Hill. 1930.

North Carolina Arts Council. "Facts & Stats About the Arts in North Carolina." http://www.ncarts.org/who_facts.cfm.

North Carolina Biotechnology Center. http://www.ncbiotech.org.

North Carolina Center for Public Policy Research, Inc. *Which Way Now? Economic Development and Industrialization in North Carolina*. The North Carolina Center for Public Policy Research, Inc. Raleigh. 1979.

North Carolina Department of Conservation and Development. *North Carolina Industrial Directory*. North Carolina Department of Conservation and Development. Raleigh. 1928.

North Carolina Department of Agriculture and Consumer Services. "Hog Numbers Up." http://www.ncagr.com/stats/livestoc/anihgi03.htm.

North Carolina Department of Agriculture and Consumer Services. http://www.ncagr.com.

North Carolina Department of Commerce. Division of Tourism, Film and Sports Development. http://www.visitnc.com.

North Carolina Department of Commerce Finance Center. "Incentives." http://www.nccommerce.com/finance/incentives/.

North Carolina Department of Commerce.

"North Carolina: The State of Minds Information & Technology." http://www.investnc.com.

North Carolina Department of Commerce. "North Carolina: The State of Minds Automotive." http://www.investnc.com.

North Carolina Department of Commerce. "North Carolina: The State of Minds Pharmaceutical, Biotechnology & Life Sciences Industry." http://www.investnc.com.

North Carolina Department of Commerce. "North Carolina: The State of Minds Plastics." http://www.investnc.com.

North Carolina Department of Commerce. "2004 Governor's Conference on Tourism Handout." April 6, 2004. http://www.nccommerce.com/tourism/govconf/hand/2004gconfpres.pdf.

North Carolina Department of Commerce. http://www.nccommerce.com.

North Carolina Department of Commerce/Film. http://www.nccommerce.com/Film/.

North Carolina Department of Revenue. "1998 Report." http://www.dor.state.nc.us/publications/1998report.html.

North Carolina Department of Transportation. *Report of Impact of the North Carolina Ports on the State Economy*. Raleigh. 1975.

North Carolina Department of Transportation. "Charting a New Direction for NCDOT: North Carolina's Long-Range Statewide Multimodal Transportation Plan" (September 2004): http://www.ncdot.org/planning/statewideplan/pdf.ncstatewidetransportationplan.pdf.

North Carolina Economic Development Board. "2004 Strategic Plan." http://www.ncedb.com.

North Carolina Flood Maps. "North Carolina Floodplain Mapping: Hurricane Floyd and 10-Year Disaster Assistance Report." http://www.ncfloodmaps.com/pubdocs/HistoricData.pdf.

North Carolina Governor's Textile Tariff Study Commission. *Supplemental Cotton Textile Tariff Study*. Raleigh. 1957.

North Carolina Grape Council and North Carolina Department of Agriculture & Consumer Services. http://www.ncwine.org.

N.C. Insight. "North Carolina: State of the Arts?" Vol. V, no. 4. February 1983. North Carolina Center for Public Policy Research. Raleigh.

North Carolina Office of the Governor. "Easley Announces NC Film Industry as Third in Nation, Bringing in $230 Million." June 5, 2003.

North Carolina Office of the Governor. "NC Film Office Honored at California Film Conference." October 14, 2003.

North Carolina Office of the Governor. "UNC-Community College Partnership means LEARN NC to Reach all Tar Heel Teachers, Students." May 26, 1999. No. 356. http://www.unc.edu/news/archives/may99/learn052699.htm.

North Carolina Public Schools. http://

www.ncpublicschools.org.

North Carolina Rural Economic Development Center. http://www.ncruralcenter.org.

North Carolina State Department of Archives and History. *A Lonesome Place Against the Sky*. Raleigh. 1971.

"North Carolina: The State of Minds." *Fortune* Special Sections. http://www.fortune.com/fortune/services/sections/fortune/region/2003_01nc.html.

North Carolina Tobacco Trust Fund Commission. http://www.tobaccotrustfund.org.

North Carolina Zoo. http://www.nczoo.org.

Orr, Douglas M. and Alfred W. Stuart, eds. *The North Carolina Atlas: Portrait for a New Century*. Chapel Hill: University of North Carolina Press, 1999.

Parramore, Thomas C. *Cradle of the Colony—The History of Chowan County and Edenton, North Carolina*. Edenton Chamber of Commerce. Edenton, North Carolina 1967.

_____. *Express Lanes and Country Roads—The Way We Lived in North Carolina, 1920-1970*. University of North Carolina Press. Chapel Hill. 1983.

Pearsall, Howard Turner. *The North Carolina Symphony Orchestra from 1932 to 1962: Its Founding, Musical Growth, and Musical Activities*. Bloomington, Indiana. Indiana University. 1969.

Perkins, Van L. *Crisis in Agriculture: The Agricultural Adjustment Administration and the New Deal, 1933*. University of California Publications in History. University of California Press. Berkeley, California. 1969.

Perry, Percival. *The Naval Stores Industry in the Old South, 1790-1860*. School of Forestry, North Carolina State University. Raleigh. 1967.

Pittman. Thomas M. "Industrial Life in Colonial Carolina." *The North Carolina Booklet*. North Carolina Society, Daughters of the Revolution. July 1907.

Pope, Liston. *Millhands and Preachers—A Study of Gastonia*. Yale University Press. New Haven. 1942.

Powell, William S. *North Carolina through the Centuries*. Chapel Hill: University of North Carolina Press, 1989.

Powell, William S. *North Carolina—A Bicentennial History*. W.W. Norton and Company, Inc. New York. 1977.

——. *The North Carolina Gazetteer*. University of North Carolina Press. Chapel Hill. 1968.

Ragan, Robert Allison. *Leading Textile Mills of Gaston County from 1904 to the Present and Gaston County Textile Leaders*. 1975.

——. *The Pioneer Cotton Mills of Gaston County, N.C.* Charlotte.

Raleigh Durham International Airport. "Fast Facts." *Airport News*. http://www.rdu.com.

Rankin, Carl E. *The University of North Carolina and the Problems of the Cotton Mill Employee*. Columbia University. New York. 1934.

Research Triangle Foundation of North Carolina. http://www.rtp.org.

Research Triangle Institute. http://www.rti.org.

Rhyne, Jennings J. *Some Southern Cotton Mill Workers and Their Villages*. University of North Carolina Press. Chapel Hill. 1930.

Rights, Burton Jones. *Economic Life in Early Wachovia*. Moravian Theological Seminary. Bethlehem, Pennsylvania. 1955.

Robert, Joseph Clarke. "The Tobacco Industry in Ante-Bellum North Carolina." *The North Carolina Historical Review*. April 1938.

——. *The Tobacco Kingdom—Plantation, Market, and Factory in Virginia and North Carolina, 1800-1860*. Duke University Press. Durham. 1938.

Robinson, John L. *Living Hard: Southern Americans in the Great Depression*. University Press of America. Washington, D.C. 1981.

Ross, Malcolm and Stewart, B. Anthony. "North Carolina, Dixie Dynamo." *National Geographic*. February 1962.

Schenck, David. *Historical Sketch of the Schenck and Bevens Families*. Thomas, Reece and Company, Book and Job Printers. Greensboro, North Carolina. 1884.

School of Public Health, University of North Carolina-Chapel Hill. *Transactions of the National Conference on Cotton Dust and Health*. Charlotte. May 2, 1970.

Silberman, Todd. "Wake County Schools: A Question of Balance." *The Century Foundation*. http://www.tcf.org/publications/education/silberman.pdf.

Simmons, Tim. "Where Do We Go From Here?" *(Raleigh) News & Observer*, February 25, 2001.

Smart Start. http://www.smartstart-nc.org.

Southern Furniture Journal. High Point, North Carolina. June 1910.

Spooner, John C. "Dell to spend $115 million on new plant" *CNN News*, November 9, 2004. http://cnn.com.

Stark, Louis. "The Meaning of the Textile Strike." *The New Republic*. May 8, 1929.

State of North Carolina Department of Transportation. "Geographic Information System." www.ncdot.org.

Stick, David. *The Outer Banks of North Carolina*. University of North Carolina Press. Chapel Hill. 1958.

Strother, David Hunter. "North Carolina Illustrated." *Harper's New Monthly Magazine*. March and August 1857.

Tar Heel. "The Future of the Public Schools." Vol. XI, no. 9.

Taylor, Harden F. *Survey of Marine Fisheries in North Carolina*. University of North Carolina Press. Chapel Hill. 1951.

Terrill, Tom E. and Hirsch, Jerrold. *Such As Us—Southern Voices of the Thirties*. University of North Carolina Press. Chapel Hill. 1978.

Thomas, David N. *Foundations of the North Carolina Furniture Industry*. School of Forestry, North Carolina State University. Raleigh. 1967.

Thompson, Holland. *From the Cotton Field to the Cotton Mill*. The Mac-Millan Company. New York. 1906.

——. *The New South*. Yale University Press. New Haven. 1919.

Tilley, Nannie May. *The Bright-Tobacco Industry 1860-1929*. University of North Carolina Press. Chapel Hill. 1948.

Troxler, Howard. "Art and Ambition—North Carolina's School of the Arts." *Tar Heel*. Vol. IX, no. 2.

Tufts, Leonard. *Pinehurst North Carolina*. Leonard Tufts. Boston. 1905.

University of North Carolina News Letter, The. Vol. XL, no. 14. December 15, 1954.

U.S. Bureau of the Census. "2000 U.S. Census." http://www.census.gov.

U.S. Department of Health & Human Services. http://www.hhs.gov.

U.S. Department of the Interior, National Park Service. *Benchmark Schedule Outlines Cape Hatteras Lighthouse Relocation*. Cape Hatteras National Seashore.

U.S. Department of the Interior, National Park Service. *The Cape Hatteras Light Station Relocation Project Named Outstanding Civil Engineering Achievement*. Cape Hatteras National Seashore. May 8, 2000.

U.S. Department of the Interior. National Park Service. *Synopsis: Cape Hatteras Lighthouse*. Cape Hatteras National Seashore. May 17, 2000.

University of North Carolina at Charlotte, Department of Geography and Earth Sciences. "North Carolina Atlas Revisited." http://www.ncatlasrevisited.org.

Unto These Hills. http://www.untothesehills.com.

Wachovia Corporation. http://www.wachovia.com.

Wake County Public School System. http://www.wcpss.net.

Wall, Bennett Harrison. *Ebenezer Pettigrew, An Economic Study of an Ante-Bellum Planter*. University of North Carolina. Chapel Hill. 1946.

Walls, Dwayne E. *The Chickenbone Special*. Harcourt Brace Jovanovich, Inc. New York. 1970.

Ward, Dorothy. "Reaching for the Stars—The North Carolina School of Science and Mathematics." *Tar Heel*. Vol. X, no. 1.

Watson, Harry L. *An Independent People—The Way We Lived in North Carolina, 1770-1820*. University of North Carolina Press. Chapel Hill. 1983.

——. "Squire Oldway and his Friends: Opposition to Internal Im-provements in Antebellum North Carolina." *The North Carolina Historical Review*. April 1977.

Webb, Elizabeth Yates. *The Develop-ment of Industry in North Carolina*.

Whittington, Dale. *Planning for the Microelectronics Industry in North Carolina*. Department of City and Regional Planning, University of North Carolina. Chapel Hill. 1981.

Wilson, Louis Round. *Campaign for Higher Education in North Carolina*. Chapel Hill. 1932.

——. *The Research Triangle of North Carolina*. The Colonial Press. Chapel Hill. 1967.

INDEX